The Human Side
of Afro-American History

Compiled and Edited by

MARGARET STIMMANN BRANSON
Supervisor of Social Sciences,
Oakland, California, Public Schools

and

EDWARD E. FRANCE, *Professor of History*
Chairman, Department of Black Studies
California State College at Hayward

GINN AND COMPANY

A Xerox Company

Table of Contents

VI RECONSTRUCTION: VICTORIES WON AND LOST

VII ON THE FRONTIER

VIII   TO SEEK A WIDER WORLD

IX BLACK AND WHITE TOGETHER—THE DRIVE FOR CIVIL RIGHTS

X BLACK POWER AND BEYOND

x

Section One

In the Beginning–Africa

I'll Make Me a Man

Evidence fully accepted by many outstanding anthropologists seems to indicate that man originated in Africa. In one of his best known poems, James Weldon Johnson gives his idea of how man was created. He does not say in what color the image was cast but simply that God made Himself a man.

Source: Johnson, James Weldon. *God's Trombones: Seven Negro Sermons in Verse.* New York: Copyright 1927 by The Viking Press, Inc., renewed 1955 by Grace Nail Johnson. Reprinted by permission of The Viking Press, Inc.

The Creation

Then God sat down—
On the side of a hill where he could think;
By a deep, wide river he sat down;
With his head in his hands,
God thought and thought,
Till he thought: I'll make me a man!

Up from the bed of the river
God scooped the clay;
And by the bank of the river
He kneeled him down;
And there the great God Almighty
Who lit the sun and fixed it in the sky,
Who flung the stars to the most far corner of the night,
Who rounded the earth in the middle of his hand;
This Great God,

Like a mammy bending over her baby,
Kneeled down in the dust
Toiling over a lump of clay
Till he shaped it in his own image
Then into it he blew the breath of life,
And man became a living soul.
Amen. Amen.

circa 1500

African Civilizations

Most Americans, at least until very recently, have thought of Africa as a "land without a past" whose peoples were "barbarians." Ralph Linton, an outstanding anthropologist, offers evidence to refute that idea. He states that Africans were in many instances not only equal to but superior to their contemporaries in Europe. Linton describes the African kingdom of Dahomey as a magnificent example of political organization.

Source: Linton, Ralph. *The Tree of Culture.* New York: Alfred A. Knopf, 1955, pp. 445, 459, 460.

Few Americans realize how rich and complex the cultures of many African societies were at the time of the first European contact. In the regions from which most of the American Negroes' ancestors were drawn, there was a series of strong and enduring kingdoms which deserved the name of civilizations on every count except that of literacy. In their arts and crafts these societies were little, if at all inferior to medieval Europeans, while, in the thoroughness of their political organization and the skill with which social institutions were utilized to lend stability to the political structure, they far exceeded anything in Europe prior to the sixteenth century. It is not too much to say that in their home territory the African Negroes have shown a genius for state-building unsurpassed by any other people, except possibly the Incas of Peru.

The kingdom was divided for administrative purposes into twelve districts, each under a hereditary district chief. Within each district there were several villages, also with hereditary chiefs. Each chief had his insignia of office: a carved staff and stool, which varied in design

2

according to the particular office and had a height proportional to its importance, a pole, and an umbrella carried over him on state occasions. The main duties of the chiefs were judicial. State finances were on a sound and regular basis, with sales taxes the most important source of income. Inheritance taxes were also levied, and the king received the confiscated estates of criminals. A commoner who had made undue display of his wealth was very likely to be condemned on some trumped-up charge. There were numerous minor officials, and the whole bureaucracy was watched by an extensive, well-organized secret service.

Census taking was a distinctive feature of the Dahomean state activities. Every year there was a careful enumeration of the Dahomean population, including reports on births and deaths. Each individual was represented by a pebble. Special officials were charged with enumerating slaves, war captives, and deaths in battle. The pebble record was divided into fifteen units, one each for adult males, adult females, and children of each age group up to thirteen. The bags of pebbles were stored in a special house at the capitol and constituted a lasting archive from which it was possible to see whether the population was increasing or diminishing and to govern policy accordingly.

circa 1790

I Meet the King of the Ebos

Unsuccessful in his attempts to run a business in Vermont, Joseph Hawkins, a native of New York, became a slave trader. He was still a teenager when he set out from Charleston bound for the Guinea coast. According to Hawkins, "Happy did I consider myself in obtaining a situation reputable in its nature and highly profitable in prospect. . . ."

However, Hawkins was not to continue trafficking in human beings for long. He was blinded on the voyage back to the United States when he was just twenty-three years old. Thus his career as a slaver began and ended with just one voyage. To raise money to support himself, Hawkins dictated a book which was then published for him by friends. His *History of a Voyage to the Coast of Africa* offers these insights into how and why some Africans sold their fellow countrymen into slavery.

Source: Hawkins, Joseph. *A History of a Voyage to the Coast of*

3

Africa and Travels into the Interior of That Country; Containing Particular Descriptions of the Climate and Inhabitants, and Interesting Particulars Concerning the Slave Trade (second edition). Troy, New York: Luther Pratt, 1797, pp. 63-67, 92-94, 109-111 *passim.*

The Capital of Ebo or Quappa Ebo, is pleasantly situated on the sides of two hills. . . . The open country along the river downward was highly cultivated, and beautifully contrasted in its verdure with the brown appearance of the town, which, excepting a few trees here and there, dispersed, exhibited a view of considerable population and regularity. The streets were laid out with a considerable regard to order . . . there was not anything of grandeur, it is true, but certainly a degree of elegant simplicity and neatness which I did not expect to find.

We were conducted to the King's hut; he received us at his door, and after shaking me by the hand very earnestly for a minute, retired, and beckoned us to follow, which we did. This hut was oblong, as large as some of our barns and divided into rooms by wicker partitions, covered with neatly coloured mats, and ornamented with cane and reed baskets, with other fancy works of the kind.

When we reached the third apartment, where there was a number of women already seated, he sat down on the bench covered with a mat, and holding out his hands to me, shook mine very earnestly again. He then shook Hurdee's [Hawkins' native interpreter and guide] speaking to him in the Ebo language. I was then directed to salute all his wives, seventeen in number. . . .

[I] was handed round to the elders, or what I suppose some subjects of an European monarch would call the NOBILITY. With all these I shook hands in turn, was then led to a mat placed for me nearly in the front of his SABLE majesty, with whom by means of Hurdee I entered into conversation on the subject of my mission.

He informed me that he had been made acquainted with the object of my journey, that he was pleased at my preferring him to his neighbors; that he was willing to trade with me in GOLD, IVORY, or PRISONERS: that he should wish to trade constantly and to be furnished with goods from the SEA COUNTRIES, as he called them, in abundance, for which he would pay largely. . . . He then entered on general conversation, enquiring into the manners, customs, and situation of my country [the United States] of which he appeared to have already had some accounts. He related some particulars concerning himself and the people of EBO, his wars with some neighboring people and frequently

4

enlivened his spirits and our conversations with draughts of excellent palm wine. . . .

[Later the King] proposed that I should go and see the prisoners. . . . We found them confined in a large area within a thick stockade, on the outside of which was a trench; the inside was divided into parcel and huts irregularly constructed; and the entrance as well as the whole circuit was guarded by men with spears.

We commonly find ourselves impressed with emotions of horror and compassion on entering places where our fellow men are doomed to punishment or thraldom [slavery]. In the scene before me, the ear was not indeed dinned with clanking of heavy fetters, but was horrible in its peculiar way. The captives were destitute for the most part of even their necessary covering, and bound indiscriminately together by the hands and legs, the cords being again fastened to the ground by stakes; they were loosed a few at a time once every day, when each was permitted to eat the only meal they were allowed, consisting of rice and palm oil. . . .

I had often in the course of the voyage and the journey, rebuked myself for having embarked in the African trade, but found a consolation in the reflection that it was not from a malicious inclination or avaricious disposition that I had embarked in it, but from the pressing call of necessity. . . . I was fully convinced the removal of these poor wretches, even into the slavery of the West Indies, would be an act of humanity, rather than one exposed to censure. . . .

Their [the Ebos'] policy is as simple as their manners, and more effective than volumes of laboured regulations. I have before noticed that offences against parents are punished by slavery or death; thefts I also said are rare. . . . Stealing and such petty offences are generally punished by selling the offender into slavery. When a thief is detected, the neighborhood assemble, and are bound to make it a common affair; if convicted, the full value of the thing stolen is made good to the person aggrieved, from the sale of the culprit, with one third of what should remain; the two other thirds are a [gift or tribute] to the King.

Black Jews Come to the New World

> Little is known of the history of the Black Jews of Africa and how and why some of them migrated to America. However, Roi Ottley, a well-known black writer, did considerable research into their fascinating history. Some of his findings follow.

> Source: Ottley, Roi. *New World A-Coming* (New York: Literary Classics, Inc. Distributed by Houghton Mifflin Company, Boston), 1943, pp. 139, 140-145, 150.

Harlem's Black Jews, in the view of Jewish scholars, are the descendants of the Falashas, whose form of worship is distinct from white Jewry, influenced as it is by African culture. As far as I can learn, white and black Jews are branches of the same tree, with striking similarities as well as curious differences.

. . . The legend—according to Jewish authorities—is that about 2,600 years ago a band of Jews, fleeing from Palestine, which was then under the oppressive rule of the Babylonians, sought refuge in Egypt and along the cataracts of the Nile. They pushed on into the deserts of Africa and ultimately penetrated the highlands of Ethiopia, where they became known as Falashas, or outsiders. They designated themselves as Beth-Israel—the house of Israel.

. . . [The Falashas] gathered in the same province . . . and fused finally into a single community. . . . [They] played a prominent role in raising the material and intellectual standards of their adopted country by strict adherence to the faith of their forefathers. A self-reliant and self-supporting people, they earned their livelihood as farmers, blacksmiths, masons, potters, weavers, tanners, saddlers, and basket-makers; and others, curiously enough, as mercenaries. Until modern times, the Falashas were virtually the only skilled workers in Ethiopia. . . .

For centuries the Black Jews regarded themselves as the only surviving Jews, living in entire ignorance of the existence of any other Jews—white or black. Nor had world Jewry at large any inkling of the Falashas' existence in the hills of Ethiopia. They were first discovered by James Bruce, a Scotch traveler who brought the story back to London in 1790. . . . He reported to white Jewry when he returned that though their skins were "black [they] possessed the characteristic of our [Jewish] race. . . ."

Arrival of the first Black Jews in America probably coincides with

6

the early days of colonization, when they might have been shipped here among other African captives to work the plantations. Only a rare handful was ever seen in this country. Yet as early as the turn of the last century, according to the records of the Common Council, Black Abyssinian Jews immigrated to the United States as free men to escape anti-Semitism abroad and opened a synagogue in lower Manhattan, where they freely observed all the traditions and customs of Judaism. There is no record of their ever having disbanded nor is there any trace of their descendants. Whether they left this city to join a Zionist movement then active that sought to establish a Promised Land outside of Buffalo, or eventually were absorbed by the black population (or the white), is a moot question. But considerable speculation surrounds the fact that in 1808, in a wooden shack on Waverly Place, eighteen black men from Abyssinia started the Abyssinian Baptist Church, a Negro institution that is in lusty existence today.

It is obviously impossible to check the numbers of Black Jews that have entered the country. But a census taken in 1938 quoted by the "Jewish Family Journal," and so far as I know the only one ever taken, estimates the Black Jewish population in New York City at 10,000, and another hundred thousand scattered throughout the United States, in such principal centers as Salt Lake City, Cincinnati, Youngstown, Philadelphia, Newark, and St. Louis. . . .

The organizer and spiritual head of Harlem's congregation, Rabbi Matthew, is . . . an intelligent black man. . . . His origins are humble. He was born of poor laboring parents in Lagos, British West Africa, now Nigeria, center of a large colony of black Jews. . . . His father was a Falasha, an African Negro Jew, and his mother a Christian whose father had been a slave in Nevis, British West Indies, and had returned to Africa with his family when the British Emancipation Act freed him. . . .

"The black man is a Jew," he [Matthew] said, "Because he is a direct lineal descendant of Abraham. Isaac, son of Abraham, was father of Esau [whose skin was hairy, like the white man's] and of Jacob [whose skin was smooth, like the black man's] . . . ."

"Don't submit meekly to being called a Negro," Rabbi Matthew has been heard to admonish his flock. "The Negro, so-called, has no history prior to the fourteenth century. And when that history began, it began in bondage, poverty, humiliation, and degradation. Insist on being called an Ethiopian, an African, or even an Afro-American. As such, yours is the most glorious history in the world. You are descended from

7

kings, and the white man knows it. It is his purpose to keep you ignorant of your past so that he can exploit you. That is why he has falsified the history of the world. . . ."

. . . Black Jews—like many of their co-religionists—seek a homeland. They await the Messiah who will re-establish a Negro nation—not a Jewish nation—through the redemption of Africa. . . .

The Black Jews, it appears, are more intensely Negro than Jew. . . . Whatever its true character and ultimate aims, the future of the Black Jews—inescapably identified as they are with the Negro people—is bound to the future of the black man. They apparently know this well!

1840's

"Few People Ever Trouble Themselves to Think About Africa At All"

Sir Henry Huntley, an Englishman, was a veteran African trader specializing in powder, dyes, and cotton goods. He was so appalled at the "completely erroneous ideas of the social condition of the African nations generally . . . and of the degree of civilization which they have attained" that he decided to write a book entitled *Sir H. Huntley's Seven Years' Service on the Slave Coast, Western Africa.*

Here are some excerpts from Sir Henry Huntley's attempt to set the record straight about Western Africa in the 1840's.

Source: *Sir H. Huntley's Seven Years Service on the Slave Coast, Western Africa,* as reviewed in "The Westminster Review" and reprinted in *Littell's Living Age.* No. 294. 6 December, 1851. pp. 449-450.

. . . Such opinions have arisen from completely erroneous ideas of the social condition of the African nations generally, and of the degree of civilization (such as it is) which they have attained. They cannot justly be regarded as savages. The greater number of the nations throughout Africa have fixed habitations; defences round their towns; cultivate their lands; wear cotton dresses of their own manufacture, dyed with native dyes; and work in gold and iron. It is true that their dwellings are generally only mud huts, not much better than some Irish cabins, though certainly cleaner; that the defences round their towns are only stockades or mud walls, some twelve feet high and two or three feet thick, only sufficient to defend them against neighboring tribes; that though the lands immediately round their towns are often cultivated with considerable care, yet that in most places there are 100 acres uncultivated for every acre that is cultivated. . . . The native loom is a very primitive concern but the native cotton is excellent, and the native dresses are often very handsome. The African indigo is said to resist the action of light and acids better than any other . . . and their dyes far brighter and more enduring. . . .

The native workmanship in iron is very rude, yet some of their agricultural implements appear to be admirably suited for their purpose. The native workmanship in gold is not merely curious, but often really beautiful. . . .

We cannot profess—who can do so?—a very accurate or extended knowledge of Africa; but we have, ourselves, been some six hundred miles into the interior; we have resided for years in the country; we have come in contact with natives from almost every part of Africa, frequently immediately on their arrival from their native countries, and before they could have been in the slightest degree influenced by European customs or habits. . . . We remember, on returning to England . . . a naval officer [who] was asked respecting the condition of the natives in the interior; he replied—"Oh, savages, perfect savages! The people along the coast have become a little civilized by coming in contact with us, but those in the interior are perfectly savage; I have seen hundreds of them taken by my own vessel from slavers." We fear the gallant officer did not know much more of Africa than he was able to learn from the deck of his vessel. But his evidence appeared to suit the preconceived opinions of [his listeners] and was met with gentle approving smiles;—a kind of "Oh, of course," look.

The chief classes from which slaves are obtained are, prisoners taken in war, the more powerful nations usually attacking the weaker and more savage tribes; criminals of certain classes, debtors—seldom, however, if ever, sold into foreign slavery; and, of course, the offspring of all slaves. Not only is the debtor liable to be seized, but if he cannot be taken, any of his family may be; and amongst some tribes or nations it is the law, that if a debt be due to any member of the tribe by a member of any other tribe, any person of the debtor's nation or tribe may be seized as a slave until the debt is paid.

The laws respecting debts throughout all the African nations are exceedingly strict: they may be, and are, very cruel and rude; but they still prove the existence of that stage of civilization in which men feel that property must be protected in most summary manner. Some months since we travelled through some hundred miles of country with a friend of ours, a merchant at the Gambia. We found his property and that of other merchants scattered over a vast extent of country, in the care of native traders. Goods, as cotton cloths, gunpowder, amber, &c., which would be of immediate value to the natives, were stored in wicker huts. There was nothing to prevent their being plundered at any moment, and yet any act of violence or robbery is exceedingly rare. The native merchants are generally able to travel amongst tribes at war with each other without being molested; and a native wealthy merchant is held in the highest honor and is more influential than most of the kings or chiefs. Certain tribes devote themselves almost entirely to commercial pursuits.

1859

Why We Should Not Go Back to Africa

Many people, both black and white, have proposed at various times that America's unwilling immigrants be returned to Africa. Henry Highland Garnet, a black abolitionist and later a United States diplomat to Liberia, at one time supported an African colonization organization. He wrote to Frederick Douglass, another black abolitionist, and asked him to "tell your readers what your objections are to the civilization and Christianization of Africa. What objection have you to colored men in this country engaging in agriculture, lawful trade, and commerce in the land of my forefathers?"

Here is part of the answer Douglass gave Garnet. It appeared in the February, 1859, issue of *Douglass' Monthly*.

Source: *Douglass' Monthly,* February, 1859. Reprinted in Foner, Philip S. *The Life and Writings of Frederick Douglass.* New York: International Publishers, 1950, Vol. II: Pre-Civil War Decade, 1850-1860, pp. 443-447 *passim*.

... The African Civilization Society says to us, go to Africa, raise cotton, civilize the natives, become planters, merchants, compete with the slave states in the Liverpool cotton market, and thus break down American slavery. To which we simply and briefly reply, "We prefer to remain in America. . . ."

Meanwhile we will state briefly for the benefit of friend Garnet, seven considerations which prevent our cooperation with the African Civilization Society.

1. No one idea has given rise to more oppression and persecution toward the colored people of this country than that which makes Africa, not America, their home. It is that wolfish idea that elbows us off the sidewalk, and denies us the rights of citizenship. The life and soul of this abominable idea would have been thrashed out of it long ago, but for the jesuitical and persistent teaching of the Society. The natural and unfailing tendency of the African Colonization Society, by sending "around the hat" in all our towns and cities for money to send colored men to Africa, will be to keep life and power in this narrow, bitter, and persecuting idea, that Africa, not America, is the Negro's true home. . . .

4. One of the chief considerations upon which the African Civilization Society is recommended to our favorable regard is its tendency to break up the slave trade. We have looked at this recommendation, and we find no reason to believe that any one man in Africa can do more for the abolition of that trade while living in Africa, than while living in America. If we cannot make Virginia, with all her enlightenment and Christianity, believe that there are better uses for her energies than employing them in breeding slaves for the market, we see not how we can expect to make Guinea, with its ignorance and savage selfishness, adopt our notions of political economy. Depend upon it, the savage chiefs on the western coast of Africa, who for ages have been accustomed to selling their captives into bondage, and pocketing the ready cash for them, will not more readily see and accept our moral and economical ideas, than the slave-traders of Maryland and Virginia. We are, therefore, less inclined to go to Africa to work against the slave-trade, than to stay here to work against it. . . .

5. There are slaves in the United States to the number of four million. They are stigmatized as an inferior race, fit only for slavery, incapable of improvement, and unable to take care of themselves. Now, it seems plain that here is the place, and we are the people to meet and put down these conclusions concerning our race. Certainly there is no place on the globe where the colored man can speak to a larger audience, either by precept or by example, than in the United States. . . .

7. We object to enrolling ourselves among the friends of that new Colonization scheme, because we believe that our people should be let

alone, and given a fair chance to work out their own destiny where they are. We are perpetually kept, with wandering eyes and open mouths, looking out for some mighty revolution in our affairs here, which is to remove us from this country. The consequence of this is, that we do not take a firm hold upon the advantages and opportunities about us. Permanent location is a mighty element of civilization. In a savage state men roam about, having no continued abiding place. They are "going, going, going." Towns and cities, houses and homes, are built by men who halt long enough to build them. There is a powerful motive for the cultivation of an honorable character, in the fact that we have a country, a neighborhood, a home. The full effect of this motive has not hitherto been experienced by our people. When in slavery, we were liable to perpetual sales, transfers, and removals; and now that we are free* we are doomed to be constantly harassed with schemes to get us out of the country. We are quite tired of all this, and wish no more of it. . . .

If colored men are convinced that they can better their condition by going to Africa, or anywhere else, we shall respect them if they will go, just as we respect others who have gone to California, Fraser Island, Oregon, and the West Indies. They are self-moved, self-sustained, and their success or failure is their own individual concern. But widely different is the case, when men combine, in societies, undertake titles, send out agents to collect money, and call upon us to help them travel from continent to continent to promote some selfish or benevolent end. In the one case, it is none of our business where our people go—they are of age and can act for themselves. But when they ask the public to go, or for money, sympathy, aid, or cooperation, or attempt to make it appear anybody's duty to go, the case ceases to be a private individual affair, and becomes a public question. . . .

* Both Douglass and Garnet were former slaves who had escaped to freedom in the North.

1903

He Would Not Africanize America

Many black Americans, including W. E. B. Du Bois, have looked with fascination and fondness upon the continent from which their ancestors came. Du Bois, born and reared in New England, was probably one of the best educated, most brilliant and active Negroes of his time (1868-1963). He was deeply affected by the racial prejudice he himself encountered; and he was equally concerned about what he felt were injustices to "native races of color" in Africa. Therefore, he joined with other thinkers and leaders of color at a world conference held in London in 1900. It was time, Du Bois said, for men of color around the world to speak out for justice with one voice.

As teacher, editor, author, and spokesman for American Negroes, Du Bois took an active part in African affairs. Many call him the "Father of Pan-Africanism." In 1962, Du Bois renounced his American citizenship and became a Ghanaian. He died in Ghana in 1963.

In the following excerpt from what is probably his most famous book, *The Souls of Black Folk,* Dr. Du Bois reveals his early views about the relationship of Africa and America.

Source: Du Bois, W. E. Burghardt. *The Souls of Black Folk: Essays and Sketches* (Eighth Edition). Chicago: A. C. McClurg and Company, 1909, pp. 3, 4, 11, 12, 13. Reprinted courtesy of Johnson Reprint Corporation, New York, New York.

Why did God make me an outcast and a stranger in mine own house? . . .

After the Egyptian and Indian, the Greek and Roman, the Teuton and Mongolian, the Negro is a sort of seventh son, born with a veil, and gifted with second-sight in this American world,—a world which yields him no true self-consciousness, but only lets him see himself through the revelation of the other world. It is a peculiar sensation, this double-consciousness, this sense of always looking at one's self through the eyes of others, of measuring one's soul by the tape of a world that looks on in amused contempt and pity. One ever feels his two-ness,—an American, a Negro; two souls, two thoughts, two unreconciled strivings; two warring ideals in one dark body, whose dogged strength alone keeps it from being torn asunder.

This history of the American Negro is the history of this strife,—this longing to attain self-conscious manhood, to merge his double self into a better and truer self. In this merging he wishes neither of the older selves to be lost. He would not Africanize America, for America has too much to teach the world and Africa. He would not bleach his Negro soul in a flood of white Americanism, for he knows that Negro blood has a message for the world. He simply wishes to make it possible for a man to be both a Negro and an American, without being cursed and spit upon by his fellows, without having the doors of Opportunity closed roughly in his face. . . .

The shadow of a mighty Negro past flits through the tale of Ethiopia the Shadowy and of Egypt the Sphinx. Throughout history, the powers of single black men flash here and there like falling stars, and die sometimes before the world has rightly gauged their brightness. . . .

We the darker ones come even now not altogether empty-handed: there are today no truer exponents of the pure human spirit of the Declaration of Independence than the American Negroes; there is no true American music but the wild sweet melodies of the Negro slave; the American fairy tales and folklore are Indian and African; and, all in all, we black men seem the sole oasis of simple faith and reverence in a dusty desert of dollars and smartness. . . .

The problem of the twentieth century is the problem of the color-line,—the relation of the darker to the lighter races of men in Asia and Africa, in America and the islands of the sea. . . .

early 1800's

Lepers or Men Returned from the Dead?

An examination of the narratives of early European explorers in Africa reveals that blacks were startled by their first encounter with whites. Their reactions to the pale-faced travelers were ones of shock, disbelief, incredulity, or even fear.

Galbraith Welch, author of the following sketch, has traveled extensively in Africa and has written several books about that continent. She has done much research into African folklore, mythology, and religion.

Source: Welch, Galbraith. *Africa Before They Came: The Continent, North, South, East, and West, Preceding the Colonial Powers.* New York: Reprinted by permission of William Morrow and Company. Copyright 1965 by Galbraith Welch, pp. 137-138.

White people were presumed to be lepers. And that, strangely, was not the worst of the notions. More disturbing was the thought that whites were returned spirits of the dead. . . . An early nineteenth century explorer, Major Gray, thrust out his hand in a friendly manner to an old, half-blind woman. When she saw that his hand was white, "shrieking, she fell to the ground."

Another old-time English traveler, Rankin, when in the back country of what is now Sierra Leone, lay resting under a tree. A child came with

14

her mother to examine him and, "discovering the monster, sprang upon her mother's back in an agony of fear and would not cease screaming." A medieval Moslem from Almeria, Spain, was shipwrecked on the African coast. The black people were astounded and "convinced that we had our bodies dyed white, [and] they scrubbed us with palm oil."

1970

Part of the Heritage of All Mankind

Ambassadors to the United States from the 34 African countries sponsored an historic diplomatic and artistic event. In February, 1970, the National Gallery of Art in Washington, D. C., opened the most extensive showing of the sculpture of Black Africa ever seen in the United States. Four galleries were cleared, and special platforms and islands were built to display masterpieces gathered from all parts of the African continent. Here is one art critic's judgment of the importance of that historic showing of Black African sculpture.

Source: "African Images, Powers, and Presences," *Time,* February 2, 1970, p. 34. Reprinted by permission from TIME, The Weekly Newsmagazine; Copyright Time Inc. 1970.

The show makes clear what many people overlook—that Black Africa developed highly organized cultures and a sophisticated naturalistic era long before the Europeans arrived. A few works survive from this era, among them the superb bronze head of a queen mother from 16th century Benin, whose kings ruled a large area of what is now southern Nigeria. There is also the portrait statue of King Bom Bosh, ruler of the Congolese kingdom of the Bakuba about 1650-1660. Most impressive of all is the famous Tada bronze from Nigeria, a relatively small (20 inches high) but monumental work that has never before been shown outside Nigeria. . . . African scholars consider it the finest surviving example of the Yoruba court art that flourished at the religious center of Ife 1000 years ago, when Europe was still sunk in the darkness of the Middle Ages.

The court art of Ife and Benin demonstrates that the ancient Africans could achieve a naturalism comparable to that of Egypt, Greece, and Renaissance Italy. But Africa's unique contribution to world art is the violently expressionistic wooden sculpture and highly stylized

15

masks of tribal art—the art that impressed and excited Picasso and Matisse and strongly deflected the course of modern art. Oddly enough, this tribal art owes much of its vitality to the wood-eating white ant of Africa. Because of its depredations [attacks]—and some help from natural decay—each generation of carvers had to create new images and new variations on traditional forms, constantly revitalizing an image that was lodged in the tribe's consciousness.

The bold dramatic carving of these masks, their extraordinary variety of styles, and their mysterious and (to uninitiated outsiders) inscrutable expressions, set them apart from anything in the traditional arts of Europe, China, or India. Even in the cloistered atmosphere of the museum, they have an inexplicable power, and when they are seen as they are meant to be seen, flashing in the sunlight, tossing, swaying and jerking with the motions of the dancers who wear them, they truly embody the presence of the sacred.

Though sometimes used in playful dances, these ritual masks are directed toward a world of spirits. Their closest Western equivalents are the miracle-working statues of Christian saints, holy objects that have supernatural powers. When the African dons a mask, he ceases to be himself and becomes the god or the force he seeks to please. "So powerful are the masks believed to be," says Keeper Fagg [an African scholar, William Fagg, Keeper of Ethnography at the British Museum], "that special precautions are taken in handling them. Many Africans believe the mere sight of one can make a woman sterile—just like radio-activity."

These deep religious roots account for the extraordinarily varied styles of African art. In Christian Europe, explains Fagg, one religion meant one style of art with comparatively minor local variations. In Africa, however, each tribe had its own gods, and consequently each had its own style of art. . . .

The show will move on to the William Rockhill Nelson Gallery of Art in Kansas City and later to the Brooklyn Museum. In a time when black pride is asserting itself, it will open many eyes. As National Gallery Director J. Carter Brown observes in his catalogue Foreword: "We are what we have been. The great images of Africa's tribal past speak to us as part of the heritage of all mankind."

Section Two

The Slave Trade

"Black Mother" Solves the Labor Shortage

Once European explorers discovered the Americas, the demands for labor grew with frantic speed. Laborers were needed, particularly in the West Indies and in the mines of Central America. At first, the European conquerors tried to enslave the natives, the "Indians" of the Americas. However, there were not enough Indians to meet their demands for labor. Furthermore, when exposed to new "white man's diseases," Indians died off in alarming proportions. So, Europeans turned to their own continent and began to ship "indentured servants" or near-slaves from home, but the supply was insufficient. At this point, the white men turned to Africa, the "Black Mother." There they found an abundant supply of workers. At last, Europeans believed they had solved their problems.

A respected authority on African history, Basil Davidson, explains the search for cheap, abundant labor as follows.

Source: Davidson, Basil. *Black Mother: The Years of the African Slave Trade.* Boston: Atlantic-Little, Brown and Company, 1961, pp. 45-48 *passim.* Reprinted by permission of Atlantic-Little, Brown and Company.

By as early as 1501, only nine years after the first voyage of Columbus, the Spanish throne had issued its initial proclamation on laws for the export of slaves to America—mainly, as yet, to Hispaniola (Haiti and the Dominican Republic today). These slaves were white—whether from Spain or North Africa—more often than black; for the black slaves it was early found, were turbulent and hard to tame. How poorly grounded in fact was the old legend of "African docility" may be seen

17

from the events of 1502. In that year the Spanish governor of Hispaniola, Ovando, complained to the Spanish Court that fugitive Negro slaves among the Indians were teaching disobedience, and that it was impossible to recapture them. Ovando asked for an end to the export of Negro slaves, and Queen Isabella consented. She seems to have decided to allow the export to the Indies only of white slaves, although her motive was no doubt different from Ovando's: she hoped that Christian slaves would help in the work of converting the heathen, [Indians], not knowing, of course, that most of the heathen would soon be dead.

Export of Christian slaves continued, though in small numbers, until the end of the seventeenth century; generally they were women. . . .

The trade in Negro captives became important as early as 1510. Before that, there had been sporadic shipments whenever the need for labor was especially acute. Ovando, in Hispaniola, had soon been forced to change his mind about suppression of the Negro trade; already in 1505, thirteen years after Columbus had made his crossing, the Spanish archives mention a caravel sailing from Seville with 17 Negro slaves and some mining equipment. Soon Ovando was asking for many more Negro workers. And in 1510 there came the beginning of the African slave trade in its massive and special form; royal orders were given for the transport first of fifty and then of two hundred slaves for *sale* in the Indies. . . .

This the Negro slaves resisted. They escaped when they could. They rose in bloody rebellion. They fought for their lives. The first notable slave revolt in Hispaniola broke out as early as 1522. Five years later there was another in Puerto Rico. A third at Santa Marta in 1529. A fourth in Panama in 1531. By 1532, the Spanish had established a special police for chasing fugitive slaves.

Yet nothing could stop the trade. There was too much money in it for the courts of Europe. . . . After 1518 the trade became increasingly an institution, a part of the Spanish economy, an absolutely essential aspect of the whole Spanish-American adventure.

1736

"Our Case Is Desprit"

Slaver Captain John Griffen sailed from Newport, Rhode Island, with a load of rum on board. He had hoped that his voyage to Africa would be short and profitable. However, nothing went well for the veteran slaver. At one port he encountered great competition with "seven sails of us Rum men" and at another nineteen sails. Time dragged on for him and his men as they languished in an unhealthy, unattractive port waiting to fill their hold with slaves. In this letter to his employer, John Griffen admits that "our case is Desprit."

Source: Spears, John Randolph. *The American Slave-Trade: An Account of Its Origin, Growth, and Suppression.* New York: Charles Scribner's Sons. 1900, pp. 31, 32.

Anamaboe, October 27th, 1736

Sir: After my Respect to you, these may Inform how it is with me at pres'nt. I bless God I Injoy my health very well as yett, but am like to have a long and trublesum voyage of it, for there never was so much Rum on the Coast at one time before. Nor ye like of ye french ships was never seen before, for ye whole Coast is full of them. for my part I can give no guess when I shall get away, for I purchest but 27 slaves since I have been here, for slaves is very scarce: we have had nineteen sails of us at one time in ye Rhoad [port], so that those ships that used to carry pryme slaves off is now forsed to take any that comes: here is 7 sails of us Rum men that we are ready to devour one another, for our Case is Desprit. Sir, I beg that you will exist my famely in what they shall want, for I no not when I shall get home to them myself. I have had the misfortin to Bury my chefe mate on ye 21st of Sept. and one man more, and Lost the negro man Prymus and Adam over board on my pasedge, one three weeks after another; that makes me now very weke handed for out of what it left thair is two that is good for nothing. Capt. Hamond has bin heare six months and has but 60 slaves on bord. My hearty servis to your spouse and famely. I am y'rs to com'd.

John Griffen

Slaves for Hire—Not for Sale

In colonial newspapers, owners frequently advertised their skilled slaves for hire by the month, quarter, or year. Dr. Marcus Wilson Jernegan, an authority on colonial America, examined the files of the South Carolina *Gazette* from 1732-1776 and found at least 28 different trades for which slaves could be hired. In the following passage, Dr. Jernegan explains why owners offered to "rent" their slaves to each other and why skilled whites sometimes objected to the economic competition of these black craftsmen.

Source: Jernegan, Marcus Wilson. *Laboring and Dependent Classes In Colonial America, 1607-1783: Studies of the Economic, Educational and Social Significance of Slaves, Servants, Apprentices, and Poor Folk.* Chicago, Illinois: The University of Chicago Press. 1931, pp. 16, 20, 21.

The practice of hiring out skilled workers must have been profitable, judging from the frequency of such advertisements. If such a man could be hired out, so that the cost of his upkeep would be met by the person who employed him, and a sum of money—say ten pounds—be paid, besides, for his work for one year, that would be a very profitable investment.... We know that the practice was in existence from an early date. For example, a master offered to hire out a bricklayer and a plasterer, by the month, quarter, or more or less time, in town or country. Another offered a negro blacksmith by the month or year....

...In South Carolina both free white laborers and the general assembly were greatly disturbed at the rapid development of the number of negro artisans, and respected their skill to the extent at least that they made vigorous complaint of the competition between white and slave artisans. For example, the South Carolina *Commons Journal* of 1744 contains an interesting petition of one Andrew Ruck, a shipwright, on behalf of himself and several other shipwrights. He complains that negro slaves worked in Charleston and other places near the same town, at the shipwright's trade, and were "chiefly employed in mending, repairing, and caulking of ships, other vessels and boats"; that, as a result, white shipwrights could meet with little or no work, were reduced to poverty, and would be obliged to leave the province if not relieved; that such a practice would discourage white shipwrights from settling in the province; and, therefore, the petitioners asked that relief be granted by the assembly. This petition was referred to a committee who reported that five other ship carpenters had sent in a petition denouncing Andrew Ruck. . . declaring that there was no lack of work; that because of scarcity of white shipwrights slaves had to do the work. . . .

A report of another committee in 1744, appointed to suggest effectual measures for increasing the number of white persons in the province, complained that one hindrance to such increase was that "a great number of negroes are brought up to and daily employed in Mechanic Trades both in Town and Country," and proposed that the negro act be amended by introducing a clause to prohibit "the bringing up of Negroes and other Slaves to Mechanic Trades in which white persons are usually employed." But the interest of many persons who were profiting from this practice prevented the passage of such a bill. . . .

1750's

The Journal of a Slave Trader

John Newton, an English sea captain, commanded slave ships when he was a young man in the 1750's. In his later life, however, he became a preacher and worked hard to abolish the slave trade. He wrote abolitionist pamphlets warning his readers that slavery was as damaging to the moral fiber of those who allowed it as it was to slaves themselves. Newton was a major influence on William Wilberforce, who became Britain's most outspoken fighter for the abolition of slavery. Wilberforce University in Ohio was named in his honor.

In the passage that follows, John Newton describes a day in the lives of captives aboard his slave ship. It was written during the time that Newton was active in the slave trade.

Source: Newton, John. *The Journal of a Slave Trader, 1750-1754.* London: Epworth Press, 1962, p. 103.

Usually, about two-thirds of a cargo of slaves are males. When a hundred and fifty or two hundred stout men, torn from their native land, many of whom never saw the sea, much less a ship, till a short space before they had embarked; who have, probably, the same natural prejudice against a white man, as we have against a black; and who often bring with them an apprehension they are bought to be eaten: I say, when thus circumstanced, it is not to be expected that they will tamely resign themselves to their situation. It is always taken for granted, that they will attempt to gain their liberty if possible. Accordingly, as we dare not trust them, we receive them on board, from the first as enemies; and, before their number exceeds, perhaps, ten or fifteen, they are all put in irons; in most ships, two and two together. And frequently, they are not thus confined, as they might most conveniently stand or move, the right hand and foot of one to the left of the other, but across; that is; the hand and foot of each on the same side, whether right or left, are fettered together: so that they cannot move either hand or foot, but with great caution, and with perfect consent. Thus they must sit, walk, and lie, for many months (sometimes for nine or ten), without any mitigation or relief, unless they are sick.

In the night, they are confined below; in the daytime (if the weather be fine) they are upon deck; and as they are brought by pairs, a chain is put through a ring upon their irons, and this likewise locked down to the ring-bolts, which are fastened, at certain intervals, upon the deck. These, and other precautions, are no more than necessary; especially as while the number of slaves increases, that of the people who are to guard them, is diminished, by sickness, or death, or by being absent in the boats; so that, sometimes, not ten men can be mustered, to watch, night and day, over two hundred, besides having all the other business of the ship to attend.

That these precautions are so often effectual, is much more to be wondered at, than that they sometimes fail. One unguarded hour, or minute, is sufficient to give the slaves the opportunity they are always waiting for. An attempt to rise upon the ship's company, brings on instantaneous and horrid war: for when they are once in motion, they are desperate; and where they do not conquer, they are seldom quelled without much mischief and bloodshed on both sides.

A Slaver Returns to America

Joseph Hawkins, the young man blinded on his first voyage to Africa on a slave ship, wrote of his meeting with the King of the Ebos which appears in Section I.

Another of his adventures from his book deals with his own reactions to the African slave trade as he saw it. Joining a slaver with dreams of getting rich quick, Hawkins was shocked by the buying and selling of black men and, according to his account, tried to escape in Africa rather than make the return voyage to America. However, his Captain found him, and Hawkins was forced to fulfill his contract. In the following excerpt from his autobiography, he tells how slaves were herded into ships and of the horrible return trip.

Source: Hawkins, Joseph. *A History of a Voyage to the Coast of Africa and Travels into the Interior of That Country; Containing Particular Descriptions of the Climate and Inhabitants, and Interesting Particulars Concerning the Slave Trade* (second edition). Troy, New York: Luther Pratt, 1797, pp. 140-142, 174, 176, 177, 179 *passim.*

. . . The slaves that I had purchased were young men, many of whom being eager to escape from their bondage in Ebo [an African country], preferred the evil that they "knew not of" to that which they then felt; but the majority were evidently affected with grief at the approaching departure.

Arrangements were made, and a sufficient body of the Ebo people undertook to accompany me as a guard to the place of embarkation; provisions were provided for the journey, so that each of the slaves was well fed, and a load of provisions or goods given him to carry. They were tied to poles in rows, four feet apart; a loose wicker bandage round the neck of each, connected him to the pole, and the arms being pinioned by a bandage affixed behind above the elbows. They had sufficient room to feed but not to loose themselves or commit any violence; and as a guard was provided with arms, we had nothing to apprehend [fear] during the night. . . .

We set out from the city about five o'clock in the morning. . . . I took my leave [of the Ebo King with whom Hawkins had become friendly] with evident marks of regret. . . . My wives [Ebo women given to him by the King] accompanied me.

This journey was extremely different in its nature from that in which I had last past this way; the dizzy pranks of the vain or the inebriated Ebo woefully contrasted by the sullen melancholy and the deep sighs of the poor Galla prisoners; often did they look back with eyes flowing with tears, turn sudden round and gaze, seeming to part with reluctance, even from their former bondage. It was excessively affecting to me, but I considered that death might have been their fate otherwise, and I endeavoured to reconcile them to their condition, by representing flattering accounts of the country to which they were going; that the bonds they then bore were only to prevent their flight; that they should be at liberty where they were going, and have plenty to eat, drink, etc. These assurances occasioned a temporary composure, and we at length arrived at the place of our embarkation; two boats had been brought up, as the shallop [a small ship, usually with two masts] drew too much water; the slaves were put on board, and necessarily in irons brought for the purpose. The measure occasioned one of the most affecting scenes I ever witnessed. Their hopes with my assurances had buoyed them up on the road; but a change from the cordage to iron fetters rent their hopes and hearts together; their wailings were torturing beyond what words can express; but delays at this crisis would have been fatal; the boat's crews were acquainted with the duty, and they were all safely embarked. . . .

The whole number of slaves that we had now on board, I found about 500, of whom above 50 were then lying in a dangerous state of illness; it was time for us to depart being now the 13th of June, 1795. . . .

We cleared the Capes without any further event worthy of notice, on the 17th of June. . . . From thence to the 27th there was little to note, but the ordinary variations of wind and weather, except the increased severity of the disorder that raged on board. It was an inflammatory fever, attended by symptoms of dysentery in some, but mostly with a violent inflammation and swelling of the eyes and eyelids. . . . The slaves were almost uniformly afflicted with this disorder in the eyes, even more than had been seized with the dysentery. Both diseases soon communicated to the crew and the 30th of June, we had scarcely men enough to work the ship.

Hitherto by exercise and open air, by keeping constantly on deck, refraining as much from salt food as possible and by frequent bathing on board, I had kept myself in perfect health, though in constant terror from the frequent deaths of the slaves, and the sickness of the crew round me.

On the 1st of July, I found my precautions had not availed, and the goodness of my constitution not sufficient to support me against the prevailing disease any longer. The fever attacked me, and my eyes swelled to such a degree that I could scarcely open them. . . . The light of the sun became to my eyes as indistinct and dark as the gloom of death; the beauties of nature to me were "blotted out forever" and in my 23rd year, when I looked forward to days of ease and comfort from the resources of my activity and industry—my path is shut up and the world become a blank of indistinctness and uncertainty.

1830-1850

For African Unbelievers—Slavery

For twenty years Captain Canot, a native of Italy who moved to Massachusetts, was an African slaver. After his "downfall," Canot tried "to mend his fortune by honorable industry in South America."

Many persons acquainted with Africa talked with Canot. Among those persons was a man named Brantz Mayer who finally was convinced that "setting aside his [Canot's] career as a slaver . . . he was a man of unquestioned integrity." Therefore, in 1854, Mayer edited Captain Canot's journals, memoranda, and conversations. Today those records provide an interesting account of how the slave trade was carried on in Africa.

While in Africa, Canot became the friend of Ahmah-De-Bellah, son of a noted Fullah chief. Nightly Canot visited in Ahmah-De-Bellah's home and pretended to be interested in becoming a "Mohametan." When the Fullah prince was sure that he had converted Canot to Islam, the two concluded a mutually profitable business deal. In this excerpt, Captain Canot recalls the reasons the "negro prince" set forth to excuse his own participation in the slave trade.

Source: *Captain Canot: Or Twenty Years Of An African Slaver; Being an Account of His Career and Adventures on the Coast, in the Interior, on Shipboard, and in the West Indies.* Written out and edited from Captain Canot's Journals, Memoranda, and Conversations by Brantz Mayer. New York: D. Appleton and Company, 1854.

While Ahmah-De-Bellah tarried at Bangalang, it was my habit to visit him every night to hear his interesting chat, as it was translated by an interpreter. Sometimes, in return, I would recount the adventure of my seafaring life. . . . Among other things, I strove to convince him of the world's rotundity [roundness] ; but to the last, he smiled incredulously at my daring assertion, and closed the argument by asking me to prove it from the Koran. He allowed me the honors due a traveller and "book-man". . . . He kindly undertook to conquer my ignorance of his creed by a careful exposition of its mysteries in several long-winded lectures, and I was so patient a listener that I believe Ahmah was entirely satisfied of my conversion. . . . He returned my nightly calls with interest; and visiting me in the warehouse during hours of business, became so fervently wrapped up in my spiritual salvation, that he would spout Mohametanism for hours through an interpreter. . . .

I learned from my intelligent Fullah, that while the Mohametan courts of his country rescued by law the people of their own faith from slavery, they omitted no occasion to inflict it, as a penalty, upon the African "unbelievers" who fell in their jurisdiction. Among these unfortunates, the smallest crime is considered capital, and a "capital crime" merits the profitable punishment of slavery. Nor was it difficult, he told me, for a country of "true believers" to acquire a multitude of bondsmen. They detested the institution, it is true, among themselves, and among their own caste, but it was both right and reputable among the unorthodox. The Koran commanded the "subjugation of the tribes to the true faith". . . . My inquisitiveness prompted me to demand whether these holy wars spoken of in the Koran were not somewhat stimulated, in our time, at least, by the profits that ensued; and I even ventured to hint that it was questionable whether the mighty chief Footha-Yallon would willingly storm a Kaffir fortification, were he not prompted by the booty of slaves!

Ahmah-De-Bella was silent for a minute, when his solemn face gradually relaxed into a quizzical smile, as he replied in truth, Mohametans were no worse than Christians . . . who knew how to make powder and guns. . . . The commands of Allah would be followed with less zeal and implements not quite so dangerous!

I could not help thinking that there was a good deal of quiet satire in the gossip of this negro prince. According to the custom of his country, we "exchanged names" at parting; and while he put in my pocket the gift of a well-thumbed *Koran,* I slung over his shoulder a double-barrelled gun. We walked side by side for some miles into the forest, as

26

he went forth from Bangalang; and as we "cracked fingers" for farewell, I promised, with my hand on my heart, that the "next dry season" I would visit his father, the venerable Ali-Mami, in his realm of Footha-Yallon.

1850's

"Good Men in Our Business Are Scarce"

Congress forbade the importation of slaves in 1808. However, men, lured by the prospects of huge profits, continued in the illegal traffic. One such man, a Captain James Smith, was finally apprehended and imprisoned in New York in the mid-1850's. The editor of The New York *Evangelist* interviewed the slaver in his prison cell and found Smith sincerely proud of his exploits. Here is what Captain Smith is reported to have told the editor.

Source: *The Suppressed Book About Slavery* (Anonymous). New York: George W. Carleton, Publisher, 1864, pp. 407-411 *passim.*

"New York," said Captain Smith, "is the chief port in the world for the Slave-Trade." He repeated two or three times, *"It is the greatest place in the universe for it. . . . "*

"But do you mean to say that this business is going on now?"

"Yes, all the while. . . ."

"Are there large shipping houses engaged in it?"

"Yes; I can go down to South Street, and go into a number of houses that help to fit out ships for the business. . . . They know me. They see me sail out of port with a ship and come back a passenger. They sometimes ask me, 'Captain, where is your ship?' (with a shrug). They know what has become of her."

"But how do you manage to get away without exciting suspicion?"

"Why, you see, we keep close, and get everything aboard, and do not ask for our out papers until we are just ready to sail. Then we go to the Custom-house, and take out papers for Rio de Janeiro, St. Helena, the Cape Verde Islands, or any port we please—it don't matter where—and instantly clear."

27

"But if you were seized at that moment, could the officers tell, by searching a ship, that she was a Slaver?"

"Oh, yes, they couldn't help knowing. Besides, they must suspect something from seeing such an almighty crew. My little brig carried but 200 tons, and could be manned by four men. But I had fourteen before the mast. The moment of leaving port is the one of danger. But we don't lose time. A steamer is kept ready, and we get away immediately...."

"But when you reach the African coast, are you not in great danger from British Ships-of-War?"

"Oh, no, we don't care a button for an English squadron. We run up the American flag, and if they come aboard, all we have to do is show our American papers, and they have no right to search us."

"That may be very well when you are going in empty. But suppose you are coming out with a cargo of Slaves on board?"

"Even then we can get along well enough, if the Niggers will keep quiet. We put them all below deck, and nail down the hatches, and then present our papers. The officers have no right to go below. The only danger in this case is that they will stay on board too long, and the Niggers begin to get smothered and make a noise."

"How many Slaves could you carry on your vessel?"

"We took on board 664. We might have stowed away 800.... The boys and women we kept on the upper deck. But all the strong men—those giant Africans that might make us trouble—we put below on the Slave deck."

"Did you chain them or put on handcuffs?"

"No never; they would die. We let them move about. We have to be pretty strict at first—for a week or so—to make them feel that we are masters. Then we lighten up for the rest of the voyage."

"How do you pack them at night?"

"They lie down upon the deck, on their sides, body to body. There would not be room enough for all to lie on their backs."

"Did many die on the passage?"

"Yes. I lost a good many the last cruise—more than ever before. Sometimes we find them dead when we go below in the morning. Then we throw them overboard."

"Are the profits of the trade large?"

"Yes, sir, very large. My brig cost $13,000 to fit her out completely. My last cargo to Cuba was worth $220,000...."

"Did you ever get chased by the English ships?"

"Yes; once a Man-of-War chased two of us. . . . It takes a man of a particular constitution to engage in our business. When once at sea with a Slave cargo, we are in free bottoms. We belong to no country. We are under the protection of no law. We must defend ourselves. A man must have a great deal of nerve in such a situation when he is liable to be chased by ships of war, or perhaps, finds himself suddenly in the midst of a whole fleet. The Mate once served me a trick for which I should have been perfectly justified in shooting him dead. We were running in between the islands of Martinique and Dominique, when suddenly there shot out from behind the land an English steamer. The Mate thought it was a Ship-of-War, and so did I. He was frightened and instantly turned the vessel off her course. This was the very movement to bring down the enemy in chase. I saw the danger and flew to the helm, and put her back again, and we passed by in safety."

"But are you not tired of this business?"

"Why, I didn't want to go out the last voyage. I tried to get another Captain to take charge of my ship. I wanted to stay at home and get married. But *good* men in our business are scarce. And I had to go."

1820's and 1830's

A Reduced Price for Those Who Run Away

Slave trading was a big business in the South until the Civil War. Traders, men who bought and sold slaves, were the middlemen of the internal slave trade. Often traders ran marketplaces where owners who wanted to sell slaves and prospective buyers gathered.

Advertising was important in the slave trader's business. With a large community circulation, the newspaper was the place to advertise needs and merchandise. Newspaper offices were often meeting places for traders and buyers and sellers of his "goods."

In general, traders were not respected as a class by slaveowning, landowning Southern gentlemen. But there were exceptions—some slave traders were of established, respected family lines and others were able to buy property and become planters

29

as well as traders. One such exception was Isaac Franklin, a trader in the New Orleans slave market. With wealth from the slave trade, he invested in land and slaves and moved in the society of the large property-owning class. In the quarter century after the War of 1812 Franklin built an estate valued at three quarters of a million dollars.

Franklin believed that advertising was important in making money. He used newspapers to inform communities of what he had to offer. Below is an advertisement and excerpts of records of Isaac Franklin.

Source: Stephenson, Wendell Homes. *Isaac Franklin, Slave Trader and Planter of the Old South with Plantation Records.* Louisiana State University Press, 1938, pp. 25, 80, 81.

This advertisement appeared in an Alexandria, Virginia, newspaper in May, 1828:

CASH IN MARKET

The subscribers having leased for a term of years the large three story brick house on Duke Street, in the town of Alexandria, D.C., formerly occupied by Gen. Young, we wish to purchase one hundred and fifty likely young negroes of both sexes between the ages of 8 and 25 years. Persons who wish to sell will do well to give us a call, as we are determined to give more than any other purchasers that are in the market, or that may hereafter come into market.

Slaves whose health was impaired, temporarily or permanently, were not warranted (guaranteed) and usually sold for less than the market value. Of ten slaves sold to Daniel Robert of Rapides Parish on March 10, 1829, William Tate "who being in bad health is not warranted against any malady, infirmity, or bodily defect" brought only about half as much as the others. The following year Franklin sold to Abner Robinson of Richmond, Virginia, three slaves who shared the name John, whose ages were 22, 24, and 32, and who brought respectively $400, $100, and $300. The three were "free from all incumbrance: but not warranted against any vice, malady or defect whatsoever, they being now sick and afflicted, and the purchaser hereby declared that he takes them as they are without any resource . . . except for validity of title."

Absconding was a habit which if known reduced the price of a slave. Among three negroes sold to William Dark of Rapides Parish on May

13, 1831, was Nancy Dines, age not recorded. She was "not warranted against any vice whatsoever, she being subject to running away, therefore health and title only guaranteed." On February 21, 1834, Peter Petrovie of Natchitoches purchased 12 slaves ranging in age from 11 to 21, all of whom were warranted free from vices save running away. A few weeks later, Franklin sold to Hudson and Kimball 10 slaves, males and females, aged 14 to 25, all "warranted against Vices and maladies prescribed by law, save and except the vice of running away. . . ."

1850's

John Lynch's Slave-Dealing Establishment

Thomas Wentworth Higginson fought against slavery with both words and deeds. He was a descendant of the Puritans, and his grandfather, Stephen Higginson, was a member of the Continental Congress of 1783.

Instead of becoming a merchant as his forebears were, Higginson chose to go to Harvard Divinity School. Soon he began to preach against slavery. He carried his antislavery crusade into politics, running unsuccessfully for Congress in 1850. He was also active in rescuing fugitive slaves. Later he went to Kansas as an agent of the National Kansas Committee. There he directed the activities of several hundred men who attempted to prevent by every means possible the extension of slavery into that territory.

When the Civil War broke out, Higginson became a Colonel, the white commander of the First South Carolina Volunteers, the 1st regiment of freed slaves to fight for the Union.

In this excerpt from his autobiography, Higginson describes the indelible impression made upon him by his first and only visit to a slave market in St. Louis, Missouri.

Source: Higginson, Thomas Wentworth. *Cheerful Yesterdays.* Boston and New York: Houghton Mifflin Company, 1898, pp. 235-236.

From the time of my Kansas visit I never had doubted that a farther conflict of some sort was impending. The absolute and increasing difference between the two sections of the nation had been most deeply impressed upon me by my first and only visit to a slave-mart. On one of my trips to St. Louis I had sought John Lynch's slave-dealing establishment, following an advertisement in a newspaper, and had found a yard full of men and women strolling listlessly about and waiting to be sold. The proprietor, looking like a slovenly horse-dealer, readily explained to me their condition and value. Presently a planter came in, having been sent on an errand to buy a little girl to wait on his wife; stating this as easily and naturally as if he had been sent for a skein of yarn. Mr. Lynch called in three sisters, the oldest perhaps eleven or twelve,— nice little mulatto girls in neat pink calico frocks suggesting a careful mother. Some question being asked, Mr. Lynch responded cheerfully, "Strip her and examine for yourself. I never have any secrets from my customers." This ceremony being waived, the eldest was chosen; and the planter, patting her on the head kindly enough, asked, "Don't you want to go with me?" when the child, bursting into a flood of tears, said, "I want to stay with my mother." Mr. Lynch's face ceased to be good-natured when he ordered the children to go out, but the bargain was finally completed. It was an epitome of slavery; the perfectly matter-of-fact character of the transaction, and the circumstance that those before me did not seem exceptionally cruel men, made the whole thing more terrible. I was beholding a case, not of special outrage, but of every-day business, which was worse. If these were the commonplaces of the institution, what must its exceptional tragedies be?

1854

"I Want You to Buy Me"

During the year 1854, the Reverend Nehemiah Adams of Boston spent three months in the South. He went there to improve his health and to find out for himself what the conditions of slavery actually were.

As a result of his stay in the South, Adams wrote a book as a "Christian . . . a lover and friend of the colored race." At the time of his visit so much was being said and written that it was hard to know what was happening. Therefore, Adams said his book contained the kind of statements he would like to have received from a friend whom he might ask, "What am I to believe? How am I to act and feel?"

Here is Dr. Adams' version of "the truth" regarding slave auctions.

Source: Adams, Nehemiah, D. D. *A South Side View of Slavery; or Three Months at the South in 1854.* (Boston: T. R. Marvin and B. B. Musey and Co., 1854), pp. 72-73.

... At home and at the south advertisements in southern papers of negroes for sale at auction, describing them minutely, have often harrowed our feelings. The minute description, they say, is, or may be, a legal defence in the way of proof and identification.

However trying a public sale may be to the feelings of the slave, they say that it is for his interest that the sale should be public.

The sale of slaves at auction in places where they are known—and this is the case everywhere except in the largest cities—excites deep interest in some of the citizens of that place. They are drawn to the sale with feeling of personal regard for the slaves, and are vigilant to prevent unprincipled persons from purchasing and carrying them away, and even from possessing them in their own neighborhood. I know of citizens combining to prevent such men from buying, and of their contributing to assist good men and women in purchasing the servants at prices greatly increased by public competition. In all such cases the law requiring and regulating public sales and advertisements of sales prevents those private transfers which would defeat the good intentions of benevolent men. It is an extremely rare case for a servant or servants who have been known in town to be removed into hands which the people of the place generally would not approve.

The sale of a negro at public auction is not a reckless, unfeeling thing in the towns at the south, where the subjects of the sale are from among themselves. In settling estates, good men exercise as much care with regard to the disposition of the slaves as though they were providing homes for white orphan children. ...

Slaves are allowed to find masters and mistresses who will buy them. Having found them, the sheriffs' and administrators' sales must by law be made public, the persons must be advertised, and everything looks like an unrestricted offer, while it is the understanding of the company that the sale has really been made in private.

Sitting in the reading-room of a hotel one morning, I saw a colored woman enter and curtsy to a gentleman opposite.

"Good morning, sir. Please, sir, how is Ben?"

"Ben—he is very well. But I don't know you."

"Ben is my husband. I heard you were in town, and I want you to buy me. My mistress is dead these three weeks, and the family is broken up."

"Well, I will buy you. Where shall I inquire?"

All this was said and done in as short a time as it takes to read it; but this woman was probably obliged by law, in the settlement of the estate, to be advertised and described.

1857

The Slave Trader an Abolitionist?

Could a slave-trader, of all people, really be an abolitionist? Here is how James Stirling, an Englishman who travelled extensively in the South, explains his statement that slave dealers were working for black freedom without realizing it.

Source: Stirling, James. *Letters from the Slave States.* London: John W. Parker & Son, 1857, pp. 298-299.

Then there is another and no less powerful Abolitionist agent constantly at work—the slave-dealer. Through his means a constant stream of Northern intelligence is spread over every plantation of the South. The most intelligent slaves are, as a rule, the most insubordinate, and these it is whom the trader purchases in the North and sells in the South. Every such slave thus bought and sold is an emissary of Abolitionism, more powerful, more subtle, and more sure of opportunities, than any whom the most rabid Abolition Society could employ. If, as is frequently the case, he can read, then he is the organ of information for the whole plantation. It needs but little of such leaven to leaven the whole mass with insubordinate and violent thoughts. Thus, by a striking retribution, the passions of men are made to recoil upon themselves: the slave-owner is made the chief of Abolitionists, and the slave-trader becomes the arch incendiary.

The danger from the insubordination of the slave population seems to me a serious and growing evil. Slave-owners, in general, affect to make light of it; but the intense eagerness with which they deny all evidences of insubordination, and the severity with which they punish supposed incendiaries, prove that a vast amount of distrust and fear lurks under their bravado. The insurrectionary movement in the Slave States during the autumn of 1856, though not formidable in itself, was alarming from the extent to which it spread, from the power of organization it evinced, and above all from the amount of disaffection it implied. The alarm in Tennessee during my visit in the beginning of December was great. At Clarksville eight or ten negroes were hanged by a Vigilance Committee, aided by impromptu Lynching by an infuriated mob. That matters were not much better in the neighbouring State of Kentucky will appear by the following: *"The Negro Insurrection.* The ringleaders of the attempted negro insurrection at Hopkinsville, Kentucky, have been hung. A white man was discovered painted black, who had been in the neighbourhood several months, and had passed off as a negro. He was sentenced to receive nine hundred lashes; he died before the whole number was inflicted."

Section Three

Those Who Endured

February, 1644

An Act Freeing Slaves in New Netherlands

> Slaves in the New Netherlands were promised freedom in the future in exchange for service to the Dutch West India Company. But this oft-promised reward was slow to come.
>
> Finally the Africans petitioned the Director and Council of the colony. Their request for manumission [to be set free] resulted in passage of the Act which follows. This Act gave birth to a free Negro class in New York. Eventually it set the pattern for the emancipation of all slaves in that colony.
>
> After the insurrection of 1712, however, the Assembly of New York passed a new Negro Law which restricted manumissions, prohibited free Negroes from holding real estate, and increased the severity of living conditions of the enslaved.
>
> Source: Laws of New York, 1691-1773, as cited in Payne, Aaron Hamlet, "The Negro in New York Prior to 1860." *The Howard Review,* Howard University, Vol. I, No. 1 (June, 1923), pp. 726-727.

We, William Kieff and Council of New Netherlands, having considered the petition of the Negroes named Paul Angola, Big Manuel, Little Manuel, Manuel de Gerrit de Reus, Simon Congo, Antony Portugis, Gracia, Peter Santomee, Jan Francisco, Little Antony, Jan Fort Orange, who have served the Company 17 or 18 years, to be liberated from their Servitude, and set at liberty, especially as they have been in the service of the Honorable West India Company here, and have long since been promised their freedom; also that they are burthened [burdened] with many children so that it is impossible for them to support their wives and children, as they have been accustomed to do, if they must continue in the CompanY's service; Therefore, we the Director and Council do release for the term of their natural lives, the above named and their wives from Slavery, hereby setting them free and at liberty, on the same footing as other Free people here in New Netherlands, where they shall be able to earn their livelihood by Agriculture, on the land shown and granted to them, on the condition that they, the above named Negroes, shall be bound to pay for the freedom they receive, each man for himself annually, as long as he lives, to the West India Company or its Deputy here, thirty skepels [barn baskets-22½ bushels] of Maize or Wheat, Pease, or Beans, and one fat hog valued at twenty guilders [$8] which thirty skepels and the hog, they, the Negroes, each for himself, promises to pay annually, beginning from the date hereof, on pain, if any one of them shall fail to pay the yearly tribute, he shall forfeit his freedom and return back into the CompanY's slavery. With the express condition that their children at present born or yet to be born, shall be bound and obliged to serve the Hon'ble West India Company as Slaves. Likewise that the above mentioned men shall be obliged to serve the Hon'ble West India Company here, by water or on land, where their services are required, on receiving fair wages from the CompanY.

June 24, 1720

You Had Better Do Something About Your Slaves

Black men were rarely content to be enslaved, and American history is full of slave revolts and attempted insurrections. Fear of slave rebellions was common in Spanish, Dutch, and English colonies. However, it was not until the early 1700's that slave uprisings became frequent in the English colonies. Here is a report of a would-be rebellion that was put down in Charleston, South Carolina. The writer of the following letter advised some absentee slaveowners in London that their slaves needed "strict management lest they be successful the next time."

Source: Public Records of South Carolina, VIII, pp. 24-27, as quoted in Aptheker, Herbert. *American Negro Slave Revolts.* New York: Columbia University Press, 1943, p. 175.

I am now to acquaint you that very lately we have had a very wicked and barbarous plott of the designe of the negroes rising with a designe to destroy all the white people in the country and then to take the town [Charleston] in full body but it pleased God it was discovered and many of them taken prisoners and some burnt some hang'd and some banish'd.

I think it proper for you to tell Mr. Percivall at home that his slaves was the principal rogues and 'tis my opinion his only way will be to sell them out singly or else I am doubtful his interest in slaves will come to little for want of strict management. Work does not agree with them. 14 of them are now at the Savanna towne and sent for [by?] white and Indians and will be executed as soon as they come down. They thought to gett to [St.] Augustine and would have got a creek [Indian] fellow to have been their pylott but the Savanna garrison tooke the negroes up half starved and the Creeke Indians would not join them or be their pylott.

1740 and 1819

Lest They Learn to Read or Write

Laws in the slave states were designed to keep blacks in bondage—mental as well as physical. Here are two examples of laws forbidding anyone to teach slaves to read or write. The first was enacted in South Carolina in 1740; the second is taken from the revised code of Virginia of 1819.

Source: Barnes, Albert. *An Inquiry into the Scriptural Views of Slavery.* Philadelphia: Perkins and Purves, 1846, pp. 92, 93.

Whereas, the having of slaves taught to write, or suffering them to be employed in writing, may be attended with great inconveniences, Be it enacted, that all and every person and persons whatsoever, who shall hereafter teach or cause any slave or slaves to be taught to write, or shall use or employ any slave as a scribe in any manner of writing whatsoever, every such person or persons shall, for every offence, forfeit the sum of one hundred pounds of current money.

2 Brevard's Digest, 243.

All meetings or assemblages of slaves, or free negroes or mulattoes mixing and associating with such slaves at any meetinghouse, or houses, or any other place, &c., in the night, or at any school or schools for teaching them reading or writing either in the day or the night, under whatever pretext, shall be deemed and considered an unlawful assembly.

1 Rev. Code, 424, 425.

1773

Care of Aged Slaves

As long as slaves were young, strong, and healthy, they were profitable to their masters. However, when they became old or disabled, some masters simply turned them out, as the following Act passed on March 8, 1773, in the Legislature of the Colony of New York makes clear.

Source: Laws of New York, 1691-1773, as cited in Payne, Aaron Hamlet, "The Negro in New York Prior to 1860." *The Howard Review,* Howard University, Vol. I, No. 1 (June, 1923), p. 764.

AN ACT TO PREVENT AGED AND DECREPIT SLAVES FROM BECOMING BURTHENSOME WITHIN THE COLONY.

From and after the passing of this Act, if any Person or Persons within this colony shall knowingly and willingly suffer and permit his, her, or their Slave and Slaves to go about begging of others their Victuals, Cloathing, or other Necessaries, such Person or Persons being thereof Convicted before two Magistrates . . . shall forfeit for every such offence the sum of ten pounds.

circa 1776

Primus Hall and General Washington Share a Blanket

Five thousand Negroes, slave and free, fought for American independence in the Revolutionary War. Blacks were in the first battles at Lexington and Concord, and they were in the last battle at Yorktown.

Here is the story of one cold night when rank was forgotten, and two soldiers struggling in a common cause sought to keep comfortable.

39

Source: Child, L. Maria. *The Freedman's Book*. Boston: Fields, Osgood and Company, 1869, p. 31.

During the War of the Revolution, Primus Hall was the colored servant of Colonel Pickering, with whom General Washington often held long consultations. One night finding they must be engaged till late, he proposed to sleep in the Colonel's tent, provided there was a spare blanket and straw. Primus, who was always eager to oblige the Commander-in-Chief, said, "Plenty of straw and blankets."

When the long conference ended, the two officers lay down to rest on the beds he had prepared. When he saw they were asleep, he seated himself on a box, and leaning his head on his hand, tried to take as comfortable a nap as he could. General Washington woke in the night, and seeing him nodding there called out, "Primus." The servant started to his feet and exclaimed, "What do you wish for, General?"

"You told me you had plenty of straw and blankets," replied Washington, "But I see you are sitting up all night for the sake of giving me your bed."

"It is no matter about me," responded Primus.

"Yes, it is," replied General Washington. "If one of us must sit up, I will take my turn. But there is no need of that. The blanket is wide enough for two. Come and lie down with me."

Primus, who reverenced the Commander-in-Chief as he did no other mortal, protested against it. But Washington threw open the blanket and said, "Come and lie down, I tell you! There is room enough for both, and I insist upon it."

The tone was too resolute to admit of further parley, and the General and his colored friend slept comfortably under the same blanket till morning.

July 30, 1776

"Sheep Will Never Make Any Insurrections"

After independence was declared on July 4, 1776, Americans found themselves fighting for the right to exist in a new, free nation. They also began debating about the kind of government the nation should establish. Delegates to the Continental Congress, therefore, had to face the issue of slavery as they searched for ways of raising money and counting voters that would be acceptable to all the colonies, small and large, North and South.

Here is part of the official records of discussions and debates of the Continental Congress. Those delegates participating were: Samuel Chase of Maryland, Thomas Lynch and Edward Rutledge of South Carolina, William Hooper of North Carolina, James Wilson and Benjamin Franklin of Pennsylvania.

Dr. Benjamin Franklin was a well-known foe of slavery. He fought against its continuation in the Continental Congresses and in the Constitutional Convention. In 1790 he asked the First Congress of the United States to abolish slavery.

Source: *Journals of the United States Continental Congress, 1774-1789.* (Edited from the Original Records in the Library of Congress by Worthington Chauncey Ford, Chief, Division of Manuscripts.) Washington, D. C.: Government Printing Office, 1909. Vol. VI (October 9-December 31, 1776), pp. 1079-1081.

July 30, 1776

Article 17. "In determining questions, each Colony shall have one vote."

Dr. Franklin: Let the smaller Colonies give equal money and men, and then have an equal vote. But if they have an equal vote without bearing equal burdens, a confederation upon such iniquitous [vicious] principles will never last long.

Wilson: We should settle upon some plan of representation.

Chase: . . . The negroes are wealth. Numbers are not a certain rule of wealth. It is the best rule we can lay down. Negroes are a species of property, personal estate. If negroes are taken into the computation of numbers to ascertain wealth, they ought to be [counted] in settling the representation. The Massachusetts fisheries, and navigation, ought to be taken into consideration. The young and old negroes are a burden to their owners. The eastern Colonies have a great advantage in trade. This will give them a superiority. We shall be governed by our interests, and ought to be. If I am satisfied in the rule of levying and appropriating money, I am willing the small Colonies should have a vote.

Wilson: If the war continues two years, each soul will have forty dollars to pay of the public debt. It will be the greatest encouragement to continue slavekeeping, and to increase it, that can be, to exempt them from the numbers which are to vote and pay. Slaves are taxables in the Southern Colonies. It will be partial and unequal. Some Colonies have as many black as white; these will not pay more than half what they ought. Slaves prevent freemen from cultivating a country.

Lynch: If it is debated, whether their slaves are their property, there is an end of the confederation. Our slaves being our property, why should they be taxed more than the land, sheep, cattle, horses, &c?

Freemen cannot be got to work in our Colonies; it is not in the ability or inclination of freemen to do the work that the negroes do. Carolina has taxed their negroes; so have other Colonies in their lands.

Dr. Franklin: Slaves rather weaken than strengthen the State, and there is therefore some difference between them and sheep; sheep will never make any insurrections.

Rutledge: I shall be happy to get rid of the idea of slavery. The slaves do not signify property; the old and young cannot work. The property of some Colonies is to be taxed, in others, not. The Eastern Colonies will become the carriers for the Southern; they will obtain wealth for which they will not be taxed.

August 1, 1776

Hooper: North Carolina is a striking exception to the general rule that was laid down yesterday, that the riches of a country are in proportion to the numbers of inhabitants. A gentleman of three or four hundred negroes don't raise more corn than feeds them. A laborer can't be hired for less than twenty-four pounds a year in Massachusetts Bay. The net profit of a negro is not more than five or six pounds per annum. I wish to see the day that slaves are not necessary. Whites and negroes cannot work together. Negroes are goods and chattels, are property. A negro works under the impulse of fear, has no care of his master's interest.

1779

"Every Negro . . . Shall Be Emancipated and Receive Fifty Dollars"

During the American Revolution, South Carolina and Georgia asked the Continental Congress for special consideration. Worried about "the desertion or insurrection" of their black slave population, representatives of those states asked to be excused from providing more troops. They also requested that some of their men then serving in the Continental Army be allowed to return home.

A committee was appointed by the Continental Congress to study their request. The committee reported that "the circumstances of the army will not admit of the detaching of any force for the defence of South Carolina and Georgia." However, because "the negro problem" along with the necessity of providing soldiers for the Continental Army "may involve inconveniences peculiarly affecting the States of South Carolina and Georgia," the Committee recommended that the United States government should at least help defray the expenses of raising troops. Accordingly, the Continental Congress adopted the following resolutions.

Source: *Secret Journals of the Acts and Proceedings of Congress From the First Meeting Thereof to the Dissolution of the Confederation.* By the Adoption of the Constitution of the United States. Published under the direction of the President of the United States, conforming to Resolutions of Congress of March 27, 1818 and of April 21, 1820. Boston: Thomas B. Wait. Vol. I, pp. 109, 110.

Resolved, That it be recommended to the states of South Carolina and Georgia, if they shall think the same expedient, to take measures immediately for raising three thousand able-bodied negroes.

That the said negroes be formed into separate corps, as battalions, according to the arrangements adopted for the main army, to be commanded by white commissioned and non-commissioned officers . . . and to appoint such . . . officers to command the said negroes as shall choose to go into that service.

Resolved, that Congress will make provision for paying the proprietors of such negroes as shall be enlisted for the service of the United States during the war, a full compensation for the property, at a rate not exceeding one thousand dollars for each active able-bodied negro man of standard size, not exceeding 35 years of age, who shall be so enlisted and pass muster.

That no pay or bounty be allowed to the said negroes; but that they be clothed and subsisted at the expense of the United States.

That every negro who shall well and faithfully serve as a soldier to the end of the present war, and shall then return his arms, be emancipated and receive the sum of fifty dollars.

1792 and later

Lest They Learn Their Numbers and Strength

If slaves were to learn their own numbers, they might seek strength in those numbers and unite to demand freedom. That was the reasoning and fear which prompted many slave states to pass laws that forbade all gatherings of blacks—even meetings of worship. The first law restricting assembly was enacted by Georgia in 1792. Later South Carolina, Virginia, Mississippi, and Missouri enacted similar laws.

Source: Barnes, Albert. *An Inquiry into the Scriptural Views of Slavery*. Philadelphia: Perkins and Purves, 1846, pp. 93-94.

No congregation or company of negroes shall, under pretence of divine worship, assemble themselves contrary to the act regulating patrols.

Prince's Digest, 342

No meeting whatever of slaves is to be allowed of such a number as could acquaint themselves of their own strength, or make combination possible. If a slave shall presume to come upon the plantation of any person, without leave in writing from his master, employer, &c., not being sent on lawful business, the owner of the plantation may inflict ten lashes for every such offence.

1 Virginia Rev. Code, 422; 3 Mississippi Rev. Code, 371;
2 Litt. and Swi. Digest, 1150; 2 Missouri Laws, 741.

It shall be lawful for any person who shall see more than seven men slaves, without some white person with them, travelling or assembled together, in any high road, to apprehend such slaves, and to inflict a whipping on such of them, not exceeding twenty lashes apiece.

2 Brevard's Digest, 243; Prince's Digest, 554

For keeping or carrying a gun, or powder, or shot, or a club, or other weapon whatever, offensive or defensive, a slave incurs for each offence, thirty-nine lashes, by order of a justice of the peace.

2 Litt. and Swi. Digest, 1150;
1 Virginia Rev. Code, 423;
2 Missouri Laws, 741; Haywood's Manual, 521.

I Learn I Am a Slave

How did children learn they were slaves? Most black young-sters became aware of their bondage very early in life, but Linda Brent did not. Her able and understanding family was able to shield her from that painful knowledge until her mother died. Then her "kind mistress" cushioned the shock of slavery for another six years. Linda firmly believed that when her good mistress died, she would be set free by the terms of her owner's will. Such was not the case, however. In this excerpt from her autobiography written long after she had escaped from slavery, Linda Brent laments her mistress' "one great wrong."

Source: Jacobs, Harriet (Linda) Brent. *Incidents in the Life of a Slave Girl Written By Herself.* (Edited by L. Maria Child.) Boston: 1861, pp. 11-16.

I was born a slave; but I never knew it till six years of happy childhood had passed away. My father was a carpenter, and considered so intelligent and skillful in his trade, that when buildings out of the common line were to be erected, he was sent for from long distances, to be head workman. On condition of paying his [owner] two hundred dollars a year, and supporting himself, he was allowed to work at his trade and manage his own affairs. His strongest wish was to purchase his children; but though he several times offered his hard earnings for that purpose, he never succeeded.

In complexion my parents were a light shade of brownish yellow, and were termed mulattoes. They lived together in a comfortable home; and though we were all slaves, I was so fondly shielded that I never dreamed I was a piece of merchandise, trusted to them for safekeeping, and liable to be demanded of them at any moment. I had one brother, William, who was two years younger than myself, a bright, affectionate child. I had also a great treasure in my maternal grandmother, who was a remarkable woman in many respects. She was the daughter of a planter in South Carolina, who at his death left her mother and her three children free, with money to go to St. Augustine [Florida], where they had relatives. It was during the Revolutionary War and they were captured on their passage, carried back and sold to different purchasers. Such was the story my grandmother used to tell me. . . . To this good grandmother I was indebted for many comforts. My brother Willie and I often received portions of the crackers, cakes, and preserves she made to sell; after we ceased to be children we were indebted to her for more important services.

... When I was six years old, my mother died, and then for the first time I learned by the talk around me that I was a slave. ... I was told that my home was now to be with her [my deceased mother's] mistress; and I found it a happy one. No toilsome or disagreeable duties were imposed upon me. My mistress was so kind to me that I was always glad to do her bidding, and proud to labor for her. I could sit by her side for hours, sewing diligently, with a heart as free from care as that of any free-born child. When she thought I was tired, she would send me out to run and jump. ... Those were happy days—too happy to last.

When I was nearly twelve years old, my kind mistress sickened and died. ... I loved her; for she had been almost like a mother to me. ...

I was sent to spend a week with my grandmother. I was old enough now to begin to think of the future; and again and again I asked myself what they would do with me. ...

After a brief period of suspense, the will of my mistress was read and we learned she had bequeathed me to her sister's daughter, a child of five years old. ...

I would give much to blot out from memory that one great wrong. As a child, I loved my mistress; and looking back on the happy days I spent with her I try to think with less bitterness of this act of injustice. While I was with her, she taught me to read and spell; and for this privilege, which so rarely falls to the lot of the slave, I bless her memory.

1830's

Class Ties Stronger Than Race

An aspect of the slave system not often mentioned in the history of slavery is the fact that class was sometimes a stronger tie among people than was color. This was especially true in colonial America and in the first fifty years following the American Revolution.

A person's social position depended upon the amount of property he owned. And in the South, property meant land and slaves. A few free blacks in the South became quite wealthy. In Louisiana, Cyprien Ricaud owned ninety-one slaves and a plantation worth a quarter of a million dollars, and Martin Donatto owned seventy-five slaves. But most black slaveowners in the South owned a small number of slaves. Often these slaves were the owner's relatives, family, or friends who would face white ownership or would have to leave the state if freed.

As the following article shows, some landowning and slaveowning blacks achieved social and political positions similar to propertied whites in their communities.

Source: *Free Negro Owners of Slaves in the United States Together With Absentee Ownership of Slaves in the United States in 1830.* Compiled under the direction of and edited by Carter G. Woodson. New York: Negro Universities Press, 1958, pp. vi, vii, viii.

Having economic interests in common with the white slaveholders, the Negro owners of slaves often enjoyed the same social standing. It was not exceptional for them to attend the same church, to educate their children in the same private school, and to frequent the same places of amusement. Under such circumstances miscegenation [mixing of races] easily followed. While those taking the census of 1830 did not generally record such facts, the few who did, as in the case of Nansemond County, Virginia, reported a situation which today would be considered alarming. In this particular County there appeared among the slaveholders free Negroes designated as Jacob of Read and white wife and Syphe of Matthews and white wife. Others reported with white wives were not slaveholders.

Practically all of these Negro slaveholders were in the South. Slavery, however, at that time had not been exterminated altogether in the North, and even there the Negro was following in the footsteps of the white man, as this report will show.

In the South where almost all of the Negro slaveholders were, moreover, we find some of them competing with the large planters in the number of slaves they owned. Most of such Negro proprietors lived in Louisiana, South Carolina, Maryland, and Virginia, as did the majority of all such slave owners. There are, moreover, a few instances of confusing absentee ownership with Negro ownership. Sometimes a free Negro had charge of a plantation, but did not own the slaves himself, and the enumerator returned him as the owner. . . .

Human, All Too Human

Often in the South, a free Negro could own property, even if that property sometimes was his own wife or child. The passage which follows reveals that all men are human—perhaps all too human.

Source: *Free Negro Owners of Slaves in the United States in 1830 Together with Absentee Ownership of Slaves in the United States in 1830.* Compiled under the direction of and edited by Carter G. Woodson. New York: Negro Universities Press, division of the Greenwood Publishing Corporation, 1968, pp. v, vi.

The census records show that the majority of the Negro owners of slaves were such from the point of view of philanthropy. In many instances the husband purchased the wife or vice versa. The slaves belonging to such families were few compared with the large numbers found among the whites on the well-developed plantations. Slaves of Negroes were in some cases the children of a free father who had purchased his wife. If he did not thereafter emancipate the mother, as so many such husbands failed to do, his own children were born his slaves and were thus reported by the enumerators.

Some of these husbands were not anxious to liberate their wives immediately. They considered it advisable to put them on probation for a few years, and if they did not find them satisfactory they would sell their wives as other slaveholders disposed of Negroes. For example, a Negro shoemaker in Charleston, South Carolina, purchased his wife for $700; but, on finding her hard to please, he sold her a few months thereafter for $750, gaining $50 by the transaction. The editor personally knew a man in Cumberland County, Virginia, whose mother was purchased by his father who had first bought himself. Becoming enamored of a man slave, she gave him her husband's manumission papers that they might escape together to free soil. Upon detecting this plot, the officers of the law received the impression that her husband had turned over the papers to the slave and arrested the freedman for the supposed offense. He had such difficulty in extricating himself from this complication that his attorney's fees amounted to $500. To pay them he disposed of his faithless wife for that amount.

Slave Days

It Was His Turkey

For years Professor Thomas W. Talley of Fisk University collected and pieced together "every attainable scrap and fragment" of non-religious or secular folk rhymes of black people. He wanted to interpret "the inner life of his own people" so that their contribution to the literary heritage of folk literature in the United States might be better understood.

Here is Professor Talley's interpretation of "justice" in slave days as revealed by the rhyme "Christmas Turkey."

Source: Talley, Thomas W. *Negro Folk Rhymes: Wise and Otherwise.* Port Washington, N.Y.: © Kennikat Press Inc. 1968, Pp. 98, 324, 325.

In a few Rhymes the vice of stealing is either laughed at, or apparently laughed at. Such Rhymes carry on their face a strictly American slave origin. An example is found in "Christmas Turkey." If one asks how I know its origin to be American, the answer is that the native African had no such thing as Christmas, and turkeys are indigenous [native] to America. In explanation of the origin of these "stealing" Rhymes I would say that it was never the Negro slave's viewpoint that his hard-earned productions righteously belonged to another. His whole viewpoint in all such cases, where he sang in this kind of verse, is well summed up in the last two lines of this little Rhyme itself.

Christmas Turkey

I prayed to de Lawd fer tucky-o.
Dat tucky wouldn't come.
I prayed, an' I prayed 'til I'se almos' daid.
No tucky at my home.

Chrismus Day, she almos' here;
My wife, she mighty mad.
She want dat tucky mo' an' mo'.
An' she want 'im mighty bad.

I prayed 'til de scales come on my knees,
An' still no tucky come.
I tuck myself to my tucky roos',
An' I brung my tucky home.

To the Negro it was his turkey. This was the Negro slave view and accounts for the origin and evolution of such verse. We leave to others a fair discussion of the ethics and a righteous conclusion; only asking them in fairness to conduct the discussion in the light of slave conditions and slave surroundings.

1832

I'm Going to Learn How to Read and Write

Thomas L. Johnson, author of this excerpt, was a slave in Virginia for 28 years. His mother told him that his grandfather had come to America from Africa and was of the Guinea Tribe.

Young Thomas burned with a desire for learning. In this selection from his autobiography, he tells how he learned to read and write.

Eventually Johnson made his way to the North and then to England. At the age of forty he became a student at Spurgeon's College, an English Baptist school for ministers. His evangelist work took him back to the land of his ancestors; he returned to Africa as a missionary.

The first edition of Johnson's autobiography, telling of his life on three continents, was published in 1882.

Source: Johnson, Thomas L. *Twenty-Eight Years a Slave Or The Story of My Life on Three Continents* (7th edition). Bourneworth (England): W. Mate and Sons, 1909, pp. 11, 12, 13.

There was a slave on our lot named Anthony Burnes who managed to get to Boston under the fugitive slave law. He was brought back to Richmond, Virginia, and put into the slave pen for sale. Young Mr. Brent came to me one day when Burnes was in the trader's pen, and told me that Anthony was in gaol [jail]. He knew how to write, and had written himself a pass and had gone to the north, and that his master and other gentlemen had brought him back, and now he would be sold to Georgia. All this, said he, Burnes brought upon himself because he knew how to write. "Lor's o'er me," I said, "is dat so?" He answered very gravely, "Yes, that is so."

When I got by myself, I said, "If dat is so, I am going to learn how to write, and if I can get to Boston, I know I can get to Canada." With this resolve, I struggled hard to learn how to write.

I began by pocketing the nice-looking letters I saw, and go to my room and try to make letters like them. I remember being in a church once, where I saw a lot of letters in a box. The writing looked so plain and nice, it seemed that I could not do better than take a few of the nicest looking ones to help me in my writing lessons. But this did not do, for although some of the letters were very nice, I did not know what to call them.

The youngest son of the master had a copy book. When I saw it I decided to have one like it. The first time after this when I had five cents, I went to a book store and asked for a copy book. I had made up my mind what to say if the bookseller should ask me for whom I wanted it. I intended telling him that it was for my master. But fortunately he did not question me in that direction. I told him in answer to his question as to what kind of copy book I wanted, to put them down that I might see them, and I would tell him.

I went home and began to learn from this book how to write. The letters were alphabetically arranged. I got on very well, but another difficulty presented itself—I could not spell.

I purchased a spelling-book in the course of time, kept it in my pocket, and at every opportunity I looked into it. But there were so many words I could not understand. At night, when the young master would be getting his lessons, I used to choose some word I wanted to know how to spell, and say, "Master, I'll bet you can't spell 'looking-glass.'" He would at once spell it. I would exclaim, "Lor's o'er me, you can spell nice." Then I would go out and spell the word over and over again. I knew that once it was in my head it would never be got out again.

This young man was very kind, and was always willing to answer my questions. But sometimes he would ask why I wanted to know, and I would say, "I want to see how far you are." In the course of time he would often read portions of his lessons to me. If I liked this and wanted to hear it again, I would say, "Lor's o'er me, read that again," which he often did. In this way each week I added a little to my small store of knowledge about the great world in which I lived.

But the door of freedom seemed as fast closed against me as ever. There was a large map of the United States hanging on the wall of the dining room, and each day as I attended to my duties I would stop a few minutes and look at the map. In the course of time I learned to spell the names of nearly all the cities along the railway route from Richmond to Boston, wondering whether I should ever see those cities where all were free. Never shall I be able to express my intense longing for freedom in those long, long days of slavery.

An Overseer Reports to His Employer

Plantation overseers enjoyed little respect from the planters they served. To the slaves, they were symbols of the worst aspects of the slavery system. Slaves despised their overseers; they even had a special name for them. Overseers were "Buckras," men of no social standing—outcasts.

Most of these overseers or managers came from the ranks of lower class, landless whites. Many were descendants of indentured servants. Most overseers had little education, and not a few were illiterate. However, as plantation managers, they had many responsibilities. They received salaries varying from $250 to $600 per year, good pay for those times. When James K. Polk, later a President of the United States, paid his overseer, Ephraim Beanland, $350 yearly in the 1830's, he considered it a high salary.

Beanland was first hired by Polk and his brother-in-law, Dr. Silas M. Caldwell, to operate their Fayette County, Tennessee, plantation. Later Beanland was sent to Mississippi to break ground for a new plantation for them. Beanland exercised strict control over the slaves in his charge. He worked them hard and was known as a man who enforced his orders with profanity, a ready fist, or a whip.

Each month Polk required a written report from Beanland. Here is one of his letters and a sample expense account. They are reprinted *exactly* as Beanland wrote them.

In the letter, the overseer informs his employer that two slaves, Jack and Ben, had run away after he "corrected" them. A white man named Hughes found Jack in the Arkansas territory and sent word back to the plantation. Meanwhile authorities, believing that Hughes and his other white companions had stolen the slaves, put them all in jail in St. Helena. Therefore, Beanland had to go to "arcensis" [Arkansas] to bail them out of jail. Furthermore, Beanland had to take a "George More" with him because Arkansas required two men to prove property ownership. As the records show, it was an expensive operation.

Source: Bassett, John Spencer. *The Southern Plantation Overseer As Revealed in His Letters*. Northampton, Massachusetts: printed for Smith College (Smith College Fiftieth Anniversary Publications), 1925, pp. 53-54, 60.

Dear Sir:

We are all well and lisbeth and mriah (sic) has both fine living children, and garisan and the mule has come long since, and I am sorry to tell you that Jack and Ben hath left the plantation on the 28 of Novemeber and I have not heard from them since on the night before I was a bailing until a 11 o'clock and Jack went alf and broke into a grocery which he was caught and when I was thorely convinced that it was him I corected and I corected him for telling em 5 or 6 positif lyes and whilste I went to diner they boath left the fields and I have not heard of them since sir I dont say I am able to advise you but I do not want any arrangements maid for either of them. I want them boath brought back if they aint the rest will leave me also I have sent to Maury after them by George More if they are there he will fetch them back and I also I sent Sillva and her family to Maury and on crist mas day I am going to see George More he is going to be back.

January 3, 1834

Expensis going to the arcensis and back

At hals in Sumerville	$ 1.62½
pasage by stage to Memphis, 3 fares	8.75
Hus [Hughes'] bill of faire at the first stand	1.12½
Hus bill of faire in rally	1.12½
Hus passage by steam bote from memphis to healeney	15.00
Jaile fease and balcksmiths acount	11.86
The first nite at Clarksvill	.75
And on monday bill of feriage	1.75
And on tuesday bill of feriage	1.75
And on wensday bill of feriage	1.25
And Jacks tavern bill	.75
And the hyring of an yawl	1.00
Hus bill of fair at hermete	0.75
Hus bill at the woad yarde and the race ground	2.50
Pasage on steam bote from healeney aup to memphis	18.00
Hus bill of faire at moshis [?]	00.75
The hire of horsis	4.00
The hire of 2 mules	2.00
Hus bill of faire at arnets	1.37
And Hues expensiss	50.00

1835

"A Reasonable Request"

Peter Williams was an educated churchman in New York. In 1796, he and three other black leaders withdrew from the John Street Methodist Church and organized the African Methodist Episcopal Church. As an Episcopal clergyman, Williams was a tireless speaker and teacher. In addition to his parish duties, he conducted a school for Negro children in New York City in the early 1800's.

Here is a brief but pointed public notice which Williams published. He asked that "native" African-Americans be treated at least as well as the foreigners who were beginning to come to America from North Europe in increasing numbers.

Source: Child, L. Maria. *The Freedman's Book.* Boston: Fields, Osgood, and Company, 1869, p. 110.

A Reasonable Request

We are natives of this country; we ask only to be treated *as well* as foreigners. Not a few of our fathers suffered and bled to purchase its independence; we ask to be treated *as well* as those who fought against it. We have toiled to cultivate it, and to raise it to its present prosperous condition; we ask only to share *equal* privileges with those who have come from distant lands to enjoy the fruits of our labor.

(signed)   Reverend Peter Williams
Colored Rector of St.
Philip's Church, 1835

October 21, 1835

"We Must Have Garrison! Lynch Him!"

William Lloyd Garrison was a white abolitionist who founded an antislavery journal called "The Liberator." For thirty-five years he published that paper and spoke against slavery. Frequently Garrison shared the lecture platform with Frederick Douglass, the prominent black abolitionist.

Not only was Garrison an enemy of slaveowning whites of the South; many citizens in his home city, Boston, Massachusetts, were not in sympathy with his views. They regarded him as a radical and dangerous man because he advocated immediate freeing of all slaves. Once when he was lecturing to the Boston Female Antislavery Society, a group of black and white women, he was attacked by a mob and led through the streets with a rope around his neck. Here is an account of his hairbreadth escape from that angry crowd.

Source: Johnson, Oliver. *William Lloyd Garrison and His Times.* Boston: Houghton Mifflin and Company, 1881, pp. 197-199.

The mob having bravely demolished the anti-slavery sign . . . next turned their attention to Mr. Garrison, whose place of retreat was easily discovered. "We must have Garrison! Out with him! Lynch him!," they cried. By advice of the mayor he attempted to escape at the rear of the building. He got safely from the back window on to a shed, making, however, a narrow escape from falling headlong to the ground. He reached a carpenter's shop, where a friend tried to conceal him, but in vain. The rioters, uttering a yell, furiously dragged him to a window, with the intention of throwing him from that height to the ground. But one of them relented and said, "Don't kill him outright." So they drew him back, and coiled a rope around his body. . . . He descended to the street by a ladder raised for the purpose. He . . . was seized by two or three of the leading rioters, powerful and athletic men. . . . Blows, however, were aimed at his head by such as were of a cruel spirit, and at last they succeeded in tearing nearly all the clothes from his body. . . .

At the south door of the City Hall the mayor attempted to protect him; but as he was unassisted by any show of authority or force, he was quickly thrust aside. There was a tremendous rush to prevent him from being taken into the hall. For a time the conflict was desperate; but at length a rescue was effected by a posse that came to the help of the mayor, and he was taken up to the mayor's room. Here he was furnished with needful clothing, the mayor and his advisers declaring that the only way to preserve his life was to commit him to jail as a disturber of the peace! Accordingly a hack [wagon] was got ready at the door, and . . . he was put into the vehicle without much difficulty; the crowd not recognizing him at first in his new garb.

"But now," says Mr. Garrison, "A scene occurred that baffles description. As the ocean, lashed into fury by the spirit of the storm, seeks to whelm the adventurous bark beneath the mountain waves, so did the mob, enraged by a series of disappointments, rush like a whirlwind upon the frail vehicle in which I sat, and endeavor to drag me out of it. Escape seemed a physical impossibility. They clung to the wheels, dashed open the doors, seized hold of the horses, and tried to upset the carriage. They were, however, vigorously repulsed by the police—a constable sprung in by my side—the doors were closed—and the driver, lustily using his whip upon the bodies of his horses and the heads of the rioters, happily made an opening through the crowd. . . . In a few moments I was locked up in a cell, safe from my persecutors. . . . I threw myself upon my prison-bed and slept tranquilly."

1840

I Am Chosen to Be Young Master's "Play Boy"

> Young slaves who served as "playmates" or companions for their future masters were chosen with great care. William W. Brown, who was born a slave on Dr. John Young's plantation in Fayette County, Kentucky, describes the day he was chosen as a "play boy."
>
> Source: Brown, William W. *The Black Man, His Antecedents, His Genius, and His Achievements.* Boston: 1847, pp. 11, 12.

When the planter's son became old enough to need a playmate to watch over him, mistress called all the young slaves together, to select one for that purpose. We were all ordered to run, jump, wrestle, turn somersets [somersaults], walk on our hands, and go through the various gymnastic exercises that the imagination of our brain could invent, or the strength and activity of our limbs could endure.

The selection was to be an important one, both to the mistress and to the slave. Whoever should gain the place was in the future to become a house servant; the ash-cake thrown aside, that unmentionable garment that buttons around the neck, which we all wore, and nothing else, was to give way to a whole suit of linen. Every one of us joined heartily in the contest while old mistress sat on the piazza watching our every movement—some 15 of us, each dressed in his one garment, sometimes standing on our head with feet in the air—still the lady looked on.

With me it seemed a matter of life and death; for, being blood kin to master, I felt that I had more at stake than my companions. At last the choice was made, and I was told to step aside as the "lucky boy," which order I obeyed with an alacrity seldom surpassed. That night I was put to soak, after which I was scraped, scrubbed, washed and dried.

The next day, a new suit came down to the quarters; I slipped into it; the young slaves gathered around me, and I was the star of the plantation! With his mother's blessing, William bade farewell to the log cabin and dirt floor of the quarters and started for the big house, where his mistress received him and sharply "laid down the law" which was to govern his future actions.

"I give your young master over to you," cautioned his mistress, "And if you let him hurt himself, I'll pull your ears; if you let him cry, I'll pull your ears, and if he wants anything and you don't let him have it, I'll pull your ears." And according to William, "right well did she keep her promise."

January 25, 1843

Who Can Ride on the Railroad?

As the following Senate Bill makes clear, railroad passengers of "colour" had problems in the North as early as the 1840's.

Source: *Correspondence with Foreign Powers Not Parties to Treaties or Conventions Giving a Mutual Right of Search of Vessels Suspected of the Slave Trade* (Class D). From January 1-December 31, 1843 inclusive. Presented by Both Houses of Parliament by Command of her Majesty, 1844. London: William Clowes and Sons, pp. 122-123.

Senate No. 9

Commonwealth of Massachusetts
Senate, January 25, 1843

The Committee was referred the Petition of Francis Jackson and others, and sundry other petitions, relating to the rights of rail-road passengers, have considered the same, and report the accompanying bill.

By order of the Committee
George Hood, Chairman

Commonwealth of Massachusetts
Eighteen Hundred and Forty-three

An Act relating to the Rights of Rail-road Passengers.

Be it enacted by the Senate and House of Representatives, in General Court assembled, and by the authority of the same, as follows:

Sect.1. No rail-road corporation shall by themselves, their directors, or others, make or establish any by-law or regulation, which shall make any distinction, or give preference in accommodation to any one or more persons over others, on account of descent, sect, or colour.

Sect.2. Any officer or servant of any rail-road corporation, who shall assault any person for the purpose of depriving him or her of any right or privilege, in any car or other rail-road accommodation, on account of descent, sect, or colour, or shall aid or abet any person in committing such assault, shall be punished by imprisonment in the county jail, not less than six days, or by fine of not less than ten dollars; and shall also be answerable to the person assaulted, to the full amount of his damage in an action of trespass.

1844

"In His Will He Give Me and My Husband Free"

Even those slaves fortunate enough to be owned by kind masters could never be certain of their positions. The following story written by Charity Bower, born in North Carolina in 1799, illustrates how little control slaves had over their own lives.

Source: Hart, Albert Bushnell, ed. *Source-book of American History*. New York: The Macmillan Company, 1900, pp. 255-257.

Oh, my old mistress was a kind woman. She was all the same a mother to poor Charity. . . . I had a wedding when I was married; for mistress didn't like to have *her* people take up with one another, without any minister to marry them. When my dear good mistress died, she charged her children never to separate me and my husband; "For, said she, "If ever there was a match made in heaven, it was Charity and her husband." My husband was a nice good man; and mistress knew we set stores by one another. Her children promised they never would separate me from my husband and children [Charity had 16 children]. Indeed, they used to tell me that they would never sell me at all; and I am sure they meant what they said. But my young master got into trouble. He used to come home and sit leaning his head on his hand by the hour together without speaking to any body. I see something was the matter; and I begged of him to tell me what made him look so worried. He told me he owed 1700 dollars, that he could not pay; and he was afraid he should have to go to prison. I *begged* him to sell me and my children, rather than go to jail. I see the tears come into his eyes. "I don't know, Charity," said he; "I'll see what can be done. One thing you may feel easy about; I will never separate you from your husband and children, let what will come."

Two or three days after, he come to me, and says he: "Charity, how should you like to be sold to Mr. Kinmore?" I told him I would rather be sold to him than to any body else, because my husband belonged to him. My husband was a nice good man, and we set stores by one another. Mr. Kinmore agreed to buy us; and so I and my children went there to live. He was a kind master; but as for mistress Kinmore,—she was a divil! Mr. Kinmore died a few years after he bought us; and in his Will he give me and my husband free; but I never know anything about it, for years afterward. I don't know how they managed it. My poor husband died and *never* knowed that he was free. . . .

Well . . . after that [after she was finally given her freedom] I concluded I'd come to the Free States. Here I have taken in washing; and my daughter is smart at her needle; and we get a very comfortable living.

February 12, 1849

My Last Will and Testament

The free Negro occupied an insecure position in the South. Unwanted by whites, he was at the mercy of many people who might attempt to re-enslave him. Whites saw the free black as a threat to the slave system. Slave states developed many laws restricting the free black. Every slave state tried to restrict the number of free Negroes within their boundaries. Often laws required removal of a slave who became free and prohibited free blacks from settling in the state.

One Charles Webb of King William County, Virginia, did all that he could to write an airtight will so that his slaves would receive their freedom when he died. Freedom without money and the means to make a living would not have meant much to the Negro. Webb recognized this fact in the document that follows.

Source: Original manuscript of Will of Charles Webb in the possession of Dr. Joseph H. Stephens, San Francisco, California. Used with Dr. Stephen's permission.

IN THE NAME OF GOD, AMEN, I Charles Webb, of the County of King William and State of Virginia, do make and ordain this to be my last will and testament, in manner and form following, to wit:

I direct that all my just debts be paid. I will and direct, that at and after my death, all my slaves, James, Nat, William, Ben, Robert, Thomas, James, son of Lucy, Jack, Solomon, Lewis, Willis, Chamberlayne, Lucy, Lavina, Caty, Eve, Lucy, daughter of Lucy, Rachel, Patsey, Eliza, Kitty and her two children, named Logan and William Henry, together with all their future increase, and all others I may have at my death, be, and they are hereby declared to be, liberated and forever emancipated from the involuntary servitude of all and every person or persons whatsoever. And in order to enable the said liberated slaves and all their future increase to move themselves to some non-slaveholding State, and buy a suitable home, I give to my said slaves and their future increase, the sum of four thousand dollars cash. . . . I give . . . all the mules I may have at my death, to aid them in moving; also what plantation tools and kitchen utensils they may wish to take with them. . . . I will and direct that the said slaves be furnished with sufficient teams and waggons, or other vehicles, out of the four thousand dollars given them (including the mules,) to move themselves and baggage out in, and to become their property, and divided according to their ratable proportions. . . . I direct that at starting on their journey, the said slaves be furnished with a liberal supply of provisions, both for themselves and teams, and that the expence of their free papers and provisions at starting, be paid for out of my estate. If any of my slaves should die before I do, the portion or portions of such as die, I direct shall fall to the family of such dying slave. . . . And I further give to the said slaves, for their joint use, my two guns and two pair of pistols, with the appurtenances thereto. . . .

Now in order effectually to do away all difficulties whatever on the subject of my emancipated slaves and the money legacies, and property given them in the foregoing part of this will, I do hereby expressly and positively direct that nothing contained in this will nor any construction of any part thereof, shall be allowed to deprive the said slaves of any portion herein given them. . . . In testimony whereof, I hereunto set my hand and seal, this the eleventh day of May, in the year eighteen hundred and forty-seven.

CHARLES WEBB, (Seal.)

60

In Sickness and in Health—Rules for the Care of Slaves

Plantation owners usually insisted that overseers sign written contracts which contained a number of rules. Those regulations spelled out exactly what was expected of a competent overseer. Whether or not the overseer lived up to those rules depended upon the kind of person he was and how closely he was supervised by the plantation owner.

Here are the rules describing how overseers on the plantations of Plowden C. J. Weston, a South Carolina rice planter, were expected to care for his slaves in sickness and in health.

Source: Printed in pamphlet form by A. J. Burke: Charleston, South Carolina. Reprinted in *De Bow's Review* XXII, 38-44, XXI 617-620, December 1856 and XXII, 376-381, April, 1857. Also reprinted in Bassett, John Spencer. *The Plantation Overseer as Revealed in His Letters.* Northampton, Massachusetts: Printed for Smith College, 1925, pp. 28-29.

SICKNESS—All sick persons are to stay in the hospital night and day, from the time they first complain to the time they are able to go to work again. The nurses are to be responsible for the sick not leaving the house, and for the cleanliness of bedding, utensils, &c. The nurses are never to be allowed to give any medicine, without the orders of the Overseer or Doctor. A woman, beside the plantation nurse, must be put to nurse all persons seriously ill. In all cases *at all* serious the Doctor is to be sent for, and his orders are to be strictly attended to: no alteration is to be made in the treatment he directs. Lying-in women are to be attended by the midwife as long as is necessary, and by a woman put to nurse them for a fortnight. They will remain at the negro houses for 4 weeks, and will then work 2 weeks on the highland. In some cases, however, it is necessary to allow them to lie up longer. The health of many women has been entirely ruined by want of care in this particular. Women are sometimes in such a state as to render it unfit for them to work in water; the Overseer should take care of them at these times. The pregnant women are always to do *some* work up to the time of their confinement, if it is only walking into the field and staying there. If they are sick, they are to go to the hospital, and stay there until it is pretty certain their time is near.

Nourishing food is to be provided for those who are getting better. The Overseer will keep an account of the articles he purchases for this purpose, during the Proprietor's absence, which he will settle for as soon as he returns.

BLEEDING IS UNDER ALL CIRCUMSTANCES STRICTLY PROHIBITED, EXCEPT BY ORDER OF THE DOCTOR.—The Overseer is particularly warned not to give strong medicines, such as calomel, or tartar emetic: simple remedies such as flax-seed tea, mint water, No. 6, magnesia, &c., are sufficient for most cases, and do less harm. Strong medicines should be left to the Doctor; and since the Proprietor never grudges a Doctor's bill, however large, he has a right to expect that the Overseer shall always send for the Doctor when a serious case occurs. Dr. . . . . is the Physician of the place. When he is absent, Dr. . . . . Great care must be taken to prevent persons from lying up when there is nothing or little the matter with them. Such persons must be turned out immediately; and those somewhat sick can do lighter work, which encourages industry. Nothing is so subversive of discipline, or so unjust, as to allow people to sham, for this causes the well-disposed to do the work of the lazy.

1852

I Don't Want a Trader to Get Me

Usually no attempt was made to keep slave families together. The heartache that resulted from forced separation of husbands, wives and their children is documented in the letter which follows. This letter is one of many original manuscripts which Dr. Ulrich B. Phillips of the University of Michigan found during the many years he devoted to a study of the Old South. The letter is reprinted exactly as it was written by the unfortunate slave, Maria Perkins.

Source: Phillips, Ulrich Bonnell. *Life and Labor in the Old South.* Boston: Little, Brown and Company, 1929, p. 212.

Charlottesville, Oct. 8th, 1852

Dear Husband I write you a letter to let you know my distress my master has sold albert to a trader on Monday court day and myself and other child is for sale also and I want you to let [me] hear from you very soon before next cort if you can I don't know when I don't want you to wait till Chrismas I want you to tell dr Hamelton and your master if either will buy me they can attend to it know and then I can go afterwards. I don't want a trader to get me they asked me if I had got any person to buy me and I told them no they took me to the court houste too they never put me up a man buy the name of brady bought albert and is gone I don't know where they say he lives in Scottesville my things is in several places some is in staunton and if I should be sold I don't know what will become of them I don't expect to meet with the luck to get that way till I am quite heartsick nothing more I am and ever will be your kind wife Maria Perkins.

To Richard Perkins.

1850's

"Yes, Two Such Slaves Did Pass Our Gate"

Levi Coffin, a Quaker who spent fifty years of his life as an active abolitionist, is often called the "President of the Underground Railroad." Coffin and his wife Catherine, better known as "Aunt Katy," hid countless fugitive slaves in their home, fed and clothed them, and helped them on to Canada. The Coffin home in Cincinnati was large and ideally suited for hiding runaways. Often slaves were concealed in upper rooms for weeks without the knowledge of any of the Coffin's boarders or frequent visitors.

According to Levi Coffin, his conversion to the cause of abolition of slavery came when he was just seven years old. In North Carolina, where he spent his boyhood, he saw a slave coffle trudging down the road. He was deeply moved by the sight of those blacks in bondage and vowed to do everything in his power to fight against slavery. And throughout his long adventurous life he did just that.

Here are Levi Coffin's own words which describe a typical incident in the work he and his wife did on the Underground Railroad.

Source: *Reminiscences of Levi Coffin, The Reputed President of the Underground Railroad; Being a Brief History of the Labors of a Lifetime in Behalf of the Slave, With the Stories of Numerous Fugitives, Who Gained Their Freedom Through His Instrumentality, and Many Other Incidents* (Third Edition). Cincinnati: The Robert Clarke Company, 1898, pp. 301-302.

Scene. —Before the war; a house in Cincinnati. Two negroes newly arrived, and evidently plantation hands, eating heartily in the kitchen. Two planters and the marshal of Cincinnati, coming hastily up the street. A lady (Aunt Katy) enters the parlor hurriedly and addressing a broad brimmed Quaker, speaks, "Levi, make thee haste. I see strange men coming with that pestilent marshal." Levi goes out and meets them at the gate.

Marshal: Good Morning, Friend Coffin. We are seeking for two runaways.

Coffin: Two escaped slaves thee would recapture?

Marshal and both owners: Yes, yes. Can you tell us where they are?

Coffin: Was one boy very black and rather heavy set; the other yellow and but slightly built?

Both owners: Yes, yes! You describe them exactly.

Coffin: I saw two such boys, not half an hour since, pass this gate; they inquired where the Cincinnati, Hamilton and Dayton depot was, and if you haste you may reach the depot before the train leaves.

Away to the marshal and the slave-owners, while Coffin re-enters the house and addressing his wife, says:

"Mark, Katy, I did but say the boys passed the gate, but said not whether they went in or out. Go hurry them with their meal, while I hitch up the old bay horse to drive the poor souls a station or two beyond the city, when they can embark with safety."

Slave Days

Song to the Runaway Slave

A renowned black expert on folklore explains the origin of this "Song to the Runaway Slave" in this way:

The story went among Negroes that a runaway slave husband returned every night, and knocked on the window of his wife's cabin to get food. Other slaves having betrayed the secret that he was still in the vicinity, he was sold in the woods to a slave trader at a reduced price. This trader was to come next day with bloodhounds to hunt him down. On the night after the sale, when the runaway slave husband knocked, the slave wife pinched their baby to make it cry. Then she sang [this] song (as if singing to the baby), so that he might, if possible, effect his escape.

Source: Talley, Thomas W. *Negro Folk Rhymes: Wise and Otherwise*. Port Washington, N.Y.: © Kennikat Press Inc. 1968. Pp. 88-89.

Song to the Runaway Slave

Go 'way from dat window, "My Honey, My Love!"
Go 'way from dat window! I say.
De baby's in de bed, an' his mammy's lyin' by,
But you cain't git yo' lodgin' here.

Go 'way from dat window, "My Honey, My Love!"
Go 'way from dat window! I say;
Fer ole Mosser's got 'is gun, an' to Miss'ip' youse been sol';
So you cain't git yo' lodgin' here.

Go 'way from dat window, "My Honey, My Love!"
Go 'way from dat window! I say.
De baby keeps a-cryin'; but you'd better un'erstan'
Dat you cain't git yo' lodgin' here.

Go 'way from dat window, "My Honey, My Love!"
Go 'way from dat window! I say;
Fer de Devil's in dat man, an' you'd better un'erstan'
Dat you cain't git yo' lodgin' here.

1857

Treatment of House and Farm Servants and Field Hands

The manner in which slaves on plantations were treated depended to a large degree upon the positions which they occupied. House and farm servants were much better off than farm and field hands, as the following letter makes clear. The writer is James Stirling, an Englishman, who traveled through the slave states during the spring of 1857.

Source: Stirling, James. *Letters From the Slave States*. London: John W. Parker and Sons, 1857, pp. 287-289, 291.

Letter XXIII

Aiken, South Carolina, 23rd March, 1857

In judging of the welfare of the slaves, it is necessary to distinguish the different conditions of slavery. The most important distinction, both as regards numbers and its influence on the well-being of the slave, is that between house-servants and farm or field-hands. The house-servant is comparatively well off. He is frequently born and bred in the family he belongs to; and even when this is not the case, the constant association of the slave and his master, and master's family, naturally leads to such an attachment as ensures good treatment. There are not wanting instances of devoted attachment of both sides in such cases. There is even a danger that the affection on the part of the owner may degenerate into over-indulgence. It is no uncommon thing to make pets of slaves, as we do of other inferior animals; and when this is the case, the real welfare of the slave is sacrificed to an indiscriminating attachment. I was struck with the appearance of the slaves in the streets of Charleston on a Sunday afternoon. A large proportion of them were well dressed, and of decent bearing, and had all the appearance of enjoying a holiday. I was informed they were principally house-servants belonging to the town; and there could be no doubt the control of public opinion, natural to a large city, had exercised a favourable influence on the condition of these poor people.

The position of the field-hands is very different; of those, especially, who labour on large plantations. Here there are none of those humanizing influences at work which temper the rigour of the system, nor is there the same check of public opinion to control abuse. The "force" is worked *en masse,* as a great human mechanism; or, if you will, as a drove of cattle. The proprietor is seldom present to direct and control. Even if he were, on large estates the numbers are too great for his personal attention to details of treatment. On all large plantations the comfort of the slave is practically at the disposal of the white overseer, and his subordinate, the negro-driver. There are many estates which the proprietor does not visit at all, or visits perhaps once a year; and where, during his absence, the slaves are left to the uncontrolled caprice of the overseer and his assistants, not another white man, perhaps, being within miles of the plantation. Who can say what passes in those voiceless solitudes? Happen what may, there is none to tell. Whatever the slave may suffer there is none to bear witness to his wrong. It needs a large amount of charity to believe that power so despotic, so utterly uncontrolled even by opinion, will never degenerate into violence. It could only be so if overseers were saints, and drivers angels. . . .

Midway between house-servants and plantation-hands stand the farm-servants of small proprietors. Of all slaves these are, probably, the best off. They are neither spoiled like pet domestics, nor abused like plantation cattle. They live much in the farmer's family, work with himself and his children, take an interest in his affairs, and in return, become objects of his regard. Such is the condition of many slaves among the small farmers in the upland districts of Virginia, Kentucky, Tennessee, Georgia, and the Carolinas. The same applies also to many proprietors in Texas and, I believe, in Arkansas. In general it may be affirmed, that the welfare of the slaves is in an inverse ratio to their numbers.

While it is right to acknowledge the growing humanity of the slave-owner, it should not be forgotten that there are certain evils inherent in the system which no humanity can compensate.

1859

A Black Abolitionist Comforts John Brown's Wife

Although Harriet Tubman and Sojourner Truth are better known black women in the abolitionist camp, Frances Ellen Watkins Harper fought long and hard for an end to slavery. A teacher, poet, and lecturer, Mrs. Harper worked on the Underground Railroad.

When she learned that John Brown, a white militant abolitionist, was imprisoned for his raid on the government arsenal at Harper's Ferry, she sent the following letter of concern to his wife. After Brown was sentenced to death for treason, Frances Watkins (she was not yet married) went to Osawatomie, Kansas, for two weeks to comfort John Brown's wife while they awaited his execution, which took place on December 2, 1859.

Source: Still, William. *The Underground Railroad.* Philadelphia: Porter and Coates, 1872, p. 762.

Farmer Centre, Ohio, Nov. 14th.

My Dear Madam:—

In an hour like this the common words of sympathy may seem like idle words, and yet I want to say something to you, the noble wife of the hero of the nineteenth century. Belonging to the race your dear husband reached forth his hand to assist, I need not tell you that my sympathies are with you. I thank you for the brave words you have spoken. A republic that produces such a wife and mother may hope for better days. Our heart may grow more hopeful for humanity when it sees the sublime sacrifice it is about to receive from his hands. Not in vain has your dear husband periled all, if the martyrdom of one hero is worth more than the life of a million cowards. From the prison comes forth a shout of triumph over that power whose ethics are robbery of the feeble and oppression of the weak, the trophies of whose chivalry are a plundered cradle and a scourged and bleeding woman. Dear sister, I thank you for the brave and noble words that you have spoken. Enclosed I send you a few dollars as a token of my gratitude, reverence, and love.

Yours respectfully,

Frances Ellen Watkins

Post Office address: care of William Still, 107 Fifth St.,
Philadelphia, Penn.

May God, our own God, sustain you in the hour of trial. If there is one thing on earth I can do for you or yours, let me be apprized. I am at your service.

January 7, 1860

I Was the Only White There

An Englishwoman visited the South for several months in the early part of 1860. She attended "colored" churches in both rural and urban areas. Upon her return to England, she wrote an extensive report on religion among blacks in America. She observed, "Whatever be their form of religion, we must acknowledge that they have the religious sentiment highly developed. All consider themselves like the Hebrews in Egypt. They await their exit and deliverance from the land of slavery. This conviction, maintained by a foreign power, would become dangerous for the Union."

In the slave states in 1860, the preachers of colored churches were usually slaves, paid with goods and services from their congregations as well as with money. "The masters do not usually interfere with the preachers or their flocks. In the free states, the negroes have their private churches, in which ministers of their own race, either black or mulatto, officiate. . . ."

Here is the Englishwoman's account of a Sunday visit to a "colored" church in Louisville, Kentucky, when she was the only white in the congregation. Her words reveal concern for blacks in slavery and an attitude toward race relationships which was typical of many white reformers of that time.

Source: "Slave Preaching." *The Englishwoman's Journal* as re-printed in *The Living Age* (published every Saturday by Littell, Son, and Company, Boston), No. 832 (May 12, 1860), p. 326.

Louisville, Kentucky, Sunday 7th.

The colored church where I went this afternoon haunts me. I was there at half-past two to see the Sunday school. Saw a pretty little delicate white girl teaching five or six little boys, woolly headed but nice little fellows. The little girl was ten years old, and her pupils eight or nine; you should have seen her little motherly ways, passing her white hands over their black foreheads and wool to encourage them. I never saw a prettier sight. You think of Eva [Little Eva in Harriet Beecher Stowe's book *Uncle Tom's Cabin*]. So did I! In another pew a fine young black (quite black) with that lovely, Christ-like expression of noble patience, was telling a class of boys of God's judgments towards the righteous: he was very simple and eloquent. . . .

After the school came the service. I sat humbly down on a back seat, a negro said "Ma'am, go forward to the front, ma'am," so I moved into a pew higher up, but not quite in advance; the negroes in the pew said "Go to the front seat."

I said "No, thank you, but why?"

"Why! because whites don't like to sit with blacks."

"I am English, not American!"

Then they sang,

"He sends his word of truth and love

To all the nations from above;

Jehovah is resolved to show

What his almighty power can do." Etc.

I thought so when I heard the sermon, and saw the real religious feeling with which it was listened to. The text was, "If a man desire the office of a bishop, he desireth a good work." The black man preached upon the character of a good pastor very well, with feeling and elo-quence, then he spoke of the perfect pastor, and of aspiration in all to be like him. One sentence was remarkable and given with an astounding power of expression: *"The master passion of man is to imitate God."*

I think he believed it, and that it was felt as true by his flock. . . . I stayed and talked to the women, who were very much enchanted with me. I was the only white there.

Section Four

Slavery Attacked and Defended

January 16, 1772

How Dare the Colonists Complain About One Monarch?

Granville Sharp, an outspoken Englishman, made repeated stinging attacks on slavery wherever it existed. In speeches, letters, and pamphlets, he cried out that slavery was inhuman—"a shameless prostitution and infringement on the common and natural rights of mankind."

Sharp insisted that "the boasted liberty of our American colonies" was a sham. American colonists, he argued, had no right to complain about one monarch in England as long as they allowed each "petty planter who avails himself of the service of slaves to continue to act as lawless kings." Here is one example of Sharp's use of strong language in a searing attack upon slavery in the American colonies.

Source: Sharp, Granville. *A Representation of the Injustices and Dangerous Tendency of Tolerating Slavery; or of Admitting the Least Claim of Private Property in the Persons of Men, in England.* London: Benjamin White, Printers, 1772.

[In] Our North American colonies . . . tho' the climate in general is so wholesome and temperate that it will not authorize this plea of necessity for the employment of Slaves, any more than our own, yet the pernicious practice of Slave-holding is become almost general in those parts.

At New York, for instance, this infringement on civil or domestic liberty is become notorious and scandalous, notwithstanding that the political controversies of the inhabitants are stuffed with theatrical bombast and ranting expressions in praise of liberty. . . .

Men, who do not scruple to detain others in Slavery, have but a very partial and unjust claim to the protection of the laws of liberty: and indeed it too plainly appears, that they have no real regard for liberty, farther than their own private interests are concerned. . . .

Every petty planter, who avails himself of the service of Slaves, is an arbitrary monarch, or rather a lawless [ruler] in his own territories, notwithstanding that the imaginary freedom of the province, wherein he resides, may seem to forbid the observation.

The *boasted liberty* of our American colonies, therefore, has so little right to that sacred name, that it seems to differ from the arbitrary power of despotic monarchies only in one circumstance; . . . that it is a *many-headed monster of tyranny,* which entirely subverts our most excellent constitution; because liberty and slavery are so opposite to each other, that they cannot [exist] in the same community. . . .

Indeed I don't at present recollect, that I ever read any of the American news-papers, except one . . . the *New York Journal,* or the *General Advertiser,* for Thursday, 22d October, 1767, No. 1294. But even this one was sufficient to give me a thorough disgust, not less to their extravagant manner of reasoning in defence of liberty . . . than to their shameless infringement upon it by an open profession and toleration of Slave-holding.

This one news-paper gives notice by advertisement, of no less than eight different persons who have escaped from Slavery, or are put up to public sale for that horrid purpose.

That I may demonstrate the indecency of such proceedings in a free country, I shall take the liberty of laying some of these advertisements before my readers, by way of example.

"To be sold for want of employment.
    A likely strong active Negro man, of about 24 years of age, this country born, understands most of a Baker's trade, and a good deal of farming business, and can do all sorts of house-work; also a healthy Negro wench of about 21 years old, is a tolerable cook, and capable of doing all sorts of house-work, can be well recommended for her honesty and sobriety, she has a female child of nigh 3 years old, which will be sold with the wench, if required, &c."

Here is not the least consideration or scruple of conscience for the inhumanity of parting *the mother* and *young child.* From the style, one would suppose the advertisement to be of no more importance, than if it related merely to the sale of *a cow* and *her calf*; that *the cow* should be sold with or without *her calf*, according as the purchaser should require.

1814

We Refuse to Use Products Produced by Slave Labor

One way to attack slavery, some abolitionists argued, was to refuse to use or to buy products produced by slave labor. The "free produce movement," as the boycott was officially called, never really caught the general public's imagination. However, a number of Quakers, or members of the Society of Friends, staunchly supported the free produce movement. One Quaker who began boycotting slave products when he was just eighteen years old was William Allen, an internationally known scientist.

Source: Allen, William. *Life of William Allen, with Selections from His Correspondence* (3 volumes). London: 1846-47, II, p. 265. Reprinted in Nuermberger, Ruth Ketring. *The Free Produce Movement: A Quaker Protest Against Slavery*. Durham, North Carolina: Duke University Press, 1942, p. 8.

One of the most prominent Friends to practice abstinence was William Allen (1770-1843). At the age of 18 he expressed his opposition to slavery. Some years later he concluded that ". . . one step farther may be taken by me, which is wanting to complete my testimony [against slavery] . . . and which, if universally adopted would eventually put a stop to this enormous evil, and that is, disusing those commodities produced by the labour of slaves. And, as sugar is undoubtedly one of the chief, I resolve through divine assistance to persevere in the disuse of it until the slave trade shall be abolished."

To this resolution Allen adhered, even when the Russian emperor [Alexander I] offered him tea with sugar produced by slave labor.

1818

"A Hard Necessity"

Roger Brooke Taney, who later became Chief Justice of the United States Supreme Court, defended a client before a Maryland court in 1818. Here is part of Taney's defense of Reverend Jacob Gruber, who had been charged with "anti-slavery inculcations [forcible teaching] and acts."

Source: Greeley, Horace. *The American Conflict: A History of the Great Rebellion in the United States of America, 1860-1864.* Hartford: O. D. Case and Company, 1864, I, p. 109.

A hard necessity, indeed, compels us to endure the evils of slavery for a time. It was imposed upon us by another nation, while yet we were in a state of colonial vassalage. It cannot be easily or suddenly removed. Yet, while it continues, it is a blot on our national character, and every real lover of freedom confidently hopes that it will be effectually, though it must be gradually, wiped away and earnestly looks for the means by which this necessary object may be attained. And, until it shall be accomplished, until the time comes when we can point without a blush to the language held in the Declaration of Independence, every friend of humanity will seek to lighten the galling chain of slavery, and better, to the utmost of his power, the wretched condition of the slave.

1820

A Crimson Conscience and Polluted Hands

Daniel Bryan, a member of the Virginia Legislature in 1820, spoke out strongly against slavery. One of his most famous arguments was that if an American had the right to buy an African, then an African had the right to buy an American. Bryan often put his protests in poetic form, as in this selection.

Source: Adams, Alice Dana. *The Neglected Period of Anti-Slavery in America (1808-1831)*. Boston and London: Ginn and Company, 1908, p. 21.

Point to me the man,
Who will not lift his voice against the trade
In human souls and blood, and I pronounce,
That he nor loves his country, nor his God.
Is he a *Christian* then? who holds in bonds
His brethren; cramps the vigour of their minds;
Usurps entire dominion o'er their wills,
Bars from their souls the light of moral day,
The image of the great Eternal Spirit
Obliterating thence? Before your God,
Whose holy eye pervades the secret depths
Of every heart, do you who hold enthrall'd
Your fellow-beings liberty, believe
That you are guiltless of a DAMNING CRIME?
Be undeceived — and cleanse from guilt and blood
Your crimson'd conscience, and polluted hands.

But They Were Slaves in Africa, Also

Some defenders of the slave trade argued that Africans themselves kept slaves, and therefore, the slave was no worse off if he were carried away to America. In fact, some defenders went so far as to argue that black slaves would be better off under American than under African bondage.

Basil Davidson, noted authority on African history, condemns such justification. He claims that "slaves" in Africa were really feudal vassals whose conditions of life were similar to those of serfs and peasants in feudal Europe. Here is Davidson's explanation.

Source: Davidson, Basil. *Black Mother: The Years of the African Slave Trade.* Boston: Atlantic-Little, Brown and Company, 1961, pp. 19-21 *passim.*

Yet the "slave" people of the coastal regions, like those of the Sudanese grasslands, were in truth serfs and vassals often with valued individual rights. Their status was altogether different from the human cattle of the slave ships and the American plantations. Early European traders on the coast, though, freely misused the word "slave"....

An early American Negro explorer of southern Nigeria, Martin Delany (Delany was a serious observer who traveled in West Africa between July, 1859 and August, 1860) spoke in sharper tones. "It is simply preposterous to talk about slavery, as that term is understood, either being legalized or existing in this part of Africa," he wrote. "It is nonsense. The system is a patriarchal one, there being no actual difference socially between slaves (called by their protectors sons or daughters) and the children of the person with whom they live. Such persons intermarry and frequently become the heads of state...."

What was true of southern Nigeria was true of other "forest" peoples. In Ashanti, Rattray [R. S. Rattray, a student of the Ashanti] found "a slave might marry; own property; himself own a slave; swear an oath; be a competent witness and ultimately become heir to his master.... An Ashanti slave, in nine cases out of ten, possibly became an adopted member of the family, and in time his descendants so merged and intermarried with the owner's kinsmen that only a few would know their origin...." Captives, that is to say, became vassals; vassals became free men; free men became chiefs.

74

Set this highly mobile social order alongside the slave system of the United States, and the vital and enormous difference becomes immediately clear. There the slaves were entirely a class apart, labeled by their color, doomed to accept an absolute servitude. . . .

This is not to suggest that the life of an African vassal was one of unalloyed bliss, but that the condition he suffered was in no way the same as plantation or mining slavery in the Americas. His condition often was comparable to that of the bulk of the men and women in Western Europe throughout medieval times. In this respect Africa and Europe, at the beginning of their connection, traded and met as equals. And it was this acceptance of equality, based on the strength and flexibility of feudal systems of state organization, that long continued to govern relations between Africa and Europe. Even in the matter of slaving their attitudes were much the same.

1831

Our Nights Are Spent Listening to Noises

While some men attacked the institution of slavery with words, others took up arms against it. Nat Turner, a black man in Southampton County, Virginia, believed that a divine power had selected him to deliver his fellow slaves from bondage.

On August 21, 1831, Turner and his followers set out to get revenge. They turned their anger and violence upon white slaveholders. First, Turner's master, Joseph Travis, and his family were murdered. Within twenty-four hours sixty more whites had been killed.

Finally state and Federal troops overpowered the slaves. More than one hundred blacks were killed, and Nat Turner was captured. Two weeks later he was hanged.

But the Nat Turner Rebellion lived on in the memories of southern whites. They were frightened by the uprising, as shown by the following letter written by a Virginian to an acquaintance in Cincinnati.

Source: Cincinnati *Journal* as quoted in *The Liberator,* January 28, 1832. Reprinted in Aptheker, Herbert. *American Negro Slave Revolts.* New York: Columbia University Press, 1943, p. 307.

These insurrections have alarmed my wife so as really to endanger her health, and I have not slept without anxiety in three months. Our nights are sometimes spent in listening to noises. A corn song, or a hog call, has often been the subject of nervous terror, and a cat, in the dining room, will banish sleep for the night. There has been and there still is a *Panic* in all this country. I am beginning to lose my courage. . . .

July 4, 1842

Until They Vote Down the Declaration of Independence

William Lloyd Garrison was a white, fire-eating abolitionist who founded *The Liberator*, an antislavery journal. He demanded the immediate emancipation of all slaves. Just seven years before he gave the stirring Fourth of July oration excerpted below, Garrison had been attacked by an angry mob in Boston for his radical ideas. After the Civil War, Garrison championed the Indians' cause and campaigned for woman suffrage.

Source: "The Lessons of Independence Day," a speech delivered by William Lloyd Garrison, July 4, 1842. Reprinted in Peabody, Selim H., compiler. *American Patriotism*, New York: 1880.

I present myself as the advocate of my enslaved countrymen, at a time when their claims cannot be shuffled out of sight, and on an occasion which entitles me to a respectful hearing in their behalf. If I am asked to prove their title to liberty, my answer is, that the Fourth of July is not a day to be wasted in establishing "self-evident truths." In the name of God who has made us of one blood, and in whose image we are created; in the name of the Messiah, who came to bind up the broken-hearted, to proclaim liberty to the captives, and the opening of a prison to them that are bound; I demand the immediate emancipation of those who are pining in slavery on the American soil, whether they are fattening for the shambles [stall for marketing goods] in Maryland and Virginia, or are wasting, as with a pestilent disease, on the cotton and sugar plantations of Alabama and Louisiana; whether they are male or female, young or old, vigorous, or infirm. I make this demand, not for the children merely, but the parents also; not for one, but for all; not with restrictions and limitations, but unconditionally. I assert their perfect equality with ourselves, as a part of the human race, and their inalienable right to liberty and the pursuit of happiness. . . . And not until, by a formal vote, the people repudiate the Declaration of Independence as a false and dangerous instrument . . . not, in fine, until they deny the authority of God and proclaim themselves to be destitute of principle and humanity, will I argue the question . . . whether our slaves are entitled to the rights and privileges of freemen. That question is settled irrevocably. . . .

1845

Frederick Douglass Laments His Grandmother's Fate

Frederick Douglass, the great black abolitionist, managed to escape from slavery. However, some other members of his family were not so fortunate. The following bitter indictment of slavery—particularly of the aged—is taken from his autobiography. In this passage, Douglass laments the fate of his aged grandmother.

Source: Douglass, Frederick. *Narrative of the Life of Frederick Douglass, An American Slave.* Boston: Published at the Anti-Slavery Office, 1845, pp. 48-49.

. . . She saw her children, her grandchildren, and her great-grandchildren, divided, like so many sheep, without being gratified with the small privilege of a single word as to their or her own destiny. And, to cap the climax of their base ingratitude and fiendish barbarity, my grandmother, who was now very old, having outlived my old master and all his children, having seen the beginning and end of all of them, and her present owners finding she was of but little value, her frame already racked with the pains of old age, and complete helplessness fast stealing over her once active limbs, they took her to the woods, built her a little hut, put up a little mud-chimney, and then made her welcome to the privilege of supporting herself there in perfect loneliness; thus virtually turning her out to die! If my poor old grandmother now lives, she lives to suffer in utter loneliness; she lives to remember and mourn over the loss of great-grandchildren. They are, in the language of the slave's poet, Whittier,—

> Gone, gone, sold, and gone
> To the rice swamp dank and lone,
> Where the slave-whip ceaseless swings,
> Where the noisome insect stings,
> Where the fever-demon strews
> Poison with the falling dews,
> Where the sickly sunbeams glare

Through the hot and misty air:—
Gone, gone, sold and gone
To the rice swamp dank and lone,
From Virginia hills and waters—
Woe is me, my stolen daughters!

The hearth is desolate. The children, the unconscious children, who once sang and danced in her presence, are gone. She gropes her way, in the darkness of age, for a drink of water. Instead of the voices of her children, she hears by day the moans of the dove, and by night the screams of the hideous owl. All is gloom. The grave is at the door. And now, when weighed down by the pains and aches of old age, when the head inclines to the feet, when the beginning and ending of human existence meet, and helpless infancy and painful old age combine together—at this time, this most needful time, the time for the exercise of that tenderness and affection which children only can exercise towards a declining parent—my poor old grandmother, the devoted mother of twelve children, is left all alone, in yonder little hut, before a few dim embers. She stands—she sits—she staggers—she falls—she groans—she dies—and there are none of her children or grandchildren present, to wipe from her wrinkled brow the cold sweat of death, or to place beneath the sod her fallen remains. Will not righteous God visit for these things? . . .

February 18, 1851

Shadrach's Case

One of the many exciting fugitive slave cases concerned a man called Shadrach. In May, 1850, Frederic Wilkins, a Virginia slave, made his escape and found his way to Boston. There he was able to get a job using the name Shadrach. However, he was soon discovered, arrested and imprisoned for violation of the fugitive slave law. A crowd of blacks aided by sympathetic whites liberated him and helped him flee to Canada.

Intense excitement spread through Boston and over the entire country. Henry Clay asked President Millard Fillmore to inform Congress of the facts of the case. President Fillmore responded to Clay's request with the following proclamation which was a call for a return to law and order.

Source: Fillmore, Millard. *By the President of the United States: A Proclamation,* February 18, 1851. Reprinted in Richardson, James D. *A Compilation of the Messages and Papers of the Presidents, 1789-1897.* Published under the authority of the Congress of the United States, 1900, V, pp. 109-110.

Whereas information has been received that sundry lawless persons, principally persons of color, combined and confederated together for the purpose of opposing by force the execution of the laws of the United States, did, at Boston, in Massachusetts, on the 15th of this month, make a violent assault on the marshal or deputy marshals of the United States for the district of Massachusetts, in the court-house, and did overcome the said officers, and did by force rescue from their custody a person arrested as a fugitive slave, and then and there a prisoner lawfully holden by the said marshal or deputy marshals of the United States, and other scandalous outrages did commit in violation of law:

Now, therefore, to the end that the authority of the laws may be maintained and those concerned in violating them brought to immediate and condign [deserved] punishment, I have issued this my proclamation, calling on all well-disposed citizens to rally to the support of the laws of their country ... and I do especially direct that prosecutions be commenced against all persons who shall have made themselves aiders or abettors in or to this flagitious [vicious] offense; and I do further command that the district attorney of the United States ... cause the foregoing offenders and all such as aided, abetted, or assisted them or shall be found to have harbored or concealed such fugitives contrary to law to be immediately arrested and proceeded with according to law.

Given under my hand and the seal of the United States this 18th day of February, 1851.

Millard Fillmore

(Seal)
Dan'l Webster, Secretary of State

What Are Our Churches Doing?

> Many abolitionists were angry because, in their opinion, churches were not doing all they could or should do to work for the abolition of slavery. When George W. Julian of Indiana was a candidate for Vice President on the Free-Soil Party ticket in 1852, he upbraided organized churches for loudly denouncing "minor sins," while refusing even to "whisper" against the worst of all sins—slavery.

> Source: "Speeches on Political Questions" as reprinted in Robinson, Charles, *The Kansas Conflict.* New York: Harper & Brothers, 1892, p. 12.

What are our churches doing for the anti-slavery reform? Alas! the popular religion of the country lies imbedded in the politics and trade of the country. It has sunk to a dead level with the ruling secular influences of the age. It has ceased to be a power, practically capable of saving the world from its sins.

What are these religious bodies doing for the slave? As I have already said, they are breaking bread with his owner around the communion table. They are receiving slave-holders into full fellowship. The preachers and members of our Protestant denominations alone own over six hundred thousand slaves. The Methodist, Baptist, and Presbyterian all have divided on the slavery question, but both divisions tolerate slave-holding.

In all the late publications of the American Tract Society, I am informed that not a syllable can be found against slavery. Such sins as Sabbath-breaking, dancing, fine dressing, etc., are abundantly noticed and condemned, but not even a whisper must go forth against the "sum of all villainies!"

1852

Is That Any Argument Against Marriage?

> "The time has come when the South must enter her plea of defence, not because the accusers are foreign nations ... but because our accusers are among our born brethren, bound to us by

freedom's holiest associations and religion's most sacred ties." Because he felt the time had come to defend slavery, John Fletcher compiled a 637-page series of eight studies on slavery. In his defense of slavery, he cited "Sacred Writings, Moral Philosophy, and Ancient History."

Fletcher was born and educated in the North, but he lived most of his life in the South. He claimed, therefore, that he was "amply qualified to weigh the prejudices, teachings, and the arguments of the one against the facts, the justifications, the religious and political sanctions of the other."

Source: Fletcher, John (Louisiana). *Studies on Slavery in Easy Lessons.* Natchez: Jackson Warner, Publisher, 1852, pp. 112-113.

The benefit of the slave-owner depends on a different principle, upon the wisdom, propriety, and prudence with which he governs and manages his slaves. If he neglect their morals, suffering them to become idle, runaways, dissolute, thieves, and robbers, and committers of crime, he is made to some extent, responsible; or if he neglect to supply suitable clothing, food, and medicine, attention in sickness, and all other necessary protection, he is liable to great loss; his profit may be greatly diminished; or, if he abuse his slave with undue cruelty, he may render him less fit for labour—may destroy him altogether; or the law may set in, and compel the slave to be sold to a less cruel master. *The interest of the master has become protection to the slave:* and this principle holds good in all countries, in all ages and among all men. But it is yet said, that there are men who most outrageously abuse and sometimes kill their slaves. Very true and because some men do the same to their wives, is it any argument against marriage? It proves that there are men who are not fit to be slave-owners. And what is the providence of God, as generally manifested, in these cases? That such a husband does not enjoy the full blessing designed by the institution of marriage; or such marriage is, in some way, shortly set aside. That such slave-owner does not enjoy the full benefit a different course would insure to him; or in some way, he is made to cease being a slave-owner. Such instances are most direct and powerful manifestations against the abuses,—not of the institution itself.

"You Do Not Mean Colour Exactly?"

When Abraham Lincoln wrote this short statement holding the "logic" of slavery up to scorn, he had not yet held a political office. But less than ten years after posing this argument to human bondage, he was President of the United States and had signed the Emancipation Proclamation.

Source: Roe, Merwin, ed. *Speeches and Letters of Abraham Lincoln.* New York: E. P. Dutton and Company, 1907, pp. 26-27.

A Fragment on Slavery—July 1854

If A can prove, however conclusively, that he may of right enslave B, why may not B snatch the same argument and prove equally that he may enslave A? You say that A is white and B is black. It is colour, then; the lighter having the right to enslave the darker. Take care. By this rule you are to be slave to the first man you meet with a fairer skin than your own.

You do not mean colour exactly? You mean the whites are intellectually the superiors of the blacks, and therefore have the right to enslave them? Take care again. By this rule you are to be slave to the first man you meet with an intellect superior to your own.

But you say it is a question of interest, and if you make it your interest you have the right to enslave another. Very well. And if he can make it his interest he has the right to enslave you.

1857

Where Is Justice?

James Stirling was an Englishman who traveled throughout the South in the 1850's. He comments on justice for slaves in this letter.

Source: Stirling, James. *Letters From the Slave States.* London: John W. Parker and Son, 1857, pp. 291-292.

Letter XXIII

Aiken, South Carolina, 23rd March, 1857

Of all the evils to which the slave is exposed, the most universal in its application, and the most pestilent in its effects, is the practical outlawry to which he is subjected by the refusal of his evidence in the courts of justice. He is thus exposed defenceless to oppression. For him the court of law is no sanctuary. The dominant white man is on the bench, in the jury box, and—unanswered—in the witness-box. No wonder that a conscientious Governor of South Carolina should say to his people: – "The administration of our laws, in relation to our coloured population, by our courts of magistrates and freeholders, as these courts are at present constituted, calls loudly for reform. Their decisions are rarely in conformity with justice or humanity. . . ."

1857

Why They Won't Publish My Book in the South

Hinton Helper, a poor white Southerner, wrote *The Impending Crisis of the South: How to Meet It.* In the book, Helper blasted slavery not because it harmed enslaved blacks, but because it had ill effects on poor Southern whites.

Helper's book infuriated many Southerners—especially slaveowners. It was banned in many slave states, as was Harriet Beecher Stowe's novel, *Uncle Tom's Cabin.*

In the following passage, the author explains why Baltimore would not allow the publication of his book. Once it was printed in New York, however, Helper's book was widely circulated by Republican members of Congress. Many, including John Sherman, a candidate for Speaker of the House, used their congressional franking [mailing] privileges to send Helper's words to those who would be voting in the 1860 elections.

Source: Helper, Hinton Rowan. *The Impending Crisis of the South: How to Meet It.* New York: Burdick Brothers, 1857, pp. 360-361.

WHY THIS WORK WAS NOT PUBLISHED IN BALTIMORE

A considerable portion of this work was written in Baltimore; and the whole of it would have been written and published there, but for the following odious clause, which we extract from the Statutes of Maryland:-

Be it enacted by the General Assembly of Maryland, That after the passage of this act, it shall not be lawful for any citizen of this State, knowingly to make, print or engrave, or aid in the making, printing or engraving, within this State, any pictorial representation, or to write or print, or to aid in the writing or printing any pamphlet, newspaper, handbill or other paper of an inflammatory character, and having a tendency to excite discontent, or stir up insurrection amongst the people of color of this State, or of either of the other States or Territories of the United States, or knowingly to carry or send, or to aid in the carrying or sending the same for circulation amongst the inhabitants of either of the other States or Territories of the United States, and any person so offending shall be guilty of a felony, and shall on conviction be sentenced to confinement in the penitentiary of this State, for a period not less than twenty years, from the time of sentence pronounced on such person. — *Act passed Dec. 1831. See 2nd Dorsey, page 1218.*

Now so long as slaveholders are clothed with the mantle of office, so long will they continue to make laws, like the above, expressly calculated to bring the non-slaveholding whites under a system of vassalage little less onerous and debasing than that to which the negroes themselves are accustomed. What wonder is it that there is no native literature in the South? The South can never have a literature of her own until after slavery shall have been abolished. Slaveholders are too lazy and ignorant to write it, and the non-slaveholders—even the few whose minds are cultivated at all—are not permitted even to make the attempt. Down with the oligarchy! Ineligibility of slaveholders—never another vote to the trafficker in human flesh!

December 9, 1859

"Negro Slavery Is Not Unjust"

It was not an easy matter for a man to deliver a public speech in favor of slavery in New York City in 1859. Charles O'Conor, one of New York's ablest and best known lawyers, found that out when he tried to explain to a crowd of 20,000 people who gathered to hear him why he believed Negro slavery was not unjust. Boos, hisses and some cheers interrupted O'Conor's speech time after time. Here is a portion of what happened on that tumultuous afternoon at the Union Meeting at New York City's Academy of Music.

84

Source: "Negro Slavery is Not Unjust." A speech delivered by Charles O'Conor at the Union Meeting at the Academy of Music, New York City, December 19, 1859. Reprinted in *Political Text-Book for 1860: Comprising a Brief View of Presidential Nominations and Elections: Including All the National Platforms Ever Yet Adopted: Also, A History of the Struggle Respecting Slavery in the Territories.* Compiled by Horace Greeley and John F. Cleveland. New York: The Tribune Association, 1860, pp. 166-167.

I insist that negro Slavery is not unjust. (Long continued applause.) *It is not unjust; it is just, wise, and beneficent.* (Hisses, followed by applause and cries of "Put him out." "Let him stay, gentlemen.")

President: Let him stay there. Order!

I maintain that negro Slavery is not unjust, that it is benign in its influence upon the white man and upon the black. (Voices—"That's so, that's so"—applause.) I maintain that it is ordained by nature; that it is a necessity of both races; that in climates where the black race can live and prosper, nature herself enjoins correlative duties on the black man and on the white, which cannot be performed except by the preservation, and . . . the perpetuation of negro Slavery.

I am fortified in this opinion by the highest tribunal in our country, that venerable exponent of our institutions and of the principles of justice—The Supreme Court of the United States. That court has held, on this subject, what wise men will ever pronounce to be sound and just doctrine. . . . As a white nation we made our Constitution and our laws, vesting all political rights in that race. They and they alone, constituted in every political sense the American people. (Applause.) As to the negro, why we allowed him to live under the shadow and protection of our laws. We gave him as we were bound to give him, protection against wrong and outrage; but we denied to him political rights, or the power to govern. We left him, for so long a period as the community in which he dwelt should so order, in the condition of a bondsman. Now, gentlemen, to that condition the negro is assigned by nature. (Cries of "Bravo," and "That's so.") Experience shows that this race cannot prosper—that they become extinct in any cold, or in any very temperate clime; but in the warm, the extremely warm regions, his race can be perpetuated, and with proper guardianship, may prosper. He has ample strength, and is competent to labor, but nature denies to him either the intellect to govern or the willingness to work. (Applause.) Both were denied him. That same power which deprived him of the will to labor, gave him in our country, as a recompense, a master to coerce that duty

85

and convert him into a useful and valuable servant. I maintain that it is not injustice to leave the negro in the condition in which nature placed him, and for which alone he is adapted. . . . Neither is it unjust in the master to compel him to labor, and thereby afford to that master a just compensation in return for the care and talent employed in governing him. In this way alone is the negro enabled to render himself useful to himself and to the society in which he is placed. . . .

I hold that the negro is decreed by nature to a state of pupilage under the dominion of the wiser white man, in every clime where God and nature meant the negro should live at all. I say that it is the duty of the white man to treat him kindly; that it is the interest of the white man to treat him kindly. (Applause.) And further, it is my belief that if the white man in the States where Slavery exists, is not interfered with by the fanatics who now are creating these disturbances . . . humanity between the white man and the black man will be faithfully and fairly carried out. . . . . . It is not pretended that the master has the right to slay his slave; it is not pretended that he has a right to be guilty of harshness and inhumanity to his slave. The laws of all the Southern States forbid that; we have not the right here at the North to be guilty of cruelty toward a horse. It is an indictable offence to commit such a cruelty. The same laws exist in the South, and if there is any failure to enforce them to the fullest extent, it is due to this external force, which is pressing upon the Southern States, and compels them to abstain perhaps from many acts beneficent toward the negro which otherwise would be performed. (Applause.) In truth, in fact, in deed, the white man in the slaveholding States has no more authority by law of the land over his slave than our laws allow to a father over his minor children. He can no more violate humanity with respect to them, than a father in any of the free States of this Union can exercise acts violative of humanity toward his own son under the age of twenty-one. So far as the law is concerned, you own your boys, and have a right to their services until they are twenty-one. You can make them work for you; you have the right to hire out their services and take their earnings; you have the right to chastise them with judgment and reason if they violate your commands; and they are entirely without political rights. Not one of them at the age of twenty years and eleven months even, can go to the polls and give a vote. Therefore, gentlemen, before the law, there is but one difference between the free white man of twenty years in the Northern States and the negro bondman in the Southern States. The white man is to be emancipated at twenty-one because his God-given

86

intellect entitles him to emancipation and fits him for the duties to devolve upon him. The negro, to be sure, is a bondman for life. He may be sold from one master to another, but where is the ill in that? One may be as good as another. If there be laws with respect to the mode of sale which by separating man and wife do occasionally lead to that which shocks humanity, and may be said to violate all propriety and all conscience—if such things are done, let the South alone and they will correct the evil.... No, if standing outside of their territory, you attack the errors of a people, you make them cling to their faults.... Let our brethren of the South alone, gentlemen, and if there be any errors of this kind, they will correct them....

May 1, 1860

"I Believe the African Slave Trader Is a True Missionary"

When the Democratic National Convention met at Charleston, South Carolina April 23, 1860, the chairman found he had an almost impossible task of trying to keep order. Six hundred delegates representing every state were present. At times it seemed as though all 600 were shouting at once in violent disagreement. Some Southerners not only wanted the Democrats to adopt a platform which supported slavery, but they favored reopening the African slave trade as well.

Finally the beleaguered chairman pounded his gavel and declared that unless the uproar stopped immediately he would leave the chair and adjourn the convention. Then slave state delegations began withdrawing from the convention in anger. Alabama walked out first, followed by most of the delegates from Mississippi, Florida, Texas, Louisiana, South Carolina, Arkansas, and Delaware. When the Georgia delegation split on the decision to withdraw, one delegate, a Mr. Gaulden, refused to leave the convention. He asked to speak to his fellow Democrats and explain why he believed in slavery.

Source: Compiled by Horace Greeley and John F. Cleveland. *Political Text-Book for 1860: Comprising a Brief View of Presidential Nominations and Elections: Including All the National Platforms Ever Yet Adopted: Also, A History of the Struggle Respecting Slavery in the Territories.* New York: The Tribune Association, 1860, pp. 39-40.

Mr. Gaulden: Mr. President and Fellow Democrats: As I stated to you a few moments ago, I have been confined to my room by severe indisposition, but, learning of the commotion and the intense excitement which were existing upon the questions before this body, I felt it to be my duty, feeble as I was, to drag myself out to the meeting of my delegation, and when there I was surprised to find a large majority of that delegation voting to secede at once from this body. I disagree with those gentlemen. I regret to disagree with my brethren from the South upon any of the great questions which interest our common country. I am a Southern States' Rights man; I am an African Slave-trader. I am one of those Southern men who believe that Slavery is right, morally, religiously, socially, and politically. (Applause.) I believe that the institution of Slavery has done more for this country, more for civilization, than all other interests put together. I believe if it were in the power of this country to strike down the institution of Slavery, it would put civilization back 200 years. . . . I believe that our Government by the Constitution never had any right to legislate upon this subject. . . .

When I look to the Northern Democrats, I see them standing up there and breasting the tide of fanaticism, oppression, wrong, and slander, with which they have to contend. I view in these men types of the old ancient Romans; I view in them all that is patriotic and noble; and for one, I am not willing to cut loose from them. (Great cheering.) I say then, that I will hold on to my Democratic friends of the North to the last day of the week—late in the evening. (Great laughter.) I am not willing to disintegrate, dismember, and turn them over to the ruthless hands of the thieving Black Republicans of the North. I would ask our Northern friends to give us all our rights and take off the ruthless restrictions which cut off our supply of slaves from foreign lands. As a matter of right and justice to the South, I would ask the Democracy of the North to grant us this thing, and I believe they have the patriotism and honesty to do it, because it is right in itself. I tell you, fellow-Democrats, that the African Slave-trader is the true Union man. (Cheers and laughter.) I tell you that the Slave-trading of Virginia is immoral, more unchristian in every possible point of view, than that African Slave-trader which goes to Africa, and brings a heathen and worthless man here, makes him a useful man, Christianizes him, and sends him and his posterity down the stream of time to join in the blessings of civilization. (Cheers and laughter.) Now, fellow-Democrats, so far as any public expression of the State of Virginia—the great Slave-trading

State of Virginia—has been given, they are all opposed to the African Slave-trade.

Dr. Reed of Indiana: I am from Indiana, and I am in favor of it.

Mr. Rynders of New York: You can get one or two recruits from New York to join with you.

The President: The time of the gentlemen has expired. (Cries of go on!)

Mr. Gaulden: Now, Fellow-Democrats, the slave-trade in Virginia forms a mighty and powerful reason for its opposition to the African slave-trade, and in this remark I do not intend any disrespect to my friends from Virginia. Virginia, the Mother of States and of statesmen, the Mother of Presidents, I apprehend may err as well as other mortals. I am afraid that her error in this regard lies in the promptings of the almighty dollar. It has been my fortune to go into that noble old State to buy a few darkies, and I have had to pay from $1,000 to $2,000 a head, when I could go to Africa and buy better Negroes for $50 apiece. (Great laughter.) Now unquestionably, it is to the interest of Virginia to break down the African slave-trade when she can sell her Negroes for $2,000. She knows that the African slave-trade would break up her monopoly, hence her objection to it. . . .

I came from the First Congressional District of the State of Georgia. I represent the African Slave-trade interests of that section. (Applause.) I am proud of the position I occupy in that respect. I believe that the African Slave-trader is the true missionary, and a true Christian, (applause) and I have pleaded with my delegation from Georgia to put this issue squarely to the Northern Democracy and say to them, are you prepared to go back to first principles, and take off your unconstitutional restrictions and leave this question to be settled by each State? Now do this, fellow citizens, and you will have peace in the country. . . .

December 3, 1860

If Northerners Would Just Mind Their Own Business

Even though the nation was trembling on the brink of the Civil War, President Buchanan insisted that it was an easy matter to settle the slavery question. All the northern people had to do was to quit stirring up trouble in the South. Here is a part of how

Buchanan analyzed the situation for Congress just a few months before the shooting began.

Source: Buchanan, James, Fourth Annual Message to Congress. Reprinted in Richardson, James D. *A Compilation of the Messages and Papers of the Presidents, 1789-1897*. Published under the Authority of the Congress of the United States, 1900, V, pp. 626-627.

Why is it, then, . . . the Union of the States . . . is threatened with destruction? I have long foreseen and often forewarned my countrymen of the now impending danger. . . . The immediate peril arises . . . from the fact that the incessant and violent agitation of the slavery question throughout the North for the last quarter of a century has at length produced its malign influence on the slaves and inspired them with vague notions of freedom. Hence a sense of security no longer exists around the family altar. . . . Many a matron throughout the South retires at night in dread of what may befall herself and children before the morning. . . .

But let us take warning in time and remove the cause of danger. It can not be denied that for five and twenty years the agitation at the North against slavery has been incessant. In 1835 pictorial handbills and inflammatory appeals were circulated extensively throughout the South of a character to excite the passions of the slaves, and, in the language of General Jackson "to stimulate them to insurrection and produce all the horrors of a servile [slave] war." This agitation has ever since been continued by the public press, by the proceedings of State and county conventions and by abolition sermons and lectures. The time of Congress has been occupied by violent speeches on this never-ending subject, and appeals, in pamphlet and other forms, endorsed by distinguished names, have been sent forth from this central point and spread broadcast over the Union.

How easy would it be for the American people to settle the slavery question forever and to restore peace and harmony to this distracted country! They, and they alone can do it. All that is necessary to accomplish the object, and all for which the slave States have ever contended, is to be let alone and permitted to manage their domestic institutions in their own way. As sovereign States, they, and they alone, are responsible before God and the world for the slavery existing among them. For this the people of the North are no more responsible and have no more right to interfere than with similar institutions in Russia or in Brazil.

"I Am a Pro-Slavery Man"

William Brownlow, editor of *The Knoxville Whig* in Tennessee, received a letter from a reader in Albany, New York. The northern reader explained to Brownlow that he was "no Lincoln man," but he wanted to know where the editor stood on the questions of slavery and secession. Here is part of William Brownlow's reply.

Source: Brownlow, William Garroway. *Sketches of the Rise, Progress, and Decline of Secession with a Narrative of Personal Adventures Among the Rebels.* Philadelphia: George W. Childs, 1862, pp. 108, 109, 111, 112.

Knoxville, May 18, 1861

To L. M. E. —

. . . I am a pro-slavery man, and so are the Union men generally of the border Slave States. I have long since made up my mind upon the slavery question, but not without studying it thoroughly. The result of my investigation is, that there is not a single passage in the New Testament, nor a single act in the records of the Church during her early history for centuries, containing any direct, professed, or *intended* censure of slavery. . . . The Saviour and his apostles exhorted owners to treat slaves as became the gospel and slaves to obedience and honesty. . . . And however much the bonds of the slaves of the South may provoke the wrath of the ultra-Abolitionists of the North, the Redeemer smiles alike upon the devout master and the pious slave!

. . . Allow me to say that the curse of the country has been that, for years, North of Mason and Dixon's line, you have kept pulpits open to the abuse of Southern slavery and of the Southern people. In like manner, the clergy of the South . . . has raised the howl of secession and it falls like an Indian war cry upon our citizens from their prostituted pulpits every Sabbath. Many of them go so far as to petition their God in public prayers to *blast* the people of the North. . . .

Lincoln Calls upon the Almighty

Carl Sandburg, the great biographer of Abraham Lincoln, once stated that Lincoln was a man soft as velvet and tough as steel. The legends about "Father Abraham" most often reveal him as one of the kindest and gentlest of men. However, in his Second Inaugural Address, Lincoln showed his strong side. In this excerpt, from that speech, he uses a religious argument as he says that the Civil War, willed by God, is to bring an end to slavery. And further, Lincoln says, there is no quarrel or argument in defense of slavery that man can raise to God, whose judgments are "true and righteous." He emphasizes that the North cannot point a finger at the "guilty South," for all people, both North and South, are responsible for the existence of slavery in the United States.

Source: Lincoln, Abraham. Second Inaugural Address. Reprinted in Richardson, James D. *A Compilation of the Messages and Papers of the Presidents, 1789-1897.* Published under the Authority of the Congress of the United States, 1900, VI, p. 277.

. . . The Almighty has His own purposes. "Woe unto the world because of offenses; for it must needs be that offenses come, but woe to that man by whom the offense cometh." If we shall suppose that American slavery is one of those offenses which, in the providence of God, must needs come, but which, having continued through His appointed time, He now wills to remove, and that He gives to both North and South this terrible war as the woe due to those by whom the offense came, shall we discern therein any departure from those divine attributes which the believers in a living God always ascribe to Him? Fondly do we hope, fervently do we pray, that this mighty scourge of war may speedily pass away. Yet, if God wills that it continue until all the wealth piled up by the bondsman's two hundred and fifty years of unrequited toil shall be sunk, and until every drop of blood drawn with the lash shall be paid by another drawn with the sword, as was said three thousand years ago, so still it must be said, "The judgments of the Lord are true and righteous altogether. . . ."

Section Five

To Make Men Free—
The Civil War

"When Dey 'Listed Colored Soldiers"

Approximately 186,000 black soldiers served in the Union Army during the Civil War—93,000 from the seceded states, 40,000 from the border states, and 52,000 from the free states. Just as statistics these numbers are quite impressive; but the significant fact is that they represent 186,000 individual decisions, individual partings from loved ones, individual courage and suffering on the fields of battle, and individual black men fighting for freedom. The slave woman whose " 'Lias" went to war expresses a feeling common to all people at all times—a sense of pride and fulfillment in a sacrifice that might better the lives of other men.

The author of "When Dey 'Listed Colored Soldiers" is Paul Lawrence Dunbar, the first of the black poets embraced by all Americans. Born in 1872 in Dayton, Ohio, Dunbar wrote novels and short stories as well as poetry. But he was primarily a poet, gaining fame that no black poet had won since the eighteenth century prominence of Phillis Wheatley. He wrote many of his poems in slave cabin dialect, a "language" quite familiar to a generation only once removed from slavery.

Source: Dunbar, Paul L. *The Complete Poems of Paul Lawrence Dunbar.* New York: Dodd, Mead and Company, 1913, pp. 182-184.

When Dey 'Listed Colored Soldiers

Dey was talkin' in de cabin, dey
    was talkin' in de hall;
But I listened kin' o' keerless, not
    a-t'inkin' 'bout it all;

An' on Sunday, too, I noticed, dey
        was whisperin' mighty much,
Stan'in' all erroun' de roadside
        w'en dey let us out o' chu'ch.
But I didn't t'ink erbout it 'twell
        de middle of de week,
An' my 'Lias come to see me, an'
        somehow he couldn't speak.
Den I seed all in a minute whut
        he'd come to see me for;—
Dey had 'listed colo'ed sojers an'
        my 'Lias gwine to wah.

Oh, I hugged him, an' I kissed
        him, an' I baiged him not to go;
But he tol' me dat his conscience,
        hit was callin' to him so,
An' he couldn't baih to lingah
        w'en he had a chanst to fight
For de freedom dey had gin him
        an' de glory of de right.
So he kissed me, an' he lef' me,
        w'en I'd p'omised to be true;
An' dey put a knapsack on him,
        an' a coat all colo'ed blue.
So I gin him pap's ol' Bible f'om
        de bottom of de draw',—
W'en dey 'listed colo'ed sojers an'
        my 'Lias went to wah.
But I t'ought of all de weary miles
        dat he would have to tramp,
An' couldn't be contented w'en
        dey tuk him to de camp.
W'y my hea't nigh broke wid
        grievin' 'twell I seed him on de street;
Den I felt lak I could go an' throw
        my body at his feet.
For his buttons was a-shinin', an'
        his face was shinin', too,
An' he looked so strong an' mighty

in his coat of sojer blue,
Dat I hollahed, "Step up, manny,"
    dough my th'oat was so' and' raw,—
W'en dey 'listed colo'ed sojers an'
    my 'Lias went to wah. . . .

Bofe my mastahs went in gray suits,
    an' I loved de Yankee blue,
But I t'ought dat I could sorrer
    for de losin' of 'em, too;
But I couldn't, for I didn't know
    de ha'f o' what I saw,
'Twell dey 'listed colo'ed sojers an'
    my 'Lias went to wah.

Mastah Jack come all sickly;
    he was broke for life, dey said;
An' dey lef' my po' young mastah
    some'r's on de roadside,—dead.
W'en de women cried and mou'ned 'em,
    I could feel it thoo an' thoo,
For I had a loved un fightin' in de
    way o' dangah, too.
Den dey tol' me dey had laid him
    some'r's down souf to res',
Wid de flag dat he had fit for
    shinin' daih acrost his breas'.
Well, I cried, but den I reckon
    dat's what Gawd had called him for,
W'en dey 'listed colo'ed sojers an'
    my 'Lias went to wah.

1855-1862

All Men Are Created Equal Except —

Abraham Lincoln insisted that the Civil War be fought primarily to save the Union. As late as the summer of 1862, he wrote to Horace Greeley, editor of The New York *Tribune:* "If I could save the Union without freeing any slave I would do it, and if I could save it by freeing all the slaves, I would do it; and if I could save it by freeing some and leaving others alone I would also do that." However, Lincoln had already made up his mind when he wrote these words that he would issue an Emancipation Proclamation when he judged the time to be ripe. As well as an expression of his own beliefs and ideals, Lincoln thought of the Proclamation in political and military terms. He planned to use it as a form of "psychological warfare" and declare slaves free at a time when manumission would cripple the South's armies and spirit most. The Proclamation would also win English and European sympathies for the North and thus keep the South from getting badly needed help from abroad.

As a politician, Lincoln's attitude toward slavery was a moderate one; he worked for years to contain rather than to abolish slavery. As a man, Lincoln was repulsed by slavery, and he condemned it. His personal feelings are revealed in this letter written in 1855 to his old friend, Joshua F. Speed.

Source: Basler, Roy P., ed. *Abraham Lincoln: His Speeches and Writings.* New York: World Book Company, 1946, p. 332.

In 1841 you and I had together a tedious low-water trip, on a Steam Boat from Louisville to St. Louis. You may remember, as I well do, that from Louisville to the mouth of the Ohio, there were, on board, ten or a dozen slaves, shackled together in irons. That sight was a continued torment to me; and I see something like it every time I touch the Ohio, or any other slave-border. It is hardly fair for you to assume that I have no interest in a thing which has, and continually exercises, the power of making me miserable. You ought rather to appreciate how much the great body of the Northern people do crucify their feelings, in order to maintain their loyalty to the Constitution and the Union.

I do oppose the extension of slavery, because my judgment and feelings so prompt me; and I am under no obligation to the contrary. If for this you and I must differ, differ we must. . . .

I am not a Know-Nothing [a third political party formed in the 1850's, a "super-patriotic" group that fought to keep "native America" from being overrun by "foreign" influences and that was hostile to many ethnic and religious groups, especially toward Roman Catholics and Irish-Americans]. That is certain. How could I be? How can anyone who abhors the oppression of Negroes be in favor of degrading classes of white people? Our progress in degeneracy appears to me to be pretty rapid. As a nation, we began by declaring that "all men are created equal." We now practically read it "all men are created equal *except Negroes*." When the Know-Nothings get control, it will read "all men are created equal, except Negroes, *and foreigners, and Catholics*." When it comes to this I should prefer emigrating to some country where they make no pretence of loving liberty—to Russia, for instance, where despotism can be taken pure, and without the base alloy of hypocrisy.

1860's

To Be Free as a Bird

Life on the plantation was not designed to prepare slaves for freedom, but it was impossible to keep the idea out of black men's minds. The great Southern statesman and philosopher Thomas Jefferson had declared that all men are created equal, and many men, both black and white, believed that he was speaking the truth. As the tides of the Civil War washed closer and closer to the plantation, the cry of "freedom now" became louder among thousands of slaves. But for some, the old familiar plantation life and the bonds of human loyalty came into painful conflict with the lure of freedom.

The moving conversation related here shows the hard decision that one young man had to make.

Source: *John Brown's Body* by Stephen Vincent Benet. Holt, Rinehart and Winston, Inc. Copyright 1927, 1928 by Stephen Vincent Benet. Copyright renewed 1955, 1956 by Rosemary Carr Benet. Reprinted by permission of Brandt & Brandt.

"What you so wakeful for, black boy?"

"Thinkin', woman."
"You got no call to be thinkin', little black boy,
Thinkin's a trouble, a h'ant lookin' over de shoulder,
Set yo' head on my breas' and forget about thinkin'."

"I got my head on yo' breas', and it's sof' dere, woman,
Sof' and sweet as a mournin' out of de Scriptures,
Sof' as two Solomon doves. But I can't help thinkin'."
"Ain't I good enough for you no more, black boy?
Don' you love me no more dat you mus' keep thinkin'?"

"You's better'n good to me and I loves you, woman,
Till I feels like Meshuck down in de fiery furnace,
Till I feels like God's own chile. But I keeps on thinkin',
Wonderin' what I'd feel like if I was free."

"Hush, black boy, hush for de Lord's sake!"

        "But listen, woman——"

"Hush yo'self, black boy, lean yo'self on my breas',
Talk like that and paterollers'll git you,
Swinge you all to bits with a blacksnake whip,
Squinch-owl carry yo' talk to de paterollers,
It ain't safe to talk like that."

        "I got to, woman,
I got a feelin' in my heart."

      "Den you set on dat feelin'!
Never heard you talk so in all my born days!
Ain't we got a good cabin here?"

      "Sho', we got a good cabin."
"Ain't we got good vittles, ain't old Mistis kind to us?"
"Sho' we got good vittles, and ole Mistis she's kind.
I'se mighty fond of ole Mistis."

      "Den what you talkin',
You brash fool-nigger?"

      "I just got a feelin', woman.
Ole Marse Billy, he's goin' away tomorrow.
Marse Clay, he's goin' with him to fight de Yankees,
All of 'em goin', yes suh."

      "And what if dey is?"
"Well, sposin' de Yankees beats?"

      "Ain't you got *no* sense,
  nigger?
Like to see any ole Yankees lick ole Marse Billy
And young Marse Clay!"

      "Hi, woman, ain't dat de trufe!"
"Well den——"

      "But I sees 'em jus' goin' and goin',
Goin' to war like Joshua, goin' like David,
And it makes me want to be free. Ain't you never thought
At all about bein' free?"

      "Sho', co'se I thought of it.
I always reckoned when ole Marse Billy died,
Old Mistis mebbe gwine to set some of us free,
Mebbe she will."

      "But we-uns gwine to be old den,

We won't be young and have the use of our hands,
We won't see our young 'uns growin' up free around us,
We won't have the strength to hoe our own co'n ourselves,
I want to be free, like me, while I got my strength."
"You might be a lot worse off and not be free,
What'd you do if ole man Zachary owned us?"

"Kill him, I reckon."
                                  "Hush, black boy, for God's sake hush!"

"I can't help it, woman. Dey ain't so many like him
But what dey is is too pizen-mean to live.
Can't you hear dat feelin' I got, woman? I ain't scared
Of talk and the paterollers, and I ain't mean.
I'se mighty fond of ole Mistis and ole Marse Billy,
I'se mighty fond of 'em all at de Big House,
I wouldn't be nobody else's nigger for nothin'.
But I hears 'em goin' away, all goin' away,
With horses and guns and things, all stompin' and wavin',
And I hears the chariot-wheels and that Jordan River,
Rollin' and Rollin' and Rollin' thu' my sleep,
And I wants to be free. I wants to see my chillun
Growin' up free, and all bust out of Egypt!
I wants to be free like an eagle in de air,
Like an eagle in de air."

December 13, 1862

Emancipation Should Be the Center of Northern Policy

The author of the following editorial, which first appeared in *The Spectator* for December 13, 1862, praised the first Negro regiments in the Union Army for their gallantry and courage. And he also condemned northern political leaders for their failure to proclaim publicly that emancipation was the very heart of their policy.

The editorial was reprinted in the January 17, 1863, edition of *The Living Age,* a widely read sort of "Reader's Digest" of the times.

Source: "The Policy of a Negro Army for the North." *The Spec-*

tator, 13 December, 1862. Reprinted in *The Living Age,* 17 January, 1863, pp. 136-137.

The first negro regiments have been raised. They have shown remarkable spirit and remarkable subordination. One of them raised by General Jim Lane, won the day against heavy odds in a little engagement at Island Mounds, on the 27th October. A company of the rawest negro recruits sailed up the Sapelo, in Florida, under Colonel Beard, early in November, twice landed under heavy fire and dispersed their enemies, and behaved altogether with the most ardent enthusiasm and courage during this, their first military trial. The negro volunteers are as eager and forward as American recruits seem now to be reluctant. What is more they are more amenable to discipline than the native Americans. . . . And for them now, even more than for the Northern white laborers, there is beginning to be a purpose in the war. . . .

None can now have the same stake in the contest as the negroes themselves. All this is beyond the possibility of question, and is quite clear to the negroes of Port Royal and of Kansas themselves. But the statesmen of the North have failed as yet to see the bearing of it. They are drifting blindly, and almost reluctantly, into an emancipation policy; and so may lose half the political fruits of it. If they make this the recognized center of their policy—as it must become if the war lasts . . . they might grasp one hundred opportunities which would otherwise escape them.

1863

Receive Them With Open Arms

"Persons of African descent" were invited to join the Union army as soldiers in 1863 after President Lincoln issued the Emancipation Proclamation. General Lorenzo Thomas was sent to the Mississippi Valley to supervise recruiting of black troops. He went about his work with great zeal. In Memphis, Helena, and elsewhere, he met with Negroes, explained the Emancipation policy, and urged them to respond to their country's call. He also spoke to white officers and soldiers at Lake Providence, Louisiana, and he minced no words.

Source: Greeley, Horace. *The American Conflict: A History of the Great Rebellion in the United States of America, 1860-1865.* Hartford, Connecticut: O. D. Case and Company, 1866, II.

You know full well—for you have been over this country—that the Rebels have sent into the field all their available fighting men—every man capable of bearing arms; and you know they have kept at home all their slaves for the raising of subsistence for their armies in the field. In this way, they can bring to bear against us all the strength of their so-called Confederate States; while we at the North can only send a portion to cultivate our army. The Administration has determined to take from the Rebels this source of supply—to take their negroes and compel them to send back a portion of the Whites to cultivate their deserted plantations—and very poor persons they would be to fill the place of the dark-hued laborer. They must do this, or their armies will starve. . . .

All of you will some day be on picket-duty; and I charge you all, if any of this unfortunate race come within your lines, that you do not turn them away, but receive them kindly and cordially. They are to be encouraged to come to us; they are to be received with open arms; they are to be fed and clothed; they are to be armed.

October 7, 1864

"Those Dainty Folks Who Object"

Not all Northerners favored the Emancipation Proclamation. Some people claimed that the government's announced anti-slavery policy had divided the North and united the South.

Speaking in Brooklyn, New York, on October 7, 1864, General Carl Schurz, who later became a newspaper editor and a Senator from Missouri, defended the Proclamation. He had harsh words for Northern whites who said they would not fight by the side of the Negro and who were thus dodging the draft by paying a sum of money required by law or by sending a substitute to serve for them.

Source: Peabody, Selim H., compiler. *American Patriotism.* New York: American Book Exchange, 1880, p. 629.

The Treason of Slavery

The Emancipation Proclamation, I say, added two hundred thousand black soldiers to our armies, and it may indeed have kept some white ones away, who merely wanted an excuse for not going anyhow. They say a white soldier cannot fight by the side of a negro. I know of white soldiers who were very glad to see the negro fight by their side. Ask our brave men at Petersburg, along the Mississippi, and on the Southern coast. Their cheers, when they saw the black columns dash upon the works of the enemy, did not sound like indignant protest against the companionship. But those dainty folks who raise the objection as a point of honor, will, I candidly believe, indeed not fight by the side of the negro, for they are just the men who will not fight at all.

1852-1863

Uncle Tom: Agitator

In 1863 when President Lincoln first met Harriet Beecher Stowe, author of *Uncle Tom's Cabin,* he remarked, "So you're the little woman who wrote the book that made this great war."

What the President meant was that in 1852 Mrs. Stowe had written a novel that had deeply stirred the hearts of the people of the North against the enslavement of blacks in America. *Uncle Tom's Cabin* was truly one of the events that led the United States into the Civil War.

Uncle Tom himself is one of the most famous of all literary characters. Some people wept about him. Others hailed him as a martyred saint. Still others branded his characterization as an outlandish lie.

In the twentieth century, "Uncle Tom" is used by many blacks as an expression of contempt to mean a person who does not stand up for his human rights, who goes along with white suppression of black. However, the author of this article insists that it is high time for those who malign Uncle Tom to reread the novel, for Harriet Beecher Stowe's character was really an agitator.

Source: Large, Arlen J. "Uncle Tom, Agitator: Mrs. Stowe's Negro Character Wasn't Really So Servile." *Wall Street Journal,* November 25, 1966.

WASHINGTON—Among the losers in the recent election was 25-year-old David Reed, a Republican running in Chicago against veteran Democratic Congressman William Dawson.

Both are Negroes. The militant Mr. Reed labeled the elderly Mr. Dawson an Uncle Tom, a satrap who cares more about staying in good graces with Mayor Richard Daley than fighting ghetto poverty. "For too long, the people of the First District have lived on Mayor Daley's plantation," said Mr. Reed.

There was no need for the candidate to stop and define the term "Uncle Tom"; its meaning has been quite plain among Negroes for decades. Not until lately, however, has the name's harsh connotation been fully recognized in standard dictionaries. Here's the entry in the brand-new Random House Dictionary of the English Language:

> Uncle Tom. (Contemptuous) A Negro who is abjectly servile or deferential to whites (so called after the leading character in "Uncle Tom's Cabin").

Uncle Tom or not, Congressman Dawson won the election big, but Uncle Tom himself remains in undeserved disgrace. And that's a shame, because a fresh reading of Harriet Beecher Stowe's 114-year-old novel suggests that its hero's good name is unjustly maligned by today's usage, that in fact Uncle Tom was a rather starchy old fellow, a trouble-maker on Simon Legree's plantation. . . .

It's easy to see why Mrs. Stowe's fictional character became a symbol of spinelessness; several scenes in the book portray a craven Tom. His first master, a relatively kindly Kentuckian, decides to sell him. Tom is summoned to the parlor by Mr. Shelby and, upon hearing the news, is told he can have the rest of the day off if he promises not to escape.

"You can have the day to yourself. Go anywhere you like, boy."

"Thank you, Mas'r," said Tom.

One doesn't have to be a Stokely Carmichael these days to wince at that "boy," or at Tom's abjectly servile reply. While Tom was meekly preparing to report to the slave trader the next day, fellow-slave Eliza was showing her spunk in her famous sprint across the Ohio River ice.

Mrs. Stowe's portrait of Tom was aimed at a 19th Century audience more susceptible to religious arguments than is today's reading public. Over and over, she scored abolitionist points by picturing Tom as spiri-tually superior to his various owners. "Pray for them that 'spitefully use you,' the good book says," declaims Tom, referring to the slave-trader. "I'm sure I'd rather be sold, ten thousand times over, than to have all that ar poor crittur's got to answer for."

Sold down the river to New Orleans, Tom is bought by the humane but dissolute father of the saintly Little Eva, who shares the old Negro's pleasure in Bible reading. Tom begins to show some backbone by gently chewing out his master for getting drunk. And when Tom is offered his choice of freedom or of continued good treatment in his cushy job as

103

coachman, the slave opts instantly for "... bein' a free man! That's what I'm joyin' for."

To Howard University's Dr. Lovell, this incident is persuasive evidence that "Uncle Tom really doesn't deserve the kind of reputation he's received."

But the kindly New Orleans master is killed in a barroom brawl, and Uncle Tom is sold to be a field hand on the cotton plantation of Simon Legree, another Stowe character whose name has become part of the language.

Uncle Tom's goodness soon has Mr. Legree climbing the walls. He orders Tom to flog a fellow slave. Looking his owner in the eye, Tom declares: "Mas'r, I never shall do it—never." Tom himself is flogged for disobedience, recovering under the ministrations of Mr. Legree's beautiful Negro mistress. Later Tom advises her and another woman slave to escape, and refuses to divulge their hiding place. In the end, a furious Simon Legree beats Tom to death for his stiff-necked attitude.

For pure starch, that's quite an example for Congressman Dawson, David Reed—or any man—to live up to.

circa 1863

Uncle Reuben: Model Negro

> This anonymous biography of "Uncle Reuben" was contained in the official report of the General Superintendent of Freedmen, United States Army, Department of Tennessee. It reveals at least one northern liberator's conception of the "ideal" Negro. While the case history undoubtedly was meant to be a tribute to "Uncle Reuben," the writer's last two sentences reveal an attitude toward blacks that was not much different from that which "Uncle Reuben's" former owners held.
>
> Source: *Report of the General Superintendent of Freedmen, Department of the Tennessee and State of Arkansas for 1864.* Memphis, Tennessee. Published in 1865.

That the negro is not wholly without ability to realize this prospect, there is convincing proof in the life of a full black, at Pine Bluff, well known as "Uncle Reuben." He was born in Georgia, and fell to a master who had but few slaves. He discovered such energy and tact, as well as complete devotion to his master's interests, that the latter entrusted everything to his management. The slave raised him from poverty to wealth. The master was enabled to buy a large plantation in Arkansas, and stock it with negroes. As his circumstances grew easier, his habits became extravagant. His estate became involved; and when overwhelmed with indebtedness, he died. The widow, helpless and without resources, called Uncle Reuben, told him that she had no one to rely upon but him, and placed her all in his hands. He was aroused by this touching confidence. He became more ambitious than ever to bring the first Bolls of Cotton to town, and to average still more to the acre than the neighboring planters. The number of bales grown on the plantation increased every year out. The children were sent North to school. His success was so remarkable, that the white overseers around became jealous of a negro's outstripping them. They compelled the mistress to place a white nominally over him. He was not, however, interfered with, until the young masters returned from the North. The fact that a negro slave had educated them, and by his own prudence and energy had amassed for them a fortune of nearly $150,000 was not as grateful to them as true. His mistress, however, always treated him as kindly as she dared. On the approach of our armies he remained till all had left but himself and family. Being assured that the President's Proclamation was true, he also quietly came in. Spirited and proud, he is the most humble of all. He refuses to sit in the presence of whites, and touches his hat to you at every address.

1827-1865

Traveling to Proclaim Truth

Although she was born a slave and named Isabella, Sojourner Truth did not keep either this name or status long. She ran away from her owners in upstate New York and then became free under that state's Emancipation Act of July 4, 1827. Deeply religious, she believed her Lord had called her to "sojourn," to travel throughout the nation speaking "truth." So she renamed herself Sojourner Truth.

Sojourner Truth was a dramatic and powerful person both in appearance and in speech. Tall and gaunt, she wore a banner across her chest with the words that are engraved on the Liberty Bell: "Proclaim Liberty throughout the land unto all the inhabitants thereof." Her voice was deep and resonant, and her words for emancipation and women's rights compelled the attention of great audiences, both black and white.

During the Civil War, Abraham Lincoln invited Sojourner Truth to the White House to honor her for services to the Union cause. She, in turn, presented the President with a Bible from the people of Baltimore.

Here is a brief account of some of her wartime activities written by the Negro historian Benjamin Quarles.

Source: Quarles, Benjamin. *The Negro in the Civil War.* Boston: Little, Brown and Company, 1953, pp. 228-229.

Another Negro woman who knew her way around an army camp was Sojourner Truth. This legendary character confined her visits to camps in the North, particularly those in Michigan—she was perhaps a bit too old to go to camps located in the South (she admitted to being over seventy, although she indignantly denied the widespread rumor that she had nursed George Washington). As a rule whenever she showed up in camp, the regiment would be ordered into line, and she would display the boxes of gifts she had solicited. Then she would distribute the contents, interspersing bits of motherly advice.

She raised money for these gifts by lecturing and singing. One of the numbers in her fund-raising repertoire was of her own composition. Written to the John Brown tune and entitled "The Valiant Soldier," its flavor may be sampled by one of its six stanzas:

"We are done with hoeing cotton, we are done with hoeing corn:
We are colored Yankee soldiers, as sure as you are born.
When Massa hears us shouting, he will think 'tis Gabriel's horn,
As we go marching on."

1861

Blacks Are "Real Soldiers" in the Rebel Army

In the early stages of the Civil War, the South called on its free blacks to volunteer for service as military laborers. In New Orleans, free men of color held a meeting and took "measures to form a military organization, and to tender their services to the Governor of Louisiana." Although voluntary offers did not give the South the number of workers needed to support the war effort, in 1861 southern states were not yet ready or forced to ask black men to fight in the Confederate Army.

106

In 1861 the states of the Confederacy passed draft laws requiring all male free Negroes between the ages of eighteen and fifty to register at their local courthouses. Workers were selected from these lists and notified by the local sheriff of their call for duty. Under Virginia law, free blacks who were so chosen could not be required to serve more than 180 days without their consent. These men were given the same rations, pay, quarters, and medical care as white laborers. As the war continued, draft laws were extended to include male slaves and, in some cases, women.

Meanwhile, the North continued to debate about using blacks to help fight the South. Frederick Douglass argued that it was ridiculous for the North to keep stalling. The South, he pointed out, had already set the precedent. Not only were free blacks and slaves serving the Confederacy as laborers, Douglass said, but also many blacks were "real soldiers."

Source: *Douglass' Monthly*, IV, September, 1861, p. 516.

It is now pretty well established that there are at the present moment many colored men in the Confederate army doing duty not only as cooks, servants, and laborers, but as real soldiers, having muskets on their shoulders, and bullets in their pockets, ready to shoot down loyal troops, and do all that soldiers may do to destroy the Federal Government and build up that of the traitors and rebels. There were such soldiers at Manassas, and they are probably there still. There is a negro in the army as well as in the field, and our Government is likely to find it out before the war comes to an end. That the negroes are numerous in the rebel army, and do for that army its heaviest work, is beyond question.

1861

Body Servants March to War with Confederates

When members of slaveholding families enlisted in the Confederate forces, they often took slaves along to serve them in camp. Some of these body servants, or valets, were free Negroes such as one John Scott, who had been through the Mexican War and then three and a half years on the Civil War front as body servant to Charles Minor Blackford of the Second Virginia Cavalry.

Some wealthy volunteers had several servants, but the usual practice was for one slave to take care of his master. There were cases in which one slave would serve a "mess" of four to eight men who all chipped in to meet the costs of keeping a valet. Body servants were responsible for cooking, washing, cleaning quarters, and caring for the masters' horses.

It would seem that the chances to desert to Union forces and the prospect of freedom would weaken the black servant's loyalty to his master. But Negro historian Benjamin Quarles claims: "Leading all other Negroes in fidelity were the body servants. They almost never deserted. If they vanished for several days, they usually showed up with forage ["borrowed" food and supplies to add to the usual scant rations issued by army commissaries]. The relationships that existed between body servants and their masters are described below.

Source: Wiley, Bell Irvin. *The Life of Johnny Reb.* New York: The Bobbs-Merrill Company, 1943, p. 328.

During battles the body servant usually remained in the rear out of reach of Federal shells. But a few became so thoroughly imbued with the martial spirit as to grab up muskets during battle and take shots at the enemy. There are several instances on record of servants thus engaged in killing and capturing Federals. On at least one occasion Confederate domestics [servants] made prisoners of Negroes serving Yankee officers. When fighting abated, the colored aide usually loaded himself with canteens and haversacks and went in search of his master. If the latter was wounded, the servant carried him to shelter and sought medical assistance; if he was killed, the domestic made arrangements for his burial or escorted the body home. The relation between master and body servant was usually marked by genuine affection. Frequently intimate association extended back to childhood days. . . .

The life of the body servant was generally not a hard one. He seldom lacked for food, and he usually recouped his wardrobe in the wake of each battle from Yankee sources. He had opportunities to earn money by doing odd jobs for his master's comrades, and the stake thus acquired could be increased or diminished by sessions with fellow servants at dice or cards. Occasional visits home for provisions made it possible for him to play the hero among less fortunate inmates of slave quarters. In camp his ready laugh . . . was a valuable stimulant to soldier morale, as was his proficiency with song and guitar.

It was with real regret, therefore, that most private soldiers dispensed with the service of their colored associates during the second and third years of conflict. But the increasing scarcity of provisions in the army and the greater need of their labor by civilians made it necessary for the Negroes to be sent home. Those who remained in camp after 1863 were largely the servants of commissioned officers or were employed by the government as musicians, cooks, nurses, hostlers [one who takes care of horses] , and wagondrivers.

1864

I Stay Where the Generals Are

> Widespread in the North was the belief that the Confederacy was using blacks as soldiers. That idea probably originated because body servants always stayed close to their masters and were thus often in the front lines. Undoubtedly some were pressed into emergency military service. Among both Confederate and Union troops, blacks were known to be accurate with a rifle and courageous in the heat of battle. But the unnamed black servant in the anecdote below is remembered for his sense of humor rather than his marksmanship.
>
> Source: Quarles, Benjamin. *The Negro in the Civil War*. Boston: Little, Brown and Company, 1953, pp. 266-267.

One of the greatest contributions by the Negro in camp was the humor and jollity that he radiated. General John B. Gordon related that Robert E. Lee often told with relish the story of his chat with an aged Negro who called to see him at headquarters. "General Lee," said the ancient one, pulling off his hat, "I been wanting to see you a long time. I'm a soldier."

"Ah? To what army do you belong—to the Union Army or the Southern Army?"

"Oh, General, I belong to your army."

"Well, have you been shot?"

"No, sir; I ain't been shot yet."

"How is that? Nearly all of our men get shot."

"Why, General, I ain't been shot 'cause I stay back whar de generals stay."

Should the Confederacy Use Blacks as Soldiers?

As the Civil War dragged on and on, military manpower became an increasingly serious problem in the South. As one high-ranking member of the Confederate cabinet put it, "I know not where white men can be found" for the armies of the South. On February 11, 1865, Judah Philip Benjamin, then Secretary of War for the Confederacy, made a speech urging slaveholders to let their slaves fight. His speech stirred up intense excitement in the country, especially among owners of black men.

Immediately following Benjamin's speech, a bill was introduced into the Confederate House of Representatives authorizing the enlistment of 200,000 slaves, with the consent of their owners. While the measure was being discussed by the South's legislature, General Robert E. Lee wrote the following letter in answer to a member of the House who had requested his opinion.

Source: Wilson, Joseph. *The Black Phalanx: A History of the Negro Soldiers of the United States in the Wars of 1775-1812, 1861-1865.* Hartford, Connecticut: American Publishing Company, 1888, pp. 492-493.

Head-quarters Confederate State Armies,
February 18th, 1865.

Hon. Barksdale, House of Representatives, Richmond.

Sir: I have the honor to acknowledge the receipt of your letter of the 12th inst. with reference to the employment of negroes as soldiers. I think the measure not only expedient but necessary. The enemy will certainly use them against us if he can get possession of them, and as his present numerical superiority will enable him to penetrate many parts of the country, I can not see the wisdom of the policy of holding them to await his arrival, when we may, by timely action and judicious management, use them to arrest his progress. I do not think that our white population can supply the necessities of a long war without over-taxing its capacity, and imposing great suffering upon our people; and I believe we should provide resources for a protracted struggle, not merely for a battle or a campaign.

In answer to your second question I can only say that, in my opinion, under proper circumstances the negroes will make efficient soldiers. I think we could at least do as well with them as the enemy, and he attaches great importance to their assistance. Under good officers and good instructions I do not see why they should not become soldiers. They possess all the physical qualifications, and their habits of obedience constitute a good formulation for discipline. They furnish a more promising material than many armies of which we read in history, which owed their efficiency to discipline alone. I think those employed should be freed. It would be neither wisdom nor justice, in my opinion, to require them to serve as slaves. The best course to pursue, it seems to me, is to call for such as are willing to come with the consent of their owners. Impressment or draft would not be likely to bring out the best class, and the use of coercion would make the measure distasteful to them and to their owners. I have no doubt if Congress would authorize their reception into service, and empower the President to call upon individuals or States for such as they are willing to contribute with the condition of emancipation to all enrolled, a sufficient number would be forthcoming to enable us to try the experiment.

If it proves successful, most of the objections to the matter would disappear, and if individuals still remained unwilling to send their negroes to the army, the force of public opinion in the States would soon bring about such legislation as would remove all obstacles. I think the matter should be left as far as possible to the people and the States, which alone can legislate as the necessities of this particular service may require. As to the mode of organizing them, it should be left as free from restraint as possible. Experience will suggest the best course, and it would be inexpedient to trammel the subject with provisions that might in the end prevent the adoption of reforms, suggested by actual trial.

With great respect,
ROBERT E. LEE, General

early 1860's

Shall Black Men Move to Haiti?

The American Colonization Society, founded in 1816, tried for years to solve race problems by encouraging free Negroes to return to Africa. Among the supporters of this idea were Henry Clay, John Randolph, some slaveowners, and some blacks. However, most blacks and abolitionists opposed a return of American Negroes to Africa.

One of the major issues leading to and coming out of the Civil War was the status of the black man. Thus, the war brought renewed interest in colonization, particularly somewhere in the Americas, as an answer to the dilemma of black and white. According to *The Liberator* for May 12, 1862, the Tammany Hall Young Men's Democratic Club passed a resolution which read, in part, "We are opposed to emancipating negro slaves, unless on some plan of colonization, in order that they may not come in contact with the white man's labor." Tammany was only one of many groups that believed colonization was *the* answer to the "Negro question."

As more and more fugitive slaves poured into Union Army camps, more and more colonization schemes were born. Some were for voluntary colonization; others suggested compulsory colonization. But all of these plans were based on the assumption that blacks and whites could never live together in peace as equals.

One of the most controversial plans involved establishment of a colony in Haiti. James Redpath, a white British-born organizer, set up an office in Boston funded with $20,000 from the Haitian Government. Redpath's title was "General Agent of the Haytian Bureau of Emigration." Several prominent blacks served as agents and spokesmen for the Bureau. Among them were James T. Holly, William Wells Brown, Henry Highland Garnet, J. B. Smith, and H. Ford Douglass.

The Haitian colonization plan stimulated great debate. Here are two reactions representative of supporters and attackers of the plan.

Sources: *Pine and Palm*, June 2, 1861. *The Liberator*, February 3, 1861.

YES (The speaker is William Wells Brown, an escaped slave who educated himself. He traveled and lectured widely and became a well-known novelist.)

I hold that the descendants of Africa, in this country, will never be respected until they shall leave the cook shop and barber's chair and the white-wash brush. . . . To emigrate to Hayti, and to develop the resources of the island, and to build up a powerful and influential government there, which shall demonstrate the genius and capabilities of the Negro, is as good an Anti-Slavery work as can be done in the Northern States of this Union. . . .

To attempt to connect the Haytian emigration movement with the old and hateful colonization scheme, is only to create a prejudice in the minds of the people. Originated by a colored nation, in the interests of the colored race, conducted and sustained exclusively by the friends or

112

members of that nation and that race, it is essentially and diametrically opposed to the colonization project, which was originated by slaveholders, in the interests of slavery, and conducted and sustained exclusively by the friends of bondage, and the haters of the Negro.

Pine and Palm, June 2, 1861

NO (Dr. John Rock was a graduate of the American Medical College in Philadelphia and a member of the Massachusetts Bar. A man of many talents and interests, by the time he was thirty-five years old he had been a schoolteacher, a dentist, and a physician, and had begun a law practice.)

There are many reasons and much philosophy in abandoning a country and people who have so diligently sought to crush us. But, then, it must be remembered that there is no other country that is particularly inviting to us, and on this account the masses of the colored people, who *think* for themselves, have believed that the same effort made in working our way up in this country, and in civilizing the whites, would accomplish our object as certain and as easy as we could by emigrating to a foreign country, and overcoming the disadvantages of language, climate, low wages, and other obstacles which would tend to embarrass us in a strange country. This being our country, we have made up our minds to remain in it, and to try to make it worth living in.

The Liberator, February 3, 1860

March 6, 1863

"Oh, Detroit! Oh, Detroit, How Thou Hast Fallen!"

Even while the Civil War was in progress anti-Negro riots took place in the North. On March 6, 1863, a screaming mob moved down Beaubien Street in Detroit. They cried, "Kill all the d----d niggers." The rioters were angry about acts allegedly committed by a man named Thomas Faulkner against both a black and a white girl. The mob claimed that Faulkner was a "nigger." But Faulkner claimed to be a white man, and he was a regular voter.

Responsible citizens of Detroit condemned the mob violence toward the city's black inhabitants. The Reverend S. S. Hunting of the Unitarian Church denounced the lawless actions from his pulpit. The Detroit *Advertiser and Tribune* praised the Reverend's sermon in an editorial. "If the houses of one class of citizens are not safe from the torch of the incendiary, is anybody's safe? If we resort to mobs where shall we stop?," asked the editors.

Here is one victim's eyewitness account of the riot.

Source: (Anonymous). *Thrilling Narrative from the Lips of Sufferers of the Late Detroit Riot, March 6, 1863 With the Hair Breadth Escapes of Men, Women, and Children and Destruction of Colored Men's Property, Not Less than $15,000.* Published by the author in 1863.

STATEMENT OF THOMAS HOLTON—I reside on Fort Street, between Beaubien and St. Antoine streets, and have a wife and one small child. We were aroused by the yells of the mob, and, on going to the street, heard windows smashing and hammering against doors, with dreadful curses of "Kill the Nigger."

A crowd rushed up to my residence and commenced their work of destruction in every possible way, with bricks, stones, and other destructive missiles, and the torch was soon set to our house. Myself and wife, with one child now, had to make the best of our efforts to escape with our lives.

They rushed after us with demoniac rage, and their curses and yells were terrifying. We would, most certainly, have fallen a prey to them, had not the hands in the Morocco Factory, just in the rear of our lot, called to us through there. We took it as a great favor, for no one could tell in what direction to go—all the streets seemed to be filled with the mob.

Without a moment's time, to even put on cloak, bonnet, or shawl, we started and wandered out to find a friend's house in the suburbs of the city, but losing our way, we found, on inquiry, way in the night, that we had been three miles and a half from the city. Being now at Cork Town, I feared to let them know who we were, for they might be a part of the number who had driven us from our homes.

We wandered all that night in the woods, with nothing to eat, nor covering from cold, till morning light. With frosted feet and our property destroyed, did the morning sun rise upon us, as destitute as when we came into the world, with the exception of what we had on, and without a friend to offer us protection, so far as we could learn. Oh, Detroit! Detroit, how hast thou fallen! No power in noonday to defend the helpless women and children from outlaws, till they have fully glutted their hellish appetites on the weak and defenseless. Humanity, where is thy blush!

Collecting the Unwritten Songs

As a young man growing up in New England, Thomas Wentworth Higginson was a student of Scottish ballads. He often said that he envied Sir Walter Scott, who had gone to Scotland, listened to the songs of the people he met in his travels, and written down these melodies. Scott's record of Scottish folk music preserved their beauty for people of other times in other places. Little did Thomas Higginson know that one day he would have an opportunity to gather and preserve some of the most beautiful Negro spirituals.

When Higginson completed college, he became an abolitionist minister. Active in the struggle for an end to slavery, he worked on the Underground Railroad and fought in the Kansas border clashes that erupted over the question of extending slavery into that territory.

During the Civil War, Higginson commanded the first regiment of ex-slaves in the Union Army. His years and travels in the South are documented in his autobiography, from which the selection about John Lynch's slave market is taken (Section 2, pp. 00-00). Colonel Higginson's military duties took him to South Carolina, Georgia, and Florida. And as he heard the songs of the black people, he began to write them down, for (he said) "history cannot afford to lose this portion of the record."

Source: Higginson, T. W. "Negro Spirituals." *The Atlantic Monthly,* Boston, June, 1867, Vol. XIX, pp. 685, 687, 689.

Often in the starlit evening I have returned from some lonely ride by the swift river, or on the plover-haunted barrens, and entering the camp, have silently approached some glimmering fire, round which the dusky figures moved in the rhythmical barbaric dance the negroes call a "shout," chanting, often harshly, but always in the most perfect time, some monotonous refrain. Writing down in the darkness, as best I could,—perhaps with my hand in the safe covert of my pocket,—the words of the song, I have afterwards carried it to my tent like some captured bird or insect, and then, after examination put it by. . . . The music I could only retain by ear. . . .

The words will be here given, as nearly as possible, in the original dialect. . . .

The favorite song in camp was the following,—sung with no accompaniment but the measured clapping of hands and the clatter of many feet. It was sung perhaps twice as often as any other. This was partly due to the fact that it properly consisted of a chorus alone, with which the verses of other songs might be combined at random.

I. HOLD YOUR LIGHT

Hold your light, Brudder Robert,—
Hold your light,
Hold your light on Canaan's shore.

What make ole Satan for follow me so?
Satan ain't got notin' for do wid me.
Hold Your light,
Hold Your light,
Hold your light on Canaan's shore.

This would be sung for half an hour at a time, perhaps, each person present being named in turn. . . .

Almost all their songs were thoroughly religious in their tone, however quaint their expression and were in a minor key, both as to words and music. The attitude is always the same, and, as a commentary on the life of the race, is infinitely pathetic. Nothing but patience for this life,—nothing but triumph in the next. Sometimes the present predominates, sometimes the future; but the combination is always implied. In the following, for instance, we hear simply the patience.

VII. THIS WORLD ALMOST DONE

Brudder, keep your lamp trimmin' and a-burnin',
Keep your lamp trimmin' and a-burnin',
Keep your lamp trimmin' and a-burnin',
For dis world most done.

So keep your lamp, &c.
Dis world most done.

But in the next, the final reward of patience is proclaimed as plaintively.

VIII. I WANT TO GO HOME

Dere's no rain to wet you,
Oh, yes, I want to go home.
Dere's no sun to burn you,
Oh, yes, I want to go home.

116

Oh, push along believers,
  Oh, yes, &c.
Dere's no hard trials,
  Oh, yes, &c.
Dere's no whips a-crackin',
  Oh, yes, &c.
My brudder on de wayside,
  Oh, yes, &c.
Oh, push along, my brudder,
  Oh, yes, &c.
Where dere's no stormy weather,
  Oh, yes, &c.
Dere's no tribulation,
  Oh, yes, &c.

But of all the "spirituals" that which surprised me the most, I think,—perhaps because it was that in which eternal nature furnished the images most directly,—was this. With all my experience of their ideals and ways of speech, I was startled when first I came on such a flower of poetry in that dark soil.

XVIII. I KNOW MOON-RISE

I know moon-rise, I know star-rise,
  Lay dis body down.

I walk in de moonlight, I walk in de starlight,
  To lay dis body down.

I'll walk in de graveyard, I'll walk through de graveyard
  To lay dis body down.

I'll lie in de grave and stretch out my arms;
  Lay dis body down.

An' my soul and your soul will meet in de day
  When I lay dis body down.

"I'll lie in de grave and stretch out my arms." Never, it seems to me, since man first lived and suffered was his infinite longing for peace uttered more plaintively than in that line.

The Black Phalanx Enters Richmond

In the last weeks of the Civil War, General Robert E. Lee and his men faced an army three times the size of their own as they attempted to defend the Confederate capital. General Sherman drove north from Savannah, Georgia, toward the city, while General Grant pressed south, crossing the Rapidan River and fighting his way through the Wilderness, west of Fredericksburg, Virginia. On April 2, 1865, Richmond was evacuated. Seven days later, Lee surrendered to Grant at the Appomattox Courthouse, eighty miles west of the smoking capital city.

Here is an account of the entry of the Black Phalanx into Richmond. Its author, Joseph Wilson, was chosen by his black comrades-in-arms after the war as their official historian.

Source: Wilson, Joseph T. *The Black Phalanx: A History of the Negro Soldiers of the United States in the Wars of 1775-1812, 1861-1865.* Hartford, Connecticut: American Publishing Company, 1888, p. 499.

The appointed time came, but instead of the draft, amid blazing roofs and falling walls, smoke and ashes, deafening reports of explosions, the frenzy of women and children, left alone not only by the negro conscripting officers and President Davis and his Cabinet, but by the army and navy; in the midst of such scenes, almost beyond description, the Black Phalanx of the Union army entered the burning city, the capital of rebeldom, scattering President Lincoln's Proclamation of Emancipation to the intended confederate black army. For twelve squares they chanted their war songs, "The Colored Volunteers," and "John Brown," in the chorus of which thousands of welcoming freedmen and freedwomen joined, making the welkin ring [filling the air] with the refrain,

> Glory, glory hallelujah,
> Glory, glory hallelujah,
> Glory, glory hallelujah,
> We is free today!

The decisive events of the next few days, following in rapid succession, culminating with Lee's surrender, on the 9th of April, at Appomattox, left no time for further action, and when the war was over, with the important and radical changes that took place, it was almost forgotten that such projects as arming and freeing the negro had ever been entertained in the South by the Confederate Government.

Section Six

Reconstruction–
Victories Won and Lost

August 14, 1862

Wouldn't You Like to Move to Central America?

President Abraham Lincoln welcomed a committee of free Negroes to the White House on the afternoon of August 14, 1862. Although the war was still going on, Lincoln already had begun to plan for the period of reconstruction that he knew must follow. He informed his visitors that Congress had appropriated money that could be used to help blacks colonize in some other country. Lincoln said that he believed their departure would be in the best interests of both races.

In the following excerpt from Lincoln's conversation with the "deputation of colored men" he had invited to the White House, the President suggests they consider a place in Central America. He knew, of course, that most of them were not keen about moving to Liberia in Africa.

Lincoln's description of a black colony in the Americas is so glowing that it sounds like "the promised land" of milk and honey. However, the President's attempt to sell his black visitors on the idea of emigrating and establishing a colony to which slaves could go when they were freed was unsuccessful.

Source: Nicolay, John G. and Hay, John, editors. *Abraham Lincoln: Complete Works.* New York: The Century Company, 1915, II, pp. 223-225.

You ought to do something to help those who are not so fortunate as yourselves. There is an unwillingness on the part of our people, harsh as it may be, for you free colored people to remain with us. Now, if you could give a start to the white people, you would open a wide door for many to be made free. If we deal with those who are not free at the

119

beginning, and whose intellects are clouded by slavery, we have very poor materials to start with. If intelligent colored men, such as are before me, would move in this matter, much might be accomplished. . . .

The place I am thinking about for a colony is in Central America. It is nearer to us than Liberia. . . . Unlike Liberia, it is a great line of travel—it is a highway. The country is a very excellent one for any people, and with great natural resources and advantages. . . . The particular place I have in view is to be a great highway from the Atlantic or Caribbean Sea to the Pacific Ocean, and this particular place has all the advantages for a colony. On both sides there are harbors—among the finest in the world. Again, there is evidence of very rich coal mines. . . .

The practical thing I want to ascertain is, whether I can get a number of able-bodied men, with their wives and children, who are willing to go when I present evidence of encouragement and protection. Could I get a hundred tolerably intelligent men . . . ? Can I have fifty? If I could have twenty-five able-bodied men, with a mixture of women and children . . . I could make a successful commencement. I want you to let me know whether this can be done or not. . . . I ask you, then, to consider seriously, not pertaining to yourselves merely, nor for your race and ours for the present time, but as one of the things, if successfully managed, for the good of mankind—not confined to the present generation. . . .

The chairman of the delegation briefly replied that they would hold a consultation, and in a short time give an answer.

The President said: "Take your full time—no hurry at all."

The delegation then withdrew.

1865

No Slaves in the Year of Jubilee

Just how destitute some former slaveowners were in the period immediately following the Civil War is reflected in this anonymous folk rhyme. One can sense the feeling of joy and of justice that must have come to many a freedman when his master had to do menial tasks and hard labor that he and his fellow slaves had once performed.

This poem is one of many collected by the black expert on folk rhymes, Thomas W. Talley of Fisk University. The use of dialect and the word "nigger" in this poem and other folk literature which is offensive to people now was regarded differently in earlier times—such techniques and devices were used to capture or recreate the mood and flavor of oral literature.

Source: Talley, Thomas W. *Negro Folk Rhymes: Wise and Otherwise.* Port Washington, N.Y.: © Kennikat Press Inc. 1968.

Destitute Former Slave Owners

Missus an' Mosser a-walkin' de street
Deir han's in deir pockets an' nothin' to eat.
She'd better be home a-washin' up de dishes,
An' a-cleanin' up de ole man's raggity britches.
He'd better run 'long an' git out de hoes
An' clear out his own crooked weedy corn rows;
De Kingdom is come, de Niggers is free.
Hain't no Nigger slaves in de Year Jubilee.

1865

"But Our Slaves Were Not So Foolish"

Victoria Hunter Clayton was the wife of Major General (C.S.A.) Henry D. Clayton. He was said to be the first man in Alabama to enlist in the Confederate Army. After the war, Clayton became Judge of the Circuit Court of Alabama and President of the University of Alabama. Clayton urged his wife to write her memoirs of their life in antebellum days. In this excerpt, Mrs. Clayton tells how her husband came home from the war to tell their slaves they were free.

Source: Clayton, Victoria V., *White and Black Under the Old Regime.* Milwaukee: The Young Churchman Company, 1899, pp. 152-153.

Ere long we received the anticipated intelligence that our slaves were all made free by the government of the United States. To this we bowed with submission. My husband said, "Victoria, I think it best for me to inform our negroes of their freedom." So he ordered all the grown slaves to come to him, and told them they no longer belonged to him as property, but were all free. He said to them, "You are not bound to remain with me any longer, and I have a proposition to make to you. If any of you desire to leave, in consideration of your faithfulness to my wife during the four years of my absence, I propose to furnish you with a conveyance to move you, and with provisions for the balance of the year."

The universal answer was, "Master, we want to stay right here with you."

The pleasure of knowing they were free seemed to be mingled with sadness. That very night, long after the usual hour for bedtime, the hum of the busy spinning wheel was heard. On inquiry in the morning I found that Nancy was the one spinning long into the night. Asking why she had been up so late at night at work, she replied:

"I have no master to feed and clothe Nancy now. She will have to look out for something for herself and look out for the rainy day."

In many instances slaves were so infatuated with the idea of being, as they said, "free as birds," that they left their homes and consequently suffered; but our slaves were not so foolish.

1865-1870

Forty Acres and a Mule

Many blacks and some whites argued that freedmen were entitled to payment in land or money for the two centuries of labor they had given to the nation. One popular suggestion was that each freedman be given forty acres and a mule so that he could start a new life as an independent farmer. The suggestion was discussed widely, and "forty acres and a mule" became so common a slogan that many blacks actually believed that they would receive such payment for their past services. However, neither the federal or state governments took any action on this idea. But there were individuals who traveled through the post-war South taking advantage of the misplaced trust of newly freed blacks. The following selection tells how cruel hoaxes were perpetrated.

Source: U. S. Congress. *Testimony Taken by the Joint Select Committee to Inquire into the Condition of Affairs in the Late Insurrectionary States.* Ku Klux Klan Report, Alabama Testimony. Statement of John G. Pierce. Vol. 13, 1872.

I can tell you from what I know and have seen myself, and also from what negroes have told me, that they have been promised land and mules—forty acres of land and a mule—on divers occasions. Many an old negro has come to me and asked me about the thing. I can illustrate it by one little thing that I saw on a visit once to Gainesville, Sumter County. At a barbecue there I saw a man who was making a speech to the negroes, telling them what good he had done for them; that he had been to Washington City and had procured from one of the Departments here certain pegs. I saw the pegs. He had about two dozen on his arm; they were painted red and blue. He said that those pegs he had obtained from here at a great expense to himself; that they had been made by the Government for the purpose of staking out the negroes' forty acres. He told the negroes that all he wanted was to have the expenses paid to him, which was about a dollar a peg. He told them that they could stick one peg down at a corner, then walk so far one way and stick another down, then walk so far another way and stick another down, till they had got the four pegs down; and that, when the four pegs were down, the negroes' forty acres would be included in that area; and all he had to say to them was, that they could stick those pegs anywhere they pleased—on anybody's land they wanted to, but not to interfere with each other; and he would advise them, in selecting the forty acres, to take half woodland and half clear; that nobody would dare to interfere with those pegs.

New Year's Day, 1866

Gray-Haired, but Too Young to Speak

The third anniversary of the Emancipation Proclamation called for a real celebration. The war, at last, was over, and black men were free. Here is an eyewitness account of one celebration. It was held on New Year's Day, 1866, in the African Baptist Church in Richmond, Virginia.

Source: Roy, Joseph E. *Pilgrim's Letters*. Boston and Chicago: Congregational Sunday School and Publishing Society, 1888.

The church was decorated with evergreens and white flowers. On the wall above the pulpit was the motto, "This is the Lord's doing; it is marvelous in our eyes." 3000 Negroes squeezed into the church. They had waited two and a half hours in the rain to get in. Many thousands more were turned away for lack of hearing room. Many newly freed Negroes spoke. All of them thanked God and Abraham Lincoln. All prayed for the soldiers. The Negro speakers urged freedmen to be hardworking and patient. Above all, they urged them to get an education. One man contrasted this New Year's day with the last one. Another man said that he had been thrown into a Richmond jail. Then he was sold and sent handcuffed to New Orleans, leaving his children whom he had never seen since. And all because his father-in-law and his mother-in-law had run away to Massachusetts and he had received a letter from them.

A gray-haired man said he was too young to speak, for he was only born on the third of last April.* Then he asked, "But where today is the auction block that stood down there worn smooth? Where is its auctioneer? He was seen the other day peddling papers!"

*The day Richmond fell. Lee surrendered to Grant officially on April 9, 1865.

1865-1877

We Remember, We Remember—Stories of Ex-Slaves

"What did it feel like to be a slave?" That was the question which Ben A. Botkin, one of America's leading authorities on folklore, asked ex-slaves. During the Depression years, Botkin headed a team of interviewers working with the WPA Writers Project. That team conducted the most extensive survey of former slaves ever made. All of the blacks with whom the writers talked were then between 75 and 105 years old.

Botkin, the son of Lithuanian immigrants who settled in Massachusetts, sympathized readily with the hard lot of those who had been born in bondage. His own father was a barber who moved from town to town trying to eke out a living for his family. Eventually, young Ben, whose real last name was Rabotnik, went to Harvard University where he became interested in folklore and social history. He was determined that first-hand observations of former slaves should not be lost; thus, he set up a massive project to find and record their life stories. Here are the reminiscences of two blacks.

Source: Botkin, Ben A. *Lay My Burden Down: A Folk History of Slavery*. Chicago: The University of Chicago Press, 1945.

When freedom came, my mama said Old Master called all of 'em to his house, and he said, "You all free, we ain't got nothing to do with you no more. Go on away. We don't whup you no more, go on your way." My mama said they go on off, then they come back and stand around, just looking at him and Old Mistress. They give 'em something to eat and he say, "Go on away, you don't belong to us no more. You been freed." They go away and they kept coming back. They didn't have no place to go and nothing to eat. From what she said, they had a terrible time. She said it was bad times. Some took sick and had no 'tention and died. Seemed like it was four or five years before they got to places they could live. They all got scattered . . . Old Master every time they go back say, "You all go on away, You been set free. You have to look out for yourselves now."

When freedom come, folks left home, out in the streets, crying, praying, singing, shouting, yelling, and knocking down everything. Some shot off big guns. Then come the calm. It was sad then. So many folks done dead, things tore up, and nowheres to go and nothing to eat, nothing to do. It got squally. Folks got sick, so hungry. Some folks starved nearly to death. . . .

I worked for Massa 'bout four years after freedom 'cause he forced me to, said he couldn't 'ford to let me go. His place [in South Carolina] was near ruint, the fences burnt, and the house would have been, but it was rock. There was a battle fought near his place, and I had taken Missy to a hideout in the mountains to where her father was, 'cause there was bullets flying everywhere. When the war was over, Massa come home and says, "You son of a gun, you's supposed to be free, but you ain't, 'cause I ain't gwine give you freedom." So I goes on working for him till I gits the chance to steal a hoss from him. The woman I wanted to marry, Govie, she 'cides to come to Texas with me. Me and Govie, we rides that hoss 'most a hundred miles, then we turned him loose . . . and come on foot the rest of the way to Texas.

All we had to eat was what we could beg, and sometimes we went three days without a bite to eat . . . When we got cold we'd crawl in a brushpile and hug up close together to keep warm. Once in a while we'd come to a farmhouse, and the man let us sleep on cottonseed in his barn, but they was few and far between, 'cause they wasn't many houses in the country them days. . . .

When we gets to Texas . . . I settled on some land, and we cut some trees and split them open and stood them on end with the tops together for our house. Then we deadened some trees, and the land was ready to farm. There was some wild cattle and hogs, and that's the way we got our start, caught some of them and tamed them.

I don't know as I 'spected nothing from freedom, but they turned us out like a bunch of stray dogs, no homes, no clothing, no nothing, not 'nough food to last us one meal. . . . All we had to farm with was sharp sticks. We'd stick holes and plant corn, and when it come up we'd punch up the dirt round it. We didn't plant cotton, 'cause we couldn't eat that. I made bows and arrows to kill wild game with, and we never went to a store for nothing. We made our clothes out of animal skins.

July 4, 1866

"And This Institute Was Our Answer"

Around their campfires, the men of the 62nd United States Colored Infantry dreamed of establishing a school for freedmen after the Civil War was over. While the 62nd was stationed at Fort McIntosh near Galveston, Texas, a committee was appointed to collect money from the soldiers for the school.

In a short time the men of the 62nd had five thousand dollars for their project. One black soldier, Samuel Sexton, gave $100 even though his earnings as a private were only $13 per month.

Major General Clinton Fisk, for whom Fisk University of Nashville, Tennessee, was later named, heartily endorsed the idea. He helped collect another $1400 from his own regiment, the 65th. In time, the soldiers raised $20,000 and made possible the building of a college in Jefferson City, Missouri—Lincoln Institute.

Today Lincoln Institute still stands as a monument to the 62nd and 65th Phalanx Regiments. It is a living symbol of the dreams of black Union soldiers and their white officers. Lieutenant Colonel David Branson, a field officer with the 62nd Regiment, dedicated Lincoln with these words.

Source: Wilson, Joseph T. *The Black Phalanx: A History of the Negro Soldiers in the Wars of 1775-1812, 1861-1865.* Hartford, Connecticut: American Publishing Company, 1888, p. 511.

MY FRIENDS:—This, with one exception, has been the happiest 4th of July in my life. That exception was in 1863, when I saw the rebel flag go down at Vicksburg. I felt the exultation of victory then, and I feel it to-day as I look upon this splendid building. Looking in the faces

126

of my old comrades of the 62nd Regiment here today, memory goes back to the past, when hundreds of you came to me at Benton Barracks, ragged, starving, and freezing—some did freeze to death—and emotions fill me that no language can express. I cannot sit down and think of those scenes of suffering without almost shedding tears. But happily those days are passed. No more marching with sluggish step and plantation gait through the streets of St. Louis, Mo., amid the jeers of your enemies; no more crossing the Mississippi on ice; no more sinking steamers, and consequent exposure on the cold, muddy banks of the river; no more killing labor on fortifications at Port Hudson, Baton Rouge and Morganza; no more voyages over the Gulf of Mexico, packed like cattle in the hold of a vessel; no more weary marches in the burning climate of Texas; no more death by the bullet, and no more afternoons on the banks of the Rio Grande, deliberating on the future education of yourselves when discharged from the army; but peace and prosperity here with the result of those deliberations before us. Our enemies predicted, that upon the disbanding of our volunteer army—particularly the colored portion of it—it would turn to bands of marauding murderers and idle vagabonds, and this Institute was our answer.

circa 1867

This Is My First Chance to Get a Start

When blacks were first offered educational opportunities, they seized them eagerly. In the following selection, eyewitnesses writing for magazines in post-Civil War years report the responses that they observed.

Source: Coulter, E. Merton. *The South During Reconstruction.* Baton Rouge: Louisiana State University Press, 1947, pp. 85-87 *passim.*

They [freedmen] felt that they could not be completely emancipated until they had attended a school; they looked upon education as having miraculous powers. Negroes "were to be seen at every street corner, and between the hours of labor, poring over the elementary pages." The porter in the store or hotel was studying his speller when

127

not busy with his work, and the washerwoman propped her reader on the fence while she labored over the washtub. They came to the schools, from the cradle to the grave; in one school it was noted that there were four generations of Negroes. One old Negro student remarked, "I'm jammed on to a hundred, and dis is my fust chance to git a start." Some teachers found that the most effective way to punish a colored child was to refuse to hear his lesson or refuse to let him come back to school. In one Georgia town where the whites were in a majority, the Negro school had 150 pupils, whereas the white school had only 35. . . .

Schoolhouses varied from palatial homes seized as abandoned property, such as the Memminger home in Charleston, to old slave markets, as in Savannah, and hovels everywhere. The methods of teachers varied widely, as indeed did the character of the schools. There were industrial schools, night schools, Sunday schools, and the elementary schools. In some schools books were used, especially the Freedmen's Book, made up of accounts of famous Negroes such as Toussaint L'Ouverture, poems and orations by Negroes, and praise of heroes like John Brown.

1867

Chicago's Integrated Schools

James Parton, a roving reporter for *The Atlantic Monthly* magazine, visited Chicago and its public schools in 1867. He reported that blacks and whites attended "common" or elementary schools, the High School, and adult evening schools together. He urged Americans to keep an eye on Chicago because "a great and splendid city is rising from the prairie, in view of all the people, who watch, criticise, compare, and suggest."

Source: Parton, James. "Chicago." *The Atlantic Monthly*. March, 1867, p. 341.

It is with pleasure that we report to the people of the United States, that their fellow-citizens of Chicago are looking well to the interests of those who are to carry on their work when they are gone. The public schools of the city are among the very best in the United States. The buildings are large, handsome and convenient...; the salaries of the teachers range from four hundred to twenty-four hundred dollars a year.... In the High School, an institution of which any city in Christendom might be justly proud, colored lads and girls may be seen in most of the classes, mingled with other pupils; and in the evening schools of the city colored men and women are received on precisely the same footing as white. Colored children also attend the common schools, and no one objects, or sees anything extraordinary in the fact. No little child is allowed to pass more than half an hour without exercise. In the higher classes, the physical exercises occur about once an hour; the windows are thrown open, the pupils rise, and all the class imitate the motions of the teacher for five minutes. The boys in the High School have a lesson daily in out-door gymnastics, skillfully taught by a gentleman who left one of his legs before Vicksburg. The girls have a variety of curious exercises, which combine work and play in an agreeable manner....

1871

To Sing of Jubilee

Fisk University in Nashville, Tennessee, was established in 1866 for freedmen by the American Missionary Society. However, the struggling young university needed money desperately during the Reconstruction years, particularly for buildings. To raise funds, a group called the Fisk Jubilee Singers began a pilgrimage of song throughout the United States and Europe. Kings and queens abroad as well as Americans heard the haunting beauty of the slave songs. In less than seven years, the Jubilee singers raised $150,000.

In the following selection, W. E. B. Du Bois tells the story of one of the world's most celebrated and dedicated musical groups.

Source: Du Bois, W. E. B. *The Souls of Black Folk: Essays and Sketches.* Chicago: A. C. McClurg and Company, 1909 (8th edition), pp. 252, 253. Reprinted courtesy of Johnson Reprint Corporation, New York, New York.

There was once a blacksmith's son born at Cadiz, New York, who in the changes of time taught school in Ohio and helped defend Cincinnati from Kirby Smith. Then he fought at Chancellorsville and Gettysburg and finally served in the Freedmen's Bureau at Nashville. Here he formed a Sunday-school class of black children in 1866, and sang with them and taught them to sing. And then they taught him to sing, and when once the glory of the Jubilee songs passed into the soul of George L. White, he knew his life-work was to let those Negroes sing to the world as they had sung to him. So in 1871 the pilgrimage of the Fisk Jubilee Singers began. North to Cincinnati they rode,—four half-clothed black boys and five girl-women,—led by a man with a cause and a purpose. They stopped at Wilberforce, the oldest of Negro schools, where a black bishop blessed them. Then they went, fighting cold and starvation, shut out of hotels, and cheerfully sneered at, ever northward; and ever the magic of their song kept thrilling hearts, until a burst of applause in the Congregational Council at Oberlin revealed them to the world. They came to New York and Henry Ward Beecher dared to welcome them, even though the metropolitan dailies sneered at his "Nigger Minstrels." So their songs conquered till they sang across the land and across the sea, before Queen and Kaiser, in Scotland and Ireland, Holland and Switzerland. Seven years they sang, and brought back a hundred and fifty thousand dollars to found Fisk University.

Since their day they have been imitated—sometimes well, by the singers of Hampton and Atlanta, sometimes ill, by straggling quartettes. Caricature has sought again to spoil the quaint beauty of the music, and has filled the air with many debased melodies which vulgar ears scarce know from the real. But the true Negro folk-song still lives in the hearts of those who have heard them truly sung and in the hearts of the Negro people.

May 30, 1872

Let Them Go to Their Own Schools

Not all the arguments about whether "colored" and white children should attend school together took place in the South. In the 1860's, Negro residents of Oakland, California, asked that schooling be provided for their children. However, there still was no school open by 1869 because "the Superintendent stated that he had not been able to open the colored school, as no provision had been made for a building in which to hold the school." The Board of Education did say that it would contribute $25 per month for maintaining a school, but that the colored people would have to furnish the building.

Finally, in 1872 the Board of Education took action to open "mixed schools." The following is an editorial which appeared in the city's daily newspaper in response to the Board's action.

Source: Editorial, Oakland *Daily Transcript*. May 30, 1872.

A Mixed Question

The recent action of the Board of Education requiring the mixing of colored with white children in public schools has naturally created much dissatisfaction. Unless the Board assumes to manage educational matters regardless of harmony, it will provide a special school for colored children.

Even though it might cost proportionately more to educate them separately (as there are so few here) we should accept this horn of the dilemma, rather than do injustice either to the colored children or to taxpayers.

Many say, "I like colored children in their place, and think they should be educated; but I object to having them brought in contact with my children, and will not send my own to any school where they are admitted." One has said, "I served through the war and helped free the contrabands, but I'm opposed to amalgamation in school or out of school—and the one will lead to the other."

Some say, "It is a good card for the private schools." Others, that "it will keep many families from settling in Oakland." And yet others, "I have no objection to my children attending a school where there are a few colored children, but I think it an injustice toward the colored children to compel them to attend schools in which they will be subjected to continual sneers, slights, and heart-burning."

An experienced teacher says, "I regret the circumstance. We are bound to protect the colored children from imposition, and it is impossible to repress the antipathies of the white children. The result will be a resort to frequent punishment. Such being the case, the result of mingling the white with colored pupils is disadvantageous to both."

The members of our Board of Education receive no compensation for their services except the gratitude of parents, the commendation of the public, and the satisfaction of deserving both.

On the one hand we hear the considerations of economy influence their action in forcing the association of colored and white; on the other hand it is said they were influenced by their own peculiar views.

If the former is the true state of the case we assure the members of the Board that Oakland *can* afford to support a public school, and will not grudge the expense. If the latter is true, we recommend those who are troubled with such peculiar views to resign their positions.

1865-1877

Reconstruction Was a Mighty Hard Pull

Reconstruction was a time filled with troubles and hardship for both blacks and whites. The war had disrupted established patterns of living, and people were struggling to build new lives. Here is a firsthand account of those difficult years given by an eighty-five year-old former slave. Although almost seventy-five years had passed between the time he gained his freedom and when he told this story, the memory of those hard years had not dimmed.

Source: Botkin, Ben A. *Lay My Burden Down: A Folk History of Slavery*. Chicago: University of Chicago Press, 1945.

Reconstruction Was a Mighty Hard Pull

I was born in Edgefield County, South Carolina. I am eighty-five years old. I was born a slave of George Strauter. I remembers hearing them say, "Thank God, I's free as a jay bird." My ma was a slave in the field. I was eleven years old when freedom was declared. When I was little, Mr. Strauter whipped my ma. It hurt me bad as it did her. I hated him. She was crying. I chunked him with rocks. He run after me, but he didn't catch me. There was twenty-five or thirty hands that worked in the field. They raised wheat, corn, oats, barley, and cotton. All the children that couldn't work stayed at one house. Aunt Mat kept the babies and small children that couldn't go to the field. He had a gin and a shop. The shop was at the fork of the roads. When the war come on, my papa went to build forts. He quit Ma and took another woman. When the war close, Ma took her four children, bundled 'em up and went to Augusta. The government give out rations there. My ma washed and ironed. People died in piles. I don't know till yet what was the matter. They said it was the change of living. I seen five or six wooden, painted coffins piled up on wagons pass by our house. Loads passed every day like you see cotton pass here. Some said it was cholera and some took consumption. Lots of the colored people nearly starved. Not much to get to do and not much houseroom. Several families had to live in one house. Lots of the colored folks went up North and froze to death. They couldn't stand the cold. They wrote back about them dying. No, they never sent them back. I heard some sent for money to come back. I heard plenty 'bout the Ku Klux. They scared the folks to death. People left Augusta in droves. About a thousand would all meet and walk going to hunt work and new homes. Some of them died. I had a sister and brother lost that way. I had another sister come to Louisiana that way. She wrote back.

I don't think the colored folks looked for a share of land. They never got nothing 'cause the white folks didn't have nothing but barren hills left. About all the mules was wore out hauling provisions in the army. Some folks say they ought to done more for the colored folks when they left, but they say they was broke. Freeing all the slaves left 'em broke.

That reconstruction was a mighty hard pull. Me and Ma couldn't live. A man paid our ways to Carlisle, Arkansas, and we come. We started working for Mr. Emerson. He had a big store, teams and land. We liked it fine, and I been here fifty-six years now. There was so much wild game, living was not so hard. If a fellow could get a little bread and a place to stay, he was all right. After I come to this state, I voted some. I have farmed and worked at odd jobs. I farmed mostly. Ma went back to her old master. He persuaded her to come back home. Me and her went back and run a farm four or five years before she died. Then I come back here.

1867

Not Even the Editors Are Foolish Enough to Believe It

"Things just aren't what they used to be in the good old days" was a theme often used by Southern newspaper editors and writers during the Reconstruction. Just two years after the Civil War ended, James Parton, an experienced reporter for *The Atlantic Monthly,* visited St. Louis. He said he was certain that not even a hundred voters in that city could have been persuaded to reestablish slavery in Missouri, even if it were possible. Nevertheless, Parton asserted, Southern editors "flatter their readers" by publishing paragraphs such as the following.

Source: Parton, James. "The City of St. Louis." *The Atlantic Monthly,* June, 1867, p. 655.

"The time was when the honest old darky got up and went to work at break of day, with a full stomach, good comfortable clothing on his back, good shoes on his feet, a heart as light and happy as the lark, and making the welkin ring with his merry songs. When the day's work was over, he laid down the shovel and the hoe, went to his comfortable log-cabin, ate the wholesome supper furnished him by his kind old master, and then lighted his pipe, took down his banjo, and played, sang, and danced until the bell rang for him to go to bed. Good, kind old master furnished him with everything necessary for his comfort, and, as he had no cares, he could sleep soundly. Alas! he cannot sing and dance with the same zest now. He has no old master to furnish him with food and raiment. No kind mistress to take care of him when he gets sick. No comfortable cabin to live in. No thick clothing to shield him from the storms. No banjo to pick, and his heart is so heavy he cannot sing and dance. Candidly, we have not heard of a real old-fashioned negro frolic since the poor darky was set free."

Very likely: people are never so merry as when they are extremely uncomfortable and know they cannot help it. Southern editors delight to print this kind of sentimental lie, but there is hardly one of them who is foolish enough to be taken in by it.

circa 1870

To Help Each Other

As slaves, blacks were denied the right of forming or belonging to clubs or societies of their own choosing. However, once slavery was outlawed, freedmen created many kinds of voluntary organizations for their own benefit similar to those whites had always enjoyed.

Not only did blacks form political associations, religious organizations, fire companies, and social societies; they also organized some labor unions. The Longshoremen's Protective Association of Charleston has been described as "the most powerful organization of the colored laboring class in South Carolina." More than 800 black men belonged to the Longshoremen's Association. Many of their strikes were successful in helping the union win better wages and improved working conditions for its members.

Another interesting voluntary association that began in the years following the Civil War is described here.

Source: Simkins, Francis B. and Woody, Robert H. *South Carolina During Reconstruction.* Gloucester, Massachusetts: Peter Smith, 1966. Copyright 1932 by the University of North Carolina.

Far more significant in the lives of the great masses were the burial aid societies. They took form in the years following the war and soon spread to every Negro community in the state. They exist today as one of the most successful experiments in cooperative societies ever known in the United States. They grew out of the inability of the Negro to provide out of his individual means the elaborate and respectable funeral each one of them sincerely desired. This difficulty was overcome by the several members of the community agreeing to create a fund by each making a small and easily paid weekly contribution to a common treasury. In this manner enough money was gathered to meet the funeral obligations when they arose from time to time. Additional dignity was insured by requiring members of the society to attend the burial of a brother in white gloves and mourning costumes, and to carry banners and badges of the organization.

The importance of these societies in the life of the Negro is made clear by the following report from Beaufort [South Carolina] in 1880: "The colored people have a number of charitable organizations for the care of their sick and the burial of their dead. Some of these are the Benevolent Society of the First Baptist Church, the Workers of Charity, The Shekinak Society, the Sons and Daughters of Zion, the Knights of Wise Men, and an Independent Order of Odd Fellows. These societies have an aggregate membership exceeding one thousand, and own eleven buildings and lots valued at $12,000."

1871

"The Impudence to Run Against a White Man"

Secret terrorist organizations roamed the South after the Civil War. The most famous of these anti-Negro groups of southern whites was the Ku Klux Klan, formed in Tennessee in 1866. But there were a number of other groups of white supremacists that fought congressional reconstruction plans and increasing black political participation with force and violence—The Knights of the White Camellia in Louisiana, The Knights of the Rising Sun in Texas, the White Brotherhood, The Pale Faces, and the '76 Association. In time, the terms "Klansman" and "Ku Klux" meant any terrorist, whether he belonged to the Ku Klux Klan or another such band.

Dressed in white robes and hoods, Klansmen broke up Republican meetings, threatened Radical leaders, and abused, lynched, and killed Negroes. Shootings, murders, whippings, plundering, and other acts of violence reached such a peak that Klan leaders themselves tried without success to disband their organizations. Congressmen became alarmed at the widespread lawlessness in the South, and they started investigations into Klan activities and membership in 1871.

Here is part of the testimony that Andrew J. Flowers, a black, gave at one of the congressional hearings. In this excerpt, Flowers tells congressmen what happened to him because he had the "impudence to run against a white man" in an election for justice of the peace.

Source: U.S. Congress. *Testimony Taken by the Joint Select Committee to Inquire into the Condition of Affairs in the Late Insurrectionary States,* Vol. XIII, *Miscellaneous and Florida,* 1872.

Washington, D.C. July 15, 1871

Andrew J. Flowers (colored) sworn and examined:

By the Chairman (Mr. Poland)

Question. Where do you live?

Answer. In Chattanooga, Tennessee.

Question. How long have you lived there?

Answer. Since July, 1865.

Question. What has been your business since you lived in Chattanooga; what trade have you followed?

Answer. The only trade I followed was coopering. I learned the trade of coopering there within the last two or three years.

Question. Do you now hold some office?

Answer. Yes, sir; I am a justice of the peace. . . .

Question. Are justices of the peace in Tennessee elected by a vote of the people?

Answer. Yes, sir; I was elected by a vote of the people. . . .

Question. You are now a justice of the peace for the whole county?

Answer. Yes, sir; for the whole county.

Question. How many justices were elected at the same time as your-self?

Answer. In our district three were elected at the same time.

Question. Were they all colored men?

Answer. No, sir; I was the only colored man; the other two were white men.

Question. Since you were elected last August, have you seen duty as a magistrate or justice of the peace?

Answer. I have. . . .

Question. I want to inquire of you particularly in reference to some violence which it has been understood was committed upon you a short time ago. Tell us the story in reference to that.

Answer. On the 17th of last month I went out from Chattanooga to Whiteside on a visit to a school which my sister was teaching. . . . I went down there on Saturday night and staid all night. My sister is teaching school there. . . .

Question. You went down on Saturday night and staid over Sun-day?

Answer. Yes, sir.

Question. State all that took place.

Answer. On Sunday night, between 11 and 12, or 10 and 11 o'clock, I cannot say exactly which. . . I woke up, and there was a crowd of men, all with masks, around me, with pistols in their hands. They waked me up. They called me by name; they took me out near a mile from the house.

Question. Tell all that they said.

Answer. They asked me what was my name. I told them. Then some of them said, "O, yes; you are the man we are looking for," and so forth. One of them told me they were going to kill me. . . . He had a pistol in his hand. After they got me out of doors, the captain of the organization (they called him "captain") told me that he was going to whip me; he said he would give me twenty-five lashes; that I had had the impudence to run against a white man for office, and beat him; that they were not going to allow it; that it was an organization organized by them to stop negroes holding office, and to put out of office those that had office; that if they did not get out of office by being told or notified or whipped, they were going to kill them. . . .

Question. They whipped you until you promised to resign your office?

Answer. Yes, sir. . . .

Question. State as much of the conversation as you can remember—all they said from the time they came until they let you go.

Answer. When they were taking me out of the door, they said they had nothing particular against me; that they didn't dispute I was a very good fellow, and they had not heard anything wrong of me; but they did not intend any nigger to hold office in the United States; that they were going to stop it, and were going to whip me to show that I was not to have the impudence to run against any white man in an election as I had done; and that I might notify a couple of other colored men that we have in our city—members of the city board—that they were going to get them. They said further that any white man who had anything to do with my election . . . if they got hold of him they would treat him just as they did me.

November 5, 1868

"I Shall Die a Republican"

Any man, black or white, who belonged to the Republican Party during the Reconstruction was a target for the hatred and violence of southern white supremacists in the Ku Klux Klan and other anti-Negro groups. In the eyes of many former Confederates, the Republican Party was for blacks and for northern carpetbaggers who they regarded as meddlers in affairs that were none of their business. As Henry Lusk, a prominent scalawag political figure in Mississippi during the Reconstruction, said: "No white man can live in the South in the future and act with any other than the Democratic Party unless he is willing to risk serious consequences."

Republicans relied on the Federal troops stationed in the South after the war for protection. Under pressure from Northern businessmen who wanted to reestablish economic ties with the

South, these troops were gradually withdrawn. Terror and violence rose and sent the white carpetbagger home and halted black economic and political progress. Eventually, "home rule" or white supremacy was restored in the South.

The following cry for help sent by a citizen to Governor Powell Clayton of Arkansas reveals just how serious were the threats to the well-being of black and white Republicans alike.

Source: U.S. Congress. *Testimony Taken by the Joint Select Committee to Inquire into the Condition of Affairs in the Late Insurrectionary States.* Letter of W. M. Harrison to Governor Clayton Powell of Arkansas. Vol. 13, 1872.

Monticello, November 5, 1868.

GOVERNOR:

I deem it my duty to lay before you a brief statement of affairs in this county.

Since the murder of William G. Dollar and of Fred. Reeves, about a month ago, our county has been remarkably quiet and peaceable until Saturday night last, when a small squad of Ku-Klux made their appearance in the neighborhood, and perhaps in the town, but did no particular mischief. About 4 o'clock Sunday evening between forty and fifty suddenly appeared in town, and, after riding around the square, as suddenly disappeared. About 11 o'clock at night ten went to the house of Abram Boler, a colored preacher, on the farm of W. T. Wells, one mile from town, broke into his house, took him off into the woods, tied him, stripped him, and gave him a very severe beating; one thrust his pistol down his throat, and the same or another stood upon his neck while he was being beaten. He had done no wrong; his only offense was, he was a radical, and could read and could give other people information. . . . Many threats were made against all, white and black, who dared vote the republican ticket. Myself and Judge Preddy and one or two others were particularly named. The word was put out by them on Sunday that the roads would be picketed, and all colored men would be killed who voted with the republicans. Some sixty-five colored men came into the election; not one dared vote the republican ticket, and not two, I believe, desired to vote the democratic. Those present that wished to decline to vote, I am told, were threatened. Levin Scott declined, and at night he was taken from his house by the Klan and cruelly beaten. . . .

Only three republican votes were cast in this town; they were given by Judge Preddy, George Crowell, and myself. . . . I am not terrified, but think it probable I shall be assassinated in a few days. I shall die a republican. I pray you send us at least ten or fifteen soldiers.

Very respectfully, &c.,

W. M. HARRISON

POWELL CLAYTON,
Governor of Arkansas

1868

Correcting South Carolina's Vocabulary

When T. J. Coglan, a white delegate from Sumter, arrived at the Constitutional Convention of South Carolina, he decided that the vocabulary of his native state needed correction. Accordingly Coglan introduced the two Resolutions which follow. They were adopted by the Convention in 1868.

Source: *Proceedings of the Constitutional Convention of South Carolina,* 1868.

RESOLVED, That this Convention take such action as it may in its wisdom deem compatible with its powers, and conducive to the public weal, to expunge [remove] forever from the vocabulary of South Carolina, the epithets "negro," "nigger," and "Yankee". . . .

RESOLVED, That the exigencies and approved civilization of the times demand that this Convention, or the Legislative body created by it, enact such laws as will make it a penal offence to use the above epithets in the manner described against an American citizen of this State, and to punish the insult by fine or imprisonment.

140

I Visit the South Carolina Legislature

Journalists and historians sympathetic to the Confederacy often labeled the South Carolina legislature as "Negro government at its worst." According to their interpretations, corruption reached its height in South Carolina.

However, many historians, for example Kenneth Stampp, who have reexamined the record since the passions of the Civil War have cooled, point out the following facts. Blacks were in the majority in the State of South Carolina and in the first radical legislature, which contained 87 Negroes and 69 whites. But blacks had a majority only in the lower house. In the Senate there were twice as many whites as blacks. While it is true that the record of the South Carolina legislature is a sorry one in many respects, it is not true that blacks were in control or solely responsible for the evils and errors of that law-making body.

The following contemporary account of the House of Representatives was written by James S. Pike, a Republican journalist. Pike was hardly sympathetic to blacks, as his opening paragraphs make clear. In fact, black scholar W. E. B. Du Bois has referred to Pike as a propagandist and has labeled the following description of Pike's as a tirade. Nonetheless, Pike's concluding paragraph does point out how much progress was made by men who "seven years ago were raising corn and cotton under the whip of the overseer."

Source: Pike, James Shepherd. *The Prostrate State: South Carolina Under Negro Government.* New York, 1874, pp. 12 ff.

In the place of this old aristocratic society stands the rude form of the most ignorant democracy that mankind ever saw, invested with the functions of government. . . .

We will enter the House of Representatives. Here sit one hundred and twenty four members. Of these, twenty-three are white men, representing the remains of the old civilization. These are good-looking, substantial citizens. . . .

This dense negro crowd . . . do the debating, the squabbling, the lawmaking, and create all the clamor and disorder of the body. . . . The Speaker is black, the Clerk is black, the doorkeepers are black, the little pages are black, the Chairman of the Ways and Means [Committee] is black, and the chaplain is coal black. . . . It must be remembered, also, that these men, with not more than a half dozen exceptions, have been

themselves slaves, and that their ancestors were slaves for generations. . . .

But the old stagers admit that the colored brethren have a wonderful
aptness at legislative proceedings. They are "quick as lightning" at de-
tecting points of order, and they certainly make incessant and extraordinary use of their knowledge. . . . The Speaker's hammer plays a
perpetual tattoo to no purpose. The talking and the interruptions from
all quarters go on with the utmost license. Everyone esteems himself as
good as his neighbor, and puts in his oar, apparently as often for love of
riot and confusion as for anything else. . . .

But underneath all this shocking burlesque upon legislative proceedings, we must not forget that there is something very real to this un-
couth and untutored multitude. It is not all sham, nor all burlesque.
They have a genuine interest and a genuine earnestness in the business
of the assembly which we are bound to recognize and respect. . . . They
have an earnest purpose, born of conviction that their position and
condition are not fully assured, which lends a sort of dignity to their
proceedings. The barbarous, animated jargon in which they so often
indulge is on occasion seen to be so transparently sincere and weighty
in their own minds that sympathy supplants disgust. The whole thing is
a wonderful novelty to them as well as to observers. Seven years ago
these men were raising corn and cotton under the whip of the overseer.
Today they are raising points of order and questions of privilege. They
find they can raise one as well as the other. They prefer the latter. It is
easier and better paid. Then, it is the evidence of an accomplished
result. It means escape and defense from old oppressors. It means
liberty. It means the destruction of prison-walls only too real to them.
It is the sunshine of their lives. It is their day of jubilee. It is their
long-promised vision of the Lord God Almighty.

February 25, 1870

The First Negro Enters the United States Senate

Hiram R. Revels, born free in North Carolina, was the first
man of African descent to serve in the United States Senate. In
fact, he was the first black man to serve in either House of Congress. To use a slogan of his time, "The bottom rail was on the
top," for Revels was a replacement for a former Mississippi

Senator, Jefferson Davis, the only President of the Confederacy.

The day Senator Revels from Mississippi arrived to claim his seat, the galleries were packed with excited people. Some were friendly; some opposed him. The cool formal statements which follow, taken from *The Congressional Globe* do not begin to tell the drama of that day. Revels served for only a very short term, but he was admitted to the Senate without serious opposition.

Since Revels was seated, only two other men of African descent have been elected to the United States Senate. Blanche K. Bruce of Mississippi went to the Senate in 1874 and Edward Brooke of Massachusetts in 1966.

Source: *The Congressional Globe,* February 25, 1870. 41st Congress, Second Session. Page 1568.

MR. WILSON: In presenting the credentials of Mr. Revels I ask that they be read, and that the oaths of office be administered to him. I now make the motion that the oaths of office be administered to him.

MR. POMEROY: On that question of administering the oaths I ask for the yeas and nays.

MR. TRUMBULL: Is there any necessity for a vote? Are not the oaths administered as a matter of course?

THE VICE PRESIDENT: There need not be a vote taken if there should be no objection.

MR. CONKLING: It is a matter of form unless there is a counter motion.

MR. TRUMBULL: We do not want any vote about it.

MR. SAULSBURY: If an objection will put it to a vote, I object.

THE VICE PRESIDENT: The Senator from Delaware objects; and that Senator and other Senators gave notice before that they would object at every stage.

MR. POMEROY: Whenever there is a contest it is customary to take a vote on it.

THE VICE PRESIDENT: The Senator from Kansas demands the yeas and nays on the motion of the Senator from Massachusetts.

The manifestations of feeling in the galleries the last hour or two have been so evident that the Chair is justified in saying to persons of all shades of opinion in the galleries that they are present under the rules of the Senate and by its courtesy, and whatever may be the result of this vote and the action of the Senate, self-respect, as well as respect to this body, demands that there shall be no expressions of approval or disapproval.

[A vote was taken then. There were 48 yeas, 8 nays. Twelve Senators were absent.]

THE VICE PRESIDENT.: The Senator-elect will present himself at the chair of the Vice President to take the oaths of office.

Mr. Revels was escorted to the desk by Mr. Wilson, and the oaths prescribed by law having been administered to him, Mr. Revels took his seat in the Senate.

March 9, 1871

"I Am No Apologist for Thieves"

Alonzo Jacob Ransier, who was born a free man in Charleston, on January 3, 1834, became one of the most able and influential black politicians of the Reconstruction period. Though he had little formal education, by the time he was sixteen years old Ransier had become the shipping clerk for a white merchant. In that post he acquired knowledge and skill in the art of business.

When the Civil War ended, General Daniel E. Sickles, military commander of South Carolina, appointed Ransier to the post of Registrar of Elections. He was also a member of the South Carolina constitutional convention.

Ransier's interests turned more and more to politics, and he decided to run for elective office. First, he was elected to the South Carolina Senate where he served ably as the presiding officer. Next he was elected Lieutenant Governor of the state, and then he was voted into the United States Congress.

Throughout his long political career, Ransier's honesty was unquestioned. When he spoke to a convention of his fellow Republicans in Charleston in 1871, he unequivocally said what he thought should be done with any man who misused public trust. Every man, black and white alike, said Ransier, bears equal responsibility for seeing that good government does in fact exist.

Source: Woodson, Carter G. *Negro Orators and Their Orations,* as reprinted in W. E. Burghardt Du Bois. *Black Reconstruction in America, 1860-1880* [1935]. New York: Russell and Russell, 1956, pp. 415-416.

I am no apologist for thieves; for if I were, I do not think I would have occupied for so long a time a place in your confidence. On the contrary, I am in favor of a most thorough investigation of the official conduct of any and every public officer in connection with the discharge of whose duties there is anything like well-grounded suspicion;

and to this effect have I spoken time and again. Nor am I lukewarm on the subject of better government in South Carolina. . . .

Let each man act as if, by his individual vote, he could wipe out the odium resting upon our party, and help to remove the evils that afflict us at present. Let him feel, black or white, that the country holds him responsible for the shortcomings of his party, and that it demands of him the elevation to public positions of men who are above suspicion. Let each man feel that upon him individually rests the work of reform; let each man feel that he is responsible for every dollar of the public money fraudulently used; for every schoolhouse closed against his children; for every dollar of taxation in excess of the reasonable and legitimate expenses of the State; in short, let every man feel that society at large will hold him and the party accountable for every misdeed in the administration of government, and will credit him with every honest effort in the interest of good government, whereby the community as a whole is best protected and the equal rights of all guaranteed and made safe.

1874

Blacks Honor a White Senator in Death

One of the most persistent and vigorous advocates of civil rights was Charles Sumner, United States Senator from Massachusetts. Before the Civil War, Sumner made such a violent attack on slavery that Representative Brooks of South Carolina physically attacked him in Congress. After the war, Sumner continued to fight for a national civil rights bill and a bill for equal rights in the schools of the District of Columbia. Although he did not live to see his bills become law, he was honored and remembered at his death by some famous black Americans.

Source: Du Bois, W. E. Burghardt. *Black Reconstruction in America, 1860-1880* [1935]. New York: Russell and Russell, 1956, p. 594.

He [Sumner] was taken ill in March, 1874; at his deathbed stood three Negroes: Frederick Douglass, George T. Downing, and Sumner Wormley, together with distinguished senators and officials. Three times he said hoarsely and in a tone of earnest entreaty: "You must take care of the civil rights bill—my bill, the civil rights bill—don't let it fail!" This was his last public message.

Frederick Douglass led his funeral procession and colored soldiers guarded his body at the State House in Boston.

September 13, 1883

"I Have Very Great Hopes for Him in the Future"

John Caldwell Calhoun, grandson of the famed South Carolina statesman, respected blacks and was in turn respected by them during the difficult Reconstruction years. When a United States Senate committee held hearings on labor and education problems in the South, Calhoun was asked to come from his home in Chicot County, Arkansas, to testify. Thomas Fortune, noted black editor of The York *Globe,* said he was glad that the Senate listened to Calhoun "because of the uniform fairness with which he treated the race and land problem."

Following is a portion of the testimony which Calhoun gave to the Senators. Calhoun explains why he had great hopes for the Negro of the future.

Source: United States Senate. Testimony of John Caldwell Calhoun before the Blair Senate Committee on Education and Labor, regarding The Relations Between Labor and Capital. Vol. II, 1883.

New York, Thursday, September 13, 1883
John Caldwell Calhoun sworn and examined by the Chairman:

... Suppose a negro comes to me to make a contract that I have written for him, and he cannot read or write. I offer that contract to him, and I read it to him. He touches a pen and signs his mark to it; there is no obligation attached at all. He says at once, "That man is an educated man; he has the advantage of me; he shows me that contract; I do not know what is in it; I cannot even read it." Therefore a contract made with a negro in that way is almost a nullity; but if he could read that contract himself and sign his own name to it, it would be a very different thing. I never allow a negro to sign a written contract with me before he has taken it home with him and had some friend to read it over and consult with him about it, because I want some obligations attached to my contracts.

Question. It is necessary for you as well as the negro?

Answer. Necessary for my protection as well as his.

Q. How many of the negroes on the plantations can comprehend a written contract by reading it, because a man may be somewhat educated and not be able to decipher a contract?

A. I cannot give you an exact proportion, for it varies to a great extent. I can only say that that number is increasing rapidly.

Q. From what circumstance comes this increase?

A. From their desire to gain knowledge.

Q. Do you find that desire strong among the colored people?

A. Very strong indeed; and there are two ideas which a negro possesses that give me great hopes for his future. If I did not believe the negro was capable of sufficient development to make him a responsible small farmer, I should not want to remain in the business that I am any longer, because I believe that the development of my business is necessarily based upon the development of the negro and the cultivation of my lands. The negro possesses two remarkable qualifications: one is that he is imitative, and the other is that he has got pride; he wants to dress well; he wants to do as well as anybody else does when you get him aroused, and with these two qualifications I have very great hopes for him in the future.

Q. What do you think of his intellectual and moral qualities and his capacity for development?

A. There are individual instances I know of where negroes have received and taken a good education. As a class, it would probably be several generations, at any rate, before they would be able to compete with the Caucasian. I believe that the negro is capable of receiving an ordinary English education, and there are instances where they enter professions and become good lawyers. For instance, I know in the town of Greenville, Mississippi, right across the river from me, a negro attorney who is a very intelligent man, and I heard one of the leading attorneys in Greenville say he would almost have anybody on the opposite side of a case rather than he would that negro. The sheriff of my county is from Ohio, and a negro; he is a man whom we all support in his office. We are anxious that the negroes should have a fair representation. For instance, you ask for the feeling existing between the proprietor and the negroes. The probate judge of my county is a negro and one of my tenants, and I am here now in New York attending to important business for my county as an appointee of that man. He has upon him the responsibilities of all estates in the county; he is probate judge.

Q. Is he a capable man?

A. A very capable man, an excellent, good man, and a very just one.

Q. Do you see any reason why with fair opportunities assured to himself and to his children, he may not become a useful and competent American citizen?

A. We already consider him so.

Q. The question is settled?

A. I thought you were speaking personally of the man I referred to.

Q. No; I was speaking of the negro generally—the negro race. . . .

A. I think they may as a class, but it will take probably generations for them. . . .

October 20, 1883

Witness Wonders

The Honorable John Mercer Langston, United States Minister and Consul General to Haiti, spoke in Washington, D. C., less than twenty years after the end of the Civil War. The son of a white plantation owner and a freed slave, Langston graduated from Oberlin College, obtained a degree in theology, and practiced law in Ohio before the Civil War. In 1868 President Johnson appointed him inspector general of the Freedmen's Bureau. Prior to his diplomatic service, Langston was a prominent Negro educator and an administrator at Howard University. Here is his estimate of the progress made by black Americans in less than a generation after freedom from bondage.

Source: "Civil Rights Law." Address by the Honorable John Mercer Langston, United States Minister and Consul General to Haiti, delivered at Washington, D. C., October 20, 1883, as reprinted in *Black and White: Land, Labor, and Politics in the South* by T. Thomas Fortune. New York: Fords, Howard, and Hulbert, 1884, pp. 183, 184.

Do you desire to witness moral wonders? Start at Chicago; travel to St. Louis; travel to Louisville; travel to Nashville; travel to Chattanooga; travel on to New Orleans, and in every State and city you will meet vast audiences, immense concourses of men and women with their children, boys and girls, who, degraded and in ignorance because of their slavery formerly, are today far advanced in general social improvement.

It would be remarkable now for you to go into the home of one of our families, and find even our daughters incompetent to discourse with you upon any subject of general interest with perfect ease and understanding. Excuse me, if I refer to the fact that some weeks ago I visited St. Louis for two reasons; first to see my son and daughter, and secondly and mainly to attend the seventy-second anniversary of the birth of perhaps the richest colored man in the State of Missouri. I went to his house, and I was surprised as I entered his doors and looked about his sitting-room and parlors, furnished in the most approved modern style, in the richest manner; but I was more surprised when I saw one hundred guests come into the house of this venerable man, to celebrate the seventy-second anniversary of his birth, all beautifully attired; and when he told me, indirectly, how much he had made, since the war, and what he was worth on the night of this celebration, I was more surprised than ever. I am surprised at the matchless progress the colored people of this country have made since their emancipation. I have traveled in the West Indies; I have seen the emancipated English, Spanish, and French Negro; but I have seen no emancipated Negro anywhere who has made the progress at all comparable with the colored people of the United States of America.

January 29, 1901

A Black Congressman Bids a Temporary Farewell

1877 is usually considered the last year of the Reconstruction period. But, like Rome, Reconstruction did not "fall" in a day. The last of the twenty-two black men to serve in the United States Congress did not leave until 1901.

A representative from North Carolina, black activist George Henry White, delivered a bitter farewell to the House of Representatives in January, 1901. He returned to his home state and practiced law and then moved to Philadelphia when blacks were disfranchised in North Carolina.

In the following speech, White predicted that the black man would return to Congress one day. His words proved to be correct; at present there are approximately a dozen black members.

Source: U.S. Congress. House. *Congressional Record.* 56th Congress, Second Session, January 29, 1901. Page 1638.

Now, Mr. Chairman, before concluding my remarks I want to submit a brief recipe for the solution of the so-called American negro problem. He asks no special favors, but simply demands that he be given the same chance for existence, for earning a livelihood, for raising himself in the scales of manhood and womanhood that are accorded to kindred nationalities. Treat him as a man; go into his home and learn of his social conditions; learn of his cares, his troubles, and his hopes for the future; gain his confidence; open the doors of industry to him; let the word "negro," "colored," and "black" be stricken from all the organizations enumerated in the federation of labor.

Help him to overcome his weaknesses, punish the crime-committing class by the courts of the land, measure the standard of the race by its best material, cease to mold prejudicial and unjust public sentiment against him, and my word for it, he will learn to support, hold up the hands of, and join in with that political party, that institution, whether secular or religious, in every community where he lives, which is destined to do the greatest good for the greatest number. Obliterate race hatred, party prejudice and help us to achieve nobler ends, greater results, and become more satisfactory citizens to our brother in white.

This, Mr. Chairman, is perhaps the negroes' temporary farewell to the American Congress; but let me say, Phoenix-like he will rise up some day and come again. These parting words are in behalf of an outraged, heart-broken, bruised, and bleeding, but God-fearing people, faithful, industrious, loyal people—rising people, full of potential force.

Mr. Chairman, in the trial of Lord Bacon, when the court disturbed the counsel for the defendant, Sir Walter Raleigh raised himself up to his full height, and addressing the court, said:

"Sir, I am pleading for the life of a human being." The only apology that I have to make for the earnestness with which I have spoken is that I am pleading for the life, the liberty, the future happiness, and manhood suffrage for one-eighth of the entire population of the United States. (LOUD APPLAUSE.)

1934

The Chief Witness Has Been Almost Barred from Court

How fair and balanced have historical accounts of the Reconstruction been? W. E. B. Du Bois, famed black historian and sociologist, claimed that "three-fourths of the testimony against the Negro in Reconstruction is on the unsupported evidence of men who hated and despised Negroes" and who tried to "discredit these black folk." To correct the historical record Du Bois undertook a lengthy study and finally wrote a book "giving the other side of the story." Here is why Du Bois said he felt compelled to write *Black Reconstruction in America.*

Source: Du Bois, W. E. Burghardt. *Black Reconstruction in America. 1860-1880* [1935]. New York: Russell and Russell, 1956, pp. 721, 725.

The chief witness in Reconstruction, the emancipated slave himself, has been almost barred from court. His written Reconstruction record has been largely destroyed and nearly always neglected. Only three or four states have preserved the debates in the Reconstruction conventions; there are few biographies of black leaders. The Negro is refused a hearing because he was poor and ignorant. It is therefore assumed that all Negroes in Reconstruction were ignorant and silly and that therefore a history of Reconstruction in any state can quite ignore him. The result is that most unfair caricatures of Negroes have been carefully preserved; but serious speeches, successful administration and upright character are almost universally ignored and forgotten. Wherever a black head rises to historic view, it is promptly slain by an adjective— "shrewd," "notorious," "cunning"—or pilloried by a sneer; or put out of view by some quite unproven charge of bad moral character. In other words, every effort has been made to treat the Negro's part in Reconstruction with silence and contempt. . . .

I write then in a field devastated by passion and belief. Naturally, as a Negro, I cannot do this writing without believing in the essential humanity of Negroes, in their ability to be educated, to do the work of the modern world, to take their place as equal citizens with others. . . . But, too, as a student of science, I want to be fair, objective and judicial. . . . But armed and warned by all this, and fortified by long study of the facts, I stand at the end of this writing, literally aghast at what American historians have done to this field.

February 16, 1965

Chimneyville—One Hundred Years Later

It was almost one hundred years to the day on which the Civil War had ended and the Reconstruction had begun. Mayor Allen

C. Thompson of Jackson, Mississippi, had been invited to give the usual welcoming speech that city officials extend to important visitors. On February 16, 1965, Mayor Thompson welcomed the United States Civil Rights Commission to the capital city of Mississippi. His words show that he and many other Southerners had not forgotten the stormy Reconstruction years of a century ago.

Source: United States Commission on Civil Rights. *Hearings Before the United States Commission on Civil Rights,* Vol. I, *Voting,* Statement of the Honorable Allen C. Thompson, Mayor of the City of Jackson, Mississippi, February 16-20, 1965.

STATEMENT OF THE HON. ALLEN C. THOMPSON, MAYOR OF THE CITY OF JACKSON, MISSISSIPPI

MAYOR THOMPSON. . . . To look at this beautiful city today it is hard to believe that a hundred years ago during the Civil War it was known as Chimneyville.

Now I am not going to go into my usual welcome and show you how the people came to the gates of Jackson and said "Surrender," and the mayor said "We're not going to do it." And they sent a letter back to General Sherman and said, "What terms will you make? The Confederate Army has left; we are defenseless." And General Sherman wrote a letter and said, "General Blair will be there with you and he will protect you."

And then to go on through the next few years to show the horror and the destruction during the Reconstruction days, you say to me, "Why bring that up? Why live in the past? Why fight the Civil War over again?" I am not doing that. I mention it first for several reasons: First, to show that Jackson and Mississippi—show what they have done over the years to rise from the ashes of disaster to one of the most glorious places in the world, in the main through the efforts of their own citizens until, of course, in recent years.

I do not have to tell you that the Federal Government has spent millions and millions of dollars putting conquered countries such as Japan and Germany back on their feet, when not one single penny was put into Jackson and Mississippi and the South during these times when we needed the money the most.

Certainly over the last four years the people of Jackson and Mississippi, as they did during the Reconstruction days, wondered whether there are any personal rights. But although most of our time has been taken up with racial problems, Jackson has made amazing progress.

152

Section Seven

On the Frontier

"This Wonderful Stranger" with Lewis and Clark

With Meriwether Lewis and William Clark on their historic transcontinental trip was an extraordinary black man, York. Frequent references are made to York and to his delightful sense of humor in the journals kept by Lewis and Clark.

The following entries from the diaries of 1805 describe the wonder and excitement that York created among the Indians, who never before had met a black man.

Source: *History of the Expedition Under the Command of Captains Lewis and Clark* to the Sources of the Missouri Then Across the Rocky Mountains and Down the River Columbia to the Pacific Ocean Performed During the Years 1804-1805-1806, By Order of the Government of the United States. (2 vols.) Philadelphia and New York, 1814, Vol. I, pp. 108-109, 113, 116, 117, 180 *passim*.

TUESDAY, 9th (October 1805) The object which appeared to astonish the Indians most was Captain Clark's servant York, a remarkable, stout, strong negro. They had never seen a being of that colour, and therefore flocked round him to examine the extraordinary monster. By way of amusement he told them that he had once been a wild animal, and caught and tamed by his master, and to convince them, showed them feats of strength, which, added to his looks, made him more terrible than we wished him to be.

FRIDAY, 12th (October 1805) The black man York ... instead of inspiring any prejudice, his colour seemed to procure him additional advantages from the Indians who desired to preserve among them some memorial of this wonderful stranger. ...

MONDAY, 15th (October 1805) We stopped at three miles on the north, a little above a camp of Ricaras. ... York was here again an object of astonishment; the children would follow him constantly, and when he chanced to turn toward them run with great terror. ...

SATURDAY, 9th (March 1806) ... In the course of the conversation the chief (Grand Chief of the Minnetarees who is called by the French "Le Borgne") observed that some foolish young men of his nation had told him there was a person among us who was quite black, and he wished to know could this be true. We assured him that it was true, and sent for York. The Borgne was very much surprised at his appearance, examined him closely and spit on his finger and rubbed his skin in order to wash off the paint; nor was it until the negro uncovered his head and showed his short hair that the Borgne could be persuaded that he was not a painted white man.

1825

James Beckwourth's "Indian Family" Finds Him

James Beckwourth lived a rugged, colorful life as a mountaineer, trader, scout, pioneer, and as a Chief of the Crow Indian nation. Few men have had more dangerous adventures.

Like most frontiersmen, Beckwourth was an excellent spinner of yarns. He never bothered to keep a journal or diary. When he finally dictated his life experiences, he undoubtedly made the most of them.

Beckwourth was born in Virginia of a Negro slave mother and an Irish overseer who had served as a major in the Revolutionary War. According to Beckwourth: "When I was but seven or eight years of age, my father removed to St. Louis, taking with him all his family and 22 Negroes. He selected a section of land between the forks of the Mississippi and Missouri Rivers, 12 miles below St. Charles, which to this day is known as 'Beckwourth's Settlement.'"

When Beckwourth was about nineteen years old he left St. Louis and a young wife for life in the West. Today a northern pass over the Sierra Nevada [Mountains], which he discovered in

1850, bears his name.

In this excerpt from Beckwourth's dictated autobiography, he tells how he came to be "reclaimed" as a Crow Indian, in a case of mistaken identity, and how he acquired a second wife. Beckwourth's "Indian family" renamed him Morning Star and eventually made him a Chief of the Crow Indians.

Source: *The Life and Adventures of James P. Beckwourth, Mountaineer, Scout, Pioneer, and Chief of the Crow Nation of Indians.* Written from his own dictation by T. D. Bonner. New York: The Macmillan Company, 1892.

[The Indians] discovered me long before I saw them. I could hear their signals to each other, and in a few moments I was surrounded by them, and escape was impossible.... To attempt to defend myself would entail inevitable death. I took the chances between death and mercy; I surrendered my gun,' traps, and what else I had, and was marched to camp under a strong escort of horse-guards.... On arriving at their village I was ushered into the chief's lodge, where there were several old men and women.... My capture was known throughout the village in five minutes; and hundreds gathered around the lodge to get a sight of the prisoner.... They at once exclaimed, "That is the lost Crow, the great brave who has killed so many of our enemies. He is our brother."

This threw the whole village into commotion; old and young were impatient to obtain a sight of the "great brave." Orders were immediately given to summon all the old women taken by the Shi-ans at the time of their captivity so many winters past, who had suffered the loss of a son at the time. The lodge was cleared for the *examining committee,* and the old women, breathless with excitement, their eyes wild and protruding, and their nostrils dilated, arrived in squads, until the lodge was filled to overflowing. I believe never was a mortal gazed at with such intense and sustained interest as I was on that occasion. Arms and legs were critically scrutinized. My face next passed the ordeal; then my neck, back, breast, and all parts of my body, even down to my feet, which did not escape the examination of these anxious matrons, in their endeavors to discover some mark or peculiarity whereby to recognize their brave son.

At length, one old woman, after having scanned my visage with the utmost intentness, came forward and said, "If this is my son, he has a mole over one of his eyes."

My eyelids were immediately pulled down to the utmost stretch of

155

their elasticity, when, sure enough, she discovered a mole just over my left eye!

Then, and oh then! Such shouts of joy as were uttered by that honest-hearted woman were seldom before heard, while all in the crowd took part in her rejoicing. . . .

All the other claimants resigning their pretension, I was fairly carried along by the excited crowd to the lodge of the "Big Bowl" who was my father. The news of my having proved to be the son of Mrs. Big Bowl flew through the village with the speed of lightning, and, on my arrival at the paternal lodge, I found it filled with all degrees of my newly-discovered relatives, who welcomed me nearly to death. . . .

My father knew me to be his son; told all the Crows that the dead was alive again and the lost one was found. . . .

While conversing to the extent of my ability with my father in the evening and affording him full information respecting the white people, their great cities, their numbers, their power, their opulence, he suddenly demanded of me if I wanted a wife; thinking, no doubt, that, if he got me married, I should lose all discontent, and forego any wish of returning to the whites.

I assented, of course.

"Very well," said he, "you shall have a pretty wife and a good one."

Away he strode to the lodge of one of the greatest braves, and asked for one of his daughters of him to bestow upon his son, who the chief must have heard was also a great brave. The consent of the parent was readily given. The name of my prospective father-in-law was Black-lodge. He had three very pretty daughters, whose names were Still-water, Black-fish, and Three-roads. . . . I was requested to take my choice. Stillwater was the eldest, and I liked her name; if it was emblematic of her disposition, she was the woman I should prefer. . . .

I was again a married man, as sacredly in their eyes as if the Holy Christian Church had fastened the irrevocable knot upon us. . . .

My brothers made me a present of twenty as fine horses as any in the nation—all trained war horses. I was also presented with all the arms and instruments requisite for an Indian campaign.

My wife's deportment coincided with her name; she would have reflected honour upon many a civilized household. She was affectionate, obedient, gentle, cheerful, and apparently quite happy. . . .

Thus I commenced my Indian life with the Crows. I said to myself, "I can trap in their streams unmolested, and derive more profit under their protection than if among my own men, exposed incessantly to assassination and alarm." I therefore resolved to abide with them, to guard my secret, to do my best in their company, and in assisting them to subdue their enemies.

There was but one recollection that troubled me, and that was my lonely one in St. Louis. My thoughts were constantly filled with her. . . .

1836 and 1849

Runaways to the Spanish Country

Many slaves who were taken to frontier areas by their masters took advantage of their opportunity to escape into the wilderness. In the following newspaper advertisements, two slaveowners reveal their fears that valued slaves may have gone off to "Spanish country."

Source: Arkansas *Gazette,* December 6, 1836, and Arkansas *State Democrat,* June 1, 1849.

$200 REWARD

Will be paid for the delivery to me, of the following described mulatto boy and the Thief who stole him, if alive—but if dead nothing, for the villain of a white man; or ONE HUNDRED DOLLARS for the delivery to me of my Negro Boy Edmond, or for securing him in Jail, so that I get him.

Said boy is a bright mulatto, about 24 years old, his hair straight, face considerably freckled . . . high cheek bones, round face, is quite talkative. . . . I think it more than likely that he has a free pass and will try to pass himself off as a white man; but if he has been sold by the villain who conveyed him off, or the one who had him conveyed away, he perhaps has none.

I have dreamed, with both eyes open, that he went toward the Spanish country; but as dreams are like some would-be-thought-honest men—quite uncertain—he may have gone some other direction.

Jeff. Col., near Pine Bluffs, Ark., Dec. 3, 1836   Thomas Bayliss

RAN AWAY

From my residence, distant one and a half miles south of Hot

Springs, State of Arkansas, a negro man named Peter, aged about forty years. . . . Yellow complexion with rather an indian and negro face. He is a good house carpenter, plays the fiddle, and speaks Spanish. His English is broken. . . . I will give ten dollars if taken in Hot Springs County; thirty if taken more than 100 miles from my residence; and seventy dollars if taken out of the state of Arkansas. . . .

A letter addressed to me here, at Hot Springs, Ark., will be promptly noticed. . . .

Any man is at liberty to whip this fellow, as I myself have never done it.

Hot Springs, May 29, 1849   John H. Ward

1840's

Life as a Free Negro on the Texas Frontier

During the 1820's the government of Mexico invited Americans to colonize in what is now the state of Texas. But in ten years more than 12,000 Americans emigrated to the territory. Fearing loss of the land to the United States, Mexico reversed its welcome policy and in 1829 forbade slavery in Mexican territory. Some free Negroes moved to the Texas frontier hoping to enjoy an equal status with other pioneers. But their hopes were not realized. When Texas became a state in 1846, slavery, of course, was protected by law. Here is a historian's account of the treatment of the free Negro in Harris County, Texas.

Source: Muir, Andrew Forest, "The Free Negro in Harris County, Texas." *Southwestern Historical Quarterly*, Vol. XLVI, January, 1943, pp. 214-215.

Viewed as competition by white labor, patronized by white benefactors, and forbidden to associate with their kinspeople, still slaves, free negroes in the South dragged out a miserable existence. So unsatisfactory was their freedom that they often voluntarily chose masters and placed themselves in servitude. . . . Despite their social and economic privation, they nevertheless enjoyed a relative security. . . . They could neither hold office, vote, sit on juries, nor give testimony against any except slaves and other free negroes. Their offenses against property and persons were penalized as though committed by slaves, more severely than the same offenses committed by whites. Despite these restrictions, they were able to live undisturbed by legal agencies, to receive justice at the criminal bar, and to assert their freedom against illegal seizure. Cases drawn from the records of Harris County doubtless typical of the South despite its late settlement, furnish proof of these conditions.

Even when it permitted free negroes, Texas strictly regulated their position. A negro, it first ruled, was one who had as much as one-fourth negro blood, but later he became one with as little as one-eighth. Negroes were punished alike, whether slave or free. While whites were punished with death, imprisonment in the penitentiary and county jail, forfeiture, and suspension of civil and political rights, and pecuniary fines, negroes were punished with death, imprisonment in the penitentiary, whipping, standing in the pillory, and labor upon public works.

"Insurrection or any attempt to excite it" by free negroes, "poisoning . . . assaulting a free white person with intent to kill, or with a weapon likely to produce death, or maiming a free white person, arson, murder, burglary"—all were punished with death. A free negro who was convicted of using insulting, abusive, or threatening language to a white person should receive between 25 and 100 lashes. He could not play cards or other games of chance with whites, for the law provided punishment for whites who so played with their inferiors. A free negro could not "preach the gospel or . . . exhort at any religious or other meeting" unless at least two slaveholders were present. An act approved on May 11, 1846, forbade a free negro to hire slaves, though no statute prevented his owning them.

On the other hand, the state insured against the sale of free persons into slavery, although the intention of the law was more likely the protection of whites than of negroes.

"Every person who shall unlawfully sell any free person for a slave, or hold any free person as a slave against his will, knowing the person so sold or held to be free, shall be punished by confinement to hard labor in the Penitentiary. . . ."

Crossing the Mighty Sierra Nevada Mountains in Midwinter

When John C. Frémont, the "Great Pathfinder," started out on his second and most important expedition, a free young Negro named Jacob Dodson volunteered to go with him. Frémont knew that difficult months lay ahead, so he chose his exploring party with care.

The small group left Kansas in 1843, crossed near the Great Salt Lake, traveled along the Columbia River in Washington, and then down the Cascade Mountains of Oregon and into Nevada.

While camped near what is now Wellington, Nevada, Frémont decided to undertake the seemingly impossible challenge of traversing the mighty Sierra Nevada Mountains in midwinter. Only twenty-five men were deemed equal to the undertaking; several of them were under twenty-one years of age. Frémont chose men of many nations—Americans, French, Germans, Canadians, and Indians. Dodson was the only black man with the party.

Probably no better testimony to the courage of Jacob Dodson, the explorer, can be found than in these entries taken from John C. Frémont's own diary.

Source: Frémont, John C. *Memoirs of My Life Including in the Narrative of Five Journeys of Western Exploration During the Years 1842, 1843-44, 1846-47, 1848-49, 1853-54.* Chicago and New York: Belford, Clarke and Company, 1887, Vol. I, pp. 275-276, 336, 337, 342, 343, 344, 351 *passim.*

FEBRUARY 11, 1844 [In the high Sierras between Nevada and California]. The meat train did not arrive this evening and I gave Godey leave to kill our little dog (Tlamath) which he prepared in Indian fashion—scorching off the hair, and washing the skin with soap and snow and then cutting it up into pieces, which were laid in the snow. Shortly afterward the sleigh arrived with a supply of horse meat; and we had tonight an extraordinary dinner—pea soup, mule, and dog.

FEBRUARY 16, 1844. We had succeeded in getting our animals safely to the first grassy hill; and this morning I started with Jacob on a reconnoitering expedition beyond the mountain. We travelled along the crest of narrow ridges, extending down from the mountain in the direction of the valley from which the snow was fast melting away.... Toward sundown we discovered some icy spots.... We started again early in the morning.... A few miles below we broke through [the ice] where the water was several feet deep; and halted to make a fire and dry our clothes. We continued a few miles farther, walking being very laborious without snow shoes.

FEBRUARY 25, 1844. I started ahead this morning with a party of eight consisting with myself of Dr. Preuss and Mr. Talbot, [Kit] Carson, Drosier, Towns, and Jacob. We took with us some of the best animals and my intention was to proceed as rapidly as possible to the house of Mr. Sutter [Sutter's Fort near Sacramento, California] and return to meet the party with a supply of provisions and fresh animals. . . .

FEBRUARY 26, 1844. We continued to follow the stream, the mountains on either hand increasing in height as we descended, and shutting up the river narrowly in precipices, along which we had great difficulty in getting our horses.

It rained heavily in the afternoon and we were forced off the river up to the heights above. . . . It was late. . . . We encamped . . . and the horses standing about in the rain looked very miserable.

FEBRUARY 27, 1844. We had a large kettle with us and a mule being killed here, his head was boiled in it for several hours and made a passable soup for famished people. . . . My favorite horse, Proveau, had become very weak. . . . Proveau could not keep up, and I left Jacob to bring him on, being obliged to press forward with the party. . . . The day was nearly gone; we had made a hard day's march and found no grass. Towns became lightheaded, wandering off into the woods without knowing where he was going, and Jacob brought him back. . . .

MARCH 1, 1844. Charles Towns, who had not yet recovered his mind, went to swim in the river, as if it were summer and the stream placid, when it was a cold mountain torrent foaming among the rocks. . . .

MARCH 6, 1844. Arrived at Sutter's Fort.

1853

There Will Be No Slavery in Oregon

Slavery was prohibited by an act of the Oregon Provisional Government in 1844, as well as by the Federal act that created the Oregon Territory in 1848. Nevertheless, proslavery men openly and vigorously tried to get the institution of slavery started in the Pacific Northwest. Their actions, of course, prompted abolitionists to form an equally determined anti-slavery bloc. It must be pointed out, however, that many anti-slavery Oregonians did not want free blacks to settle in the Territory.

The ban upon slavery did not discourage slaveholders from bringing their chattel to the Pacific Northwest. Although the number of slaves brought into the Oregon Territory was small, George Williams, Chief Justice of the Territorial Supreme Court, decided to settle the issue once and for all. In 1853 he heard what became the most famous slave case in the Pacific Northwest.

Source: Berwanger, Eugene H. *The Frontier Against Slavery: Western Anti-Negro Prejudice and the Slavery Extension Controversy.* Urbana, Illinois: University of Illinois Press, 1967, p. 82.

George Williams, chief justice of the territorial supreme court, frustrated the further importation of slaves by his decision in the most famous slave case heard in the Pacific Northwest. The situation involved Nathaniel Ford of Missouri and the Robin Holmes family, whom Ford had brought with him as slaves when he crossed the plains to Oregon in 1844. After several years the parents fled with the youngest child while Ford continued to hold the other children. Holmes sought to regain his children and to secure legally his own liberty by suing for freedom, but the courts refused to consider the suit. Finally in 1853, Williams, an Iowa Free Soil Democrat, placed the case at the head of his docket. Deciding against Ford and thereby freeing the Negroes, Williams declared that slavery could not exist in Oregon without specific legislation to protect it. Once slaves reached the territory they were automatically released from any further obligations toward their masters. . . . The decision, understandably, was not favorably received by the pro-slavery settlers, but it set a precedent, and after 1853 no attempt was again made to retain slaves through court action.

1849 and 1859

Daniel Rodgers Crosses the Continent Twice

Daniel Rodgers was an extraordinary black pioneer. Not only did he pay *twice* in dollars and cents for his freedom, but he

162

exercised that freedom by moving across mountains and plains from Arkansas to California. In 1859 Rodgers loaded his family into a wagon and set out alone to cross the continent for a second time. He lived to be over one hundred years old, but he never could understand anyone "coddling and making a lot of fuss over him" despite his remarkable achievements.

Source: Thurman, Sue Bailey. *Pioneers of Negro Origin in California.* Oakland, California: Acme Publishing Company, 1952, pp. 17, 18, 20 *passim.*

Rodgers had come first to California, in 1849, in an overland trek from Little Rock, Arkansas, in company with his master, an ambitious planter, seeking the wealth of the gold fields. ... Daniel had been promised his liberation papers providing he worked the mines and paid the customary $1000 demanded for his freedom at that time. This implied that he would toil for his master by day, and use only his "spare time" at night to raise the freedom price.

But even so, with careful saving and long hours of labor, Rodgers finally accumulated the money required, and paid in full for his release. However, the unscrupulous master gave him neither receipt nor freedom papers, and Daniel, having no legal redress, was compelled to return with his master to Little Rock.

Finding himself once more chattel [slave] property in the South, he began planning another attempt to purchase his freedom. This time he was to be aided by a group of white men in the Arkansas community. These planters came to Rodgers' rescue because they knew of the infamous treatment to which he had been subjected in California, and wanted to atone in some personal way for the dastardly deed of his master. They made up a purse among them and with it Rodgers was able to pay for himself the second time. The men who thus helped him had the following certificate drawn up—a rare and valuable document in the possession of the Rodgers family today:

Dardanell, Yell Co., Ark.
April 30, 1859

"We the undersigned citizens of Yell County, Arkansas, having been personally acquainted with the bearer, Daniel Rodgers, a free man of color, for many years past and up to the present time, take pleasure in certifying to his character for honesty, industry and integrity; also as a temperate and peaceful man, and one worthy of trust and confidence of all philanthropic and good men wherever he may go."

163

Signed by: Robert E. Walters, George Williams, Joseph Miles, W. H. Spirey, L. D. Parish, George L. Kimble, Samuel Dickens, Haunis A. Hawill, A. Feril, James A. Baird, William A. Ross, C. M. Mundock, A. H. Fulton, Joseph P. Williams, B. I. Jacoway.

(We have no record of any other incident quite like this in the struggle of the Negro for freedom in America.)

Armed with this certificate and the freedom papers given to his wife because of her kinship to her mistress, Rodgers set out for California again, exactly ten years after he made the first long journey to the Pacific. He had secured supplies of flour, meal, tea, sugar, coffee, and tobacco, calculated to last for months ahead.

He found great friendliness among the Indians, to whom he was always cordial and generous. In exchange for portions of his supplies, Rodgers received from them lodging for his family and careful directions as to the best trails to take along the way. The Indians met kindness with kindness and seemed particularly concerned for the welfare of a colored man, making his way alone with wife and small children, across the plains.

Daniel Rodgers arrived for the second time in California, after a year's travel, and located in the area of Watsonville [near the Monterey Bay]. Here he purchased land and settled down to the life of a pioneer citizen. Since there were only two colored families in the community, the Rodgers and the Derricks . . . the heads of the families applied at once for public school privileges for their offspring. The year was 1860 when colored children were not permitted to enter the white schools. In recognition of these two families, the board of education of Watsonville appointed a Caucasian woman from the east to teach in a school in which the Rodgers and the Derricks were the only pupils. Thus began one of the first "public schools" for the education of Negro youth in the state.

1852-1855

Slaves in California Purchase Their Freedom

When gold was discovered in California in 1849, men from all over the world rushed there with the hope of getting rich quick.

164

Many brought their slaves with them so that they could work in the gold fields. A number of slaves earned enough money in their "spare time" to purchase their freedom, as this document shows. Mariposa County is in the foothill "Mother Lode" country of California where extensive mining took place in the gold rush days.

Source: Beasley, Delilah L. *The Negro Trailblazers of California.* Los Angeles, 1919, pp. 84-85.

FREEDOM PAPERS

STATE OF CALIFORNIA,
COUNTY OF MARIPOSA.

Know all men to whom these presents shall come, that I, Thomas Thorn, of the State and County aforesaid, being the rightful owner of the Negro man, Peter Green, and entitled to his service as a slave during his life have this day released and do by these presents release him from any further service as a slave.

And I do by these presents from myself, my heirs, executors and administrators declare him, the said Peter Green, to be free to act for himself and no longer under bonds as a slave. Provided, however, that the said Peter Green shall pay to me the sum of one thousand dollars, good lawful money or work for the service, from the present time until the first day of April, A. D. 1854.

In Testimony whereof, I have hereunto affixed my hand and Scroll for Seal, at Quartzburge, this 5th day of February, A. D., one thousand eight hundred and fifty-three.

THOMAS THORN. (Seal)

In the presence of Benjamin F. Cadell, Jr., Joseph A. Tiry, I hereby notify that the above obligation has been complied with and that Peter Green was legally discharged.

Given under my hand at Quartzburge, this day of August, A. D. 1855.

JAMES GIVENS,
Justice of the Peace

The Golden Gate—Not a Door to Slavery

California was admitted to the Union in 1850. Under its Constitution slavery was forbidden; but men, in the spirit of the frontier, often ignored the law. Records show that many slaveowners brought their slaves to California and that, in most cases, nothing was done about it.

Archy Lee, one of the black men brought in to California in violation of the law, decided to "vote for freedom with his feet." He ran away. The story of his flight, capture, and rescue contain all the elements of the "Wild West." The case of Archy Lee is testimony of the trials and troubles of the black man on the mining frontier.

In their struggles for freedom, blacks on the frontier showed bravery and perseverance, for although slavery was illegal, the courts in 1858 usually refused to admit testimony of blacks against whites. Even so, Archy Lee's friends were able to get a legal order against his white owner and to persuade other white men to enforce the order.

The obstacles to freedom and social equality of the black in the California frontier were many and often insurmountable. But the few instances of black and white people working together, as they did for Archy Lee, gave promise of a better day ahead.

Source: Tinkham, George H. *California Men and Events.* Stockton, California: Record Publishing Company, 1919, pp. 136-137.

Another bill equally outrageous was introduced in the Assembly by A. G. Stakes, then judge of San Joaquin county. This bill "prohibited free Negroes and other obnoxious persons from immigrating to the state." It also provided that any slave escaping to this state could be reclaimed by his master without further trouble. The bill passed the Assembly by a vote of 39 to 8. It also passed the Senate by a large majority and was signed by Governor Bigler.

The last section of the law was passed to cover a special case, that of the Negro Archy Lee, who had escaped from his master while in this state. Charles Stovall in 1857 brought the boy from Mississippi, and locating at Sacramento taught school. In the meantime Archy Lee, learning that he was free, ran away. Stovall succeeded in finding and capturing him. The Negro's friends now interfered and a writ of habeas corpus was sworn out before George Penn Johnson, United States commissioner. The boy was given his freedom. Lee was again arrested by his enemies and a writ of habeas corpus issued, returnable before the Supreme Court. That profound body, Peter H. Burnett, Stephen J. Field, and David S. Terry, gave the youth to his master. According to the construction of the law, however, they declared the Negro free. This decision deeply aroused the anti-slavery whites.

Stovall took the boy to San Francisco, intending to take him back to Mississippi. The case had aroused so much excitement that Stovall traveled in a carriage by the way of Stockton to the metropolis, where he planned to quietly board the ocean liner as she passed through the Golden Gate. The Negroes of San Francisco, however, got busy and had issued habeas corpus No. 3. It was placed in the hands of the officers and they remained up all night waiting for Stovall. They expected to find him on the Stockton steamer. Suspecting, however, that Stovall was playing a strategic game, Deputy Sheriff Thompson kept watch of the outgoing steamer. As she passed Angel Island a boat put out from the shore. In the boat was Stovall, the Negro boy and four friends. The deputy intercepted the party and served on Stovall two writs, one for Archy Lee, the other for Stovall, the latter being charged with kidnapping. Stovall and his friends drew their revolvers and Stovall exclaimed, "The boy has been given to me by the Supreme Court and I'll be damned if any state court shall take him away!"

The deputy, however, returned to San Francisco with Stovall as his prisoner. Upon a technicality of the law he was acquitted of kidnapping. The writ for Archy Lee came up before Judge Freelon on March 17th. The colored men had engaged Edward D. Baker to defend the boy. He was given his freedom. Immediately he was again arrested under the fugitive slave act of 1858. In the meantime Stovall, facing a suit for damages, had left the state. Archy was again brought before Commissioner Johnson, under habeas corpus No. 4, and was discharged. The question of slavery in California was settled.

1860's

Black Miners Purchase Their Freedom Twice

"The Old Kentucky Ridge" was the name given to a mine in Nevada worked entirely by slaves. It was owned by Colonel William English and other Georgia slave owners. The Colonel promised the slaves their freedom in exchange for working in the mines. However, things did not turn out as the Colonel planned.

167

Source: Savage, W. Sherman. "The Negro on the Mining Frontier." *The Journal of Negro History,* Vol. XXX, No. 1, January, 1945, p. 36.

The slaves were promised their freedom as a compensation for working in the mines. This work was very difficult; the slaves had to carry the ore on their heads in large baskets back a half mile to the mill. The mine failed and Colonel English died destitute of funds. The slaves took what they had been able to save by working at odd jobs about the mines in their spare time and purchased land and paid for his funeral. After the death of Colonel English his nephew took over control and forced the slaves to purchase their freedom again. When they did get their freedom they settled at Grass Valley [California], where they became an important part of the community.

1870

Forty-two Days and Nights Alone on the Trail

How to get beeves to market was a major problem for the cattlemen of the West. Herds increased in size, but the market for beef and hides in the sparsely populated cattle ranch country was small.

Demand was in the more populated country east of the Mississippi. The problem was transportation—how to get the goods to the consumer. A far-sighted Texas cowman decided to drive his cattle "up the trail" to Abilene, Kansas, load them onto railroad cars there, and ship them east to the market. That venture proved so successful that almost all stockmen began moving their herds up the trail. The dangerous job of trail driving was born. Men of all colors shared the hardships and the camaraderie of the six to eight month trip to the railroad centers while they were entrusted with the safe delivery of 1500 to 3000 head of cattle.

Records of trail drivers show that black men were numerous on the trail. There was "Gov," the negro who rode with George Mohle of Lockhart, Texas, and Henry Smith of San Antonio who traveled with the C. W. Ackerman outfit. There was also "Nick," who rode out alone with Mrs. Amada Burks over the Old Kansas Trail from Banquete, Nueces County, Texas. Mrs. Burks' husband, who had started the trip up the trail, sent back an emergency message asking her to catch up to the herd as soon as possible. As Amanda Burks wrote, "So Nick and I started in my little buggy driven by two good brown ponies and overtook the herd in a day's time. . . ."

One of the bravest men to ride the trail was George Glenn, whose heroism is celebrated in this sketch.

Source: *The Trail Drivers of Texas*. Compiled and edited by John Marvin Hunter. Nashville, Tennessee: Cokesbury Press, 1925 (published under the direction of George W. Saunders, President of the Old Time Trail Drivers' Association).

In the spring of 1870 my uncle, R. B. (Bob) Johnson drove a herd of cattle up the trail to Abilene, Kansas. He took with him as one of the cow-hands a young negro whom he raised on his ranch. . . . The herd was started from Colorado County, crossing the Colorado River at La Grange and intersecting the Chisholm Trail near the Red River, and passing across the Indian Territory. Soon after reaching Abilene my uncle became ill and died. His body was embalmed, put in a metallic casket, and temporarily buried at or near Abilene about the last of July of that year, and the following September the body was disinterred and placed in a Studebaker wagon and the negro cowhand, George Glenn, as driver, started on the long trip back to Texas. It was impossible at that early date to get a dead body shipped back by rail, as there were no railroads, at least none leading from Abilene, Kansas, to Texas. This faithful negro brought his master's body back, being forty-two days and nights on the road, sleeping every night in the wagon alongside the casket. He carried the body to the cemetery at Columbus where it was laid to rest by the side of the wife who had died some years before. Of such stuff were the old trail drivers, white and black, made of.

1870's

The "Exodusters" and Nicodemus

Emancipated blacks flowed into Kansas in such numbers in the 1870's that they became known as the "Exodusters." Just as the Jews had once left Egypt in search of the promised land, so did the freedmen come to Kansas lured by the hope of a better life and the false promises of "forty acres and a mule."

Benjamin (Pap) Singleton, who called himself the father of the Exodus, persuaded more than 7000 Negroes from Tennessee alone to migrate. In 1870 there were approximately 17,000 blacks in the Sunflower State. Ten years later there were more than 43,000.

Most of the blacks who came in 1876-1878 settled in one of Singleton's three colonies: Dunlap in the Neosho Valley; Singleton in Cherokee County; and Nicodemus in Graham County. Nicodemus was the only one of the "Exoduster" communities to survive. Here is the story of the founding of that town.

Source: *Kansas: A Guide to the Sunflower State.* Written and compiled by the Federal Writers' Project of the Works Project Administration for the State of Kansas. New York: The Viking Press, 1939, pp. 329-331.

The "Exodusters" were organized in 1873 by Benjamin (Pap) Singleton. In establishing Nicodemus he was aided by Topeka Negro leaders and W. R. Hill, a white man from Indiana, who was speculating in land in western Kansas at that time and was attracted by the large fees that homesteaders paid for assistance in obtaining land and file papers. The first group reached this townsite in the autumn of 1877, too late to plant crops. Their savings had been spent for railroad fares and the payment of fees. Unable to purchase lumber or other building materials, they lived in crude dugouts or burrows. For fuel, they burned buffalo chips, sunflower stalks, and faggots cut from clumps of dwarf willows and cottonwoods. During the first year no houses of any kind were built above the ground. They received little aid from the white settlers of the county, who resented them so bitterly that Hill, blamed for bringing them in, was forced to flee. (When he returned to this section later, however, he was held in high esteem and Hill City was named for him.)

This community was named Nicodemus not for the Biblical character but for the legendary Nicodemus who came to America on a slave ship and later purchased his liberty. Of him the plantation Negroes of the South sang:

> Nicodemus was a slave of African birth,
> And was bought for a bag of gold,
> He was reckoned as a part of the salt of the earth,
> And he died years ago, very old.

> Nicodemus was a prophet, at heart he was wise,
> For he told of the battles to come;
> Now he trembled with fear when he rolled up his eyes
> And he heeded the shake of his thumb.

170

Members of the Nicodemus colony added the following hopeful chorus:

> Good time coming, good time coming,
> Long, long time on the way;
> Go tell Elijah to hurry up pomp,
> To meet us under the cottonwood tree
> In the great South Solomon Valley to build up
> The city of Nicodemus at the break of day.

Crop failures followed in monotonous succession. Even in 1883, a good crop year elsewhere in western Kansas, Nicodemus was seared by southwest winds. Many colonists, discouraged, abandoned their claims. Others found seasonal work with white farmers in the county. From a population of 500 in 1880 the town had declined to less than 200 by 1910.

One of Nicodemus' most able leaders, the Reverend Roundtree—who wore a brand on one cheek as punishment for having received educational instruction from his master's son—taught the new citizens to read and write. At a State Fair in Michigan his pleas for the colony of Nicodemus brought several carloads of food and a sum of money. Assisted by Zach Fletcher, another resident, he was successful in having Baptist and Methodist churches erected. These buildings are still used by the community. Although most of the colonists have had to begin work at an early age, some have been graduated from college and a few have held county offices. Probably the most notable of these was E. P. McCabe, state auditor (1885-1889), who later became a territorial official in Oklahoma. . . .

Kansas Negroes observe August 4 as Emancipation Day, because, according to legend, that was the day on which Nicodemus' master laid aside his whip. . . .

Late 1800's

Aunt Clara Brown Runs Her Own Gold Mine

Mining, a hard and dangerous occupation, is usually thought of as a man's work. Nonetheless, Aunt Clara Brown, who had been a slave until emancipation, became a pioneer on the mining frontier at an age when most people would have been thinking of taking life easy in a rocking chair. Her life is a reminder that persons of

171

strong will can overcome the double obstacles of being black and being a woman in a white man's world.

Source: Savage, W. Sherman. "The Negro on the Mining Frontier." *The Journal of Negro History,* Vol. XXX, No. 1, January, 1945, p. 44.

There were Negroes operating their own mines. Aunt Clara Brown, who came to Colorado with the gold seekers at the age of sixty after serving as a slave until emancipation, became one of the well known Negro citizens of Colorado. One correspondent in speaking of her said that she was a Negro woman with a state if not a national reputation as a successful miner and philanthropist. Her property was in Crisman's Camp. She was elected to membership in the Colorado Pioneer Association back in the seventies. She was one of the first Negroes elected to that association and when she died at the age of 85 she was buried with honors. She was so well known that she was considered an institution in Central City.

Section Eight

To Seek a Wider World

late 1800's

Black Men at Home on the Range

Dr. Clifford P. Westermeir, at one time the chairman of the history department at the University of Arkansas, specialized in the study of cowboy life and lore. He concluded: "Evidence of color discrimination on the part of the cowboy is not very pronounced. Difficulties between the Negro and cowboy arose only as differences between men and were probably found more often in the Southwest, although the Negro was accepted as a member of the riding fraternity in the cattle kingdom."

Why the black man was readily accepted into the "riding fraternity" is shown by these examples of courage.

Source: *Trailing the Cowboy: His Life and Lore as Told by Frontier Journalists*. Compiled and edited by Chester Peter Westermeir. Caldwell, Idaho: The Caxton Printers, Ltd., 1955, pp. 354, 365-366, 371-373 *passim.*

"Live Stock Notes," Fort Morgan *Times*
[Fort Morgan, Colorado], November 13, 1884.

A colored cowboy at Mobeetie roped, secured and tied down a steer in one minute and thirteen seconds. This is said to be the best time on record.

The Cowboy Tournament—Denver, Colorado, October, 1887.

Pinto Jim was the name of the next cowman. He was a rawboned colored man. A sorrel was pointed out to him. He made several failures in getting the rope in the right place and then had a battle that was fierce. At last, when the horse was well nigh worn out with constant

173

plunging, Jim caught a jaquima [halter] on him, had a saddle in place and was on his back in one minute more. Thirteen minutes were consumed, but the crowd (estimated at more than 8000 people) cheered the perspiring man, nevertheless, and he deserved it.

Arkansas Valley Fair, Rocky Ford, Colorado, September, 1900.
"Struggles of Man and Beast," The Denver *Republican,*
September 8, 1900.

... The largest third day crowd in its history thronged the steer throwing exhibition. ... A company of cowboys rounded up the herd in the center of the speed ring and lassoed one of the steers. Then the three Pickett brothers came forward and seized the animal by the horns. While the lasso ropes were still on him, two of them fastened a rope with hand loops around the steer's body. One of them mounted, the creature was turned loose and bounded down the race course. The crowd, safe upon the grand stands, yelled and the crowds lining the ring fence scattered indiscriminately, but he was not a very wild steer, and soon submitted to being ridden without ado. He was turned back into the herd and another selected. ...

The chief of the three performers, having got the bull finally by the horns, simply twisted his neck till he succumbed and rolled over on the ground, while the crowd applauded. Then, with the aid of the two brothers, he climbed upon the back of the beast and rode across the grounds. He had not ridden far when the animal lay down on him and refused to be further entertaining.

He was therefore abandoned and a third steer loosed from the corrals on the grounds. This one was of better mettle and at once made a spirited break for liberty, going through the first fence and gracefully over the second, out in the open country. After him rode a half dozen cowboys and he was soon brought back. The ropers held him fast until the three negroes approached him carefully from the rear. As they did so he gave one of them a ferocious kick, but did not disable him. William Pickett grasped the creature by the horns to twist, but with a ferocious rush he broke away and had to be run down again by the horses. Again the negro took him by the horns and was tossed overhead, but held his grip upon the horns. Then the mad beast rushed him to the fence, got him down and pinned him to the earth. It was one more round for the steer, but the two brothers came to the rescue again and the pinioned negro, being released, again got the animal by the horns and, securing his twist upon the steer's neck, brought him to the

174

ground and held him there. The crowd cheered and the negro let the
steer up and mounted his back. The fagged brute staggered three times
in his attempt to rise with the negro upon him, but the fourth time he
succeeded and made one more bold dash down the track. The crowd on
the railing fell back as the beast threatened to take the fence again, but
the cowboys closed in and rounded him up, and the negro slid off his
back, waved his adieus to the applauding crowd, and the show was out.

November, 1910

A Famous Black Militant's Multi-Racial Approach
to the American Dilemma

For more than 60 years W. E. B. Du Bois was the intellectual
giant among the blacks who raised their voices in protest. Long
before the slogan became popular, Du Bois wrote that "black is
beautiful." He did not hesitate to use the word black in his book
titles—for example, *Black Reconstruction,* and *Black Folk: Then
and Now.* Du Bois was proud of his black heritage. He believed
that blacks' ability to continue their rich cultural traditions and
to overcome the obstacles to their rights as men lay in knowledge
of their past and pride in their black identity.

In this first editorial of *The Crisis,* the official magazine for the
National Association for the Advancement of Colored People, Du
Bois pleads for the advancement of humanity.

Source: *The Crisis.* Editorial, November, 1910.

The First Editorial of *The Crisis,* 1910

The object of this publication is to set forth those facts and arguments which show the danger of race prejudice, particularly as manifested today toward colored people. It takes its name from the fact that
the editors believe that this is a critical time in the history of the
advancement of men. Catholicity and tolerance, reason and forebear-
ance can today make the world-old dream of human brotherhood

approach realization while bigotry and prejudice, emphasized race consciousness and force can repeat the awful history of the contact of nations and groups in the past. We strive for this higher and broader vision of Peace and Good Will.

The Policy of *The Crisis* will be simple and well defined:

It will first and foremost be a newspaper: it will record important happenings and movements in the world which bear on the great problem of interracial relations, and especially those which affect the Negro-American.

Secondly, it will be a review of opinion in the white and colored press on the race problem.

Thirdly, it will publish a few short articles.

Finally, its editorial page will stand for the rights of men, irrespective of color or race, for the highest ideals of American democracy, and for reasonable but earnest and persistent attempts to gain these rights and realize these ideals. The magazine will be the organ of no clique or party and will avoid personal rancor of all sorts. In the absence of proof to the contrary it will assume honesty of purpose on the part of all men, North and South, white and black.

early 1900's

Growing Up in a Little Southern Georgia Town

In 1934 a young man at the University of Georgia wrote his memories of growing up in a little southern Georgia town. Not only did he draw a vivid picture of the past, but he made some interesting predictions about changes to come.

Source: "What Negro Newspapers of Georgia Say About Some Social Problems, 1933." A Master's Thesis by Rollin Chambliss. Phelps-Stokes Fellowship Studies, No. 13. Athens, Georgia: *Bulletin of the University of Georgia,* Vol. XXXV, No. 2, November, 1934, pp. 4, 5, 8 *passim.*

There must have been more Negroes in the little South Georgia community in which I grew up than whites, for though there were only three or four white boys in the group with which I used to play, there were a half dozen or more Negroes. We did chores together there on the farm, and went "possum huntin' " and to the swimming hole down on the creek and played ball and did all of those things that boys do in rural Georgia.

We did them together, and yet the Negroes were always a little apart. If we were swimming, they kept downstream. If we were playing ball, they were in the outfield and we did the batting. If we were gathering plums, the Negroes always left us the best bushes. There was no ill feeling in this. Negroes were different. They knew it, and we knew it. In the fields we all drank from the same jug, but at the pump the Negroes cupped their hands and drank from them and would never have dared to use the cup hanging there. I never knew a Negro to come to the front door of my home, and I am sure that if one had done so, someone would have asked him if he minded stepping around to the back. At the age of ten I understood full well that the Negro had to be kept in his place, and I was resigned to my part in that general responsibility.

As we grew to adolescence, the relationship with Negro boys became less intimate. We began then to talk of things which the Negro could not understand—of what we were going to do in life, of our little love affairs, of school life, of our hopes for the future. In such things the Negro had no part, and gradually we played together less and less. We were more often with grown Negroes, and I think now that we were always closer to the men than we were to the boys of our own age. They knew where the rabbits were, how to tell when a dog had treed, when the wind was too high for squirrels to stir, where it was best to set a trap. I don't know how Southern white boys on the farm would learn anything without Negroes. And they sang a lot too and strummed guitars and were almost always in good humor. They never talked very much about their own affairs, and they never told things on other Negroes. I have never known a Negro to lead a white boy into anything vicious. I knew some of these old Negroes well, after a fashion, and they were in their way good people. They were friends of mine, and still are; and when I go back into my home community, I always look up those whom I knew best. I call them by their first names, as I always have; and they call me "Mister," as they always have; and I know that they are glad to see me.

But they were not like white people. There was a difference that we all recognized. It was to be expected that a Negro would steal a little now and then, not anything of consequence, of course, but petty things: watermelons, sugar cane, fresh meat, and things like that, and now and then a little corn. . . .

I am looking back to the things that I knew. In cities perhaps it was different. It may be a little different in the country now, though I don't think there has been much change. I have known Negroes who were happy, despite poverty and squalid surroundings. I have known whites who were miserable, despite wealth and culture of a kind. Old Negroes have told me, most any kind of Negro gets more out of life any day than a real, high-class white man; and I believe them. We say here in the South that we know the Negro. We believe that we have found for him a place in our culture. Education and the passing of years may change everything, but I know that there are in my community now many white people who will die perpetuating the order as they found it, the scheme of things to which they belong.

1913

A Yale Graduate Asks, "Why Am I So Treated in the South?"

William H. Ferris was the great grandson of Enoch Jefferson, who "threw off the yoke of slavery and stepped forth as a freeman" in the early 1800's. Jefferson and his son, Enoch Jefferson II, farmed near Wilmington, Delaware. When Ferris wrote the book from which the following selection was taken, he dedicated it to his grandfather and great-grandfather, who he said were "respected among white and black alike for miles around."

William Ferris attended Yale University and became a member of the Negro Society for Historical Research and a popular speaker. Despite his achievements, he was ill-treated in the South, and in this autobiographical sketch he asks why.

Source: Ferris, William H. *The African Abroad or His Evolution in Western Civilization Tracing His Development under Caucasian Milieu.* Vol. I, New Haven, Connecticut: The Tuttle, Morehouse & Taylor Press, 1913, p. 403.

When I consider that the Negro race as a race has only had 50 years of freedom; when I consider that many have forced their way up in the face of the indifference of the Anglo-Saxon race, and the opposition and jealousy of their own race, I am constrained to doff my cap to any colored man or woman who has won recognition for his deeds and achievements from his own and from the Anglo-Saxon race.

It seems hard, unjust and cruel to tell a race it must become admired, instead of a despised race, before the race problem will be solved. But it is the truth. As I travel through the South and am penned and cooped and packed like a sardine in the sweatbox known as the Jim Crow car; as I am herded, with other Negroes, as if we were all cattle; as I am denied the privilege of a sleeping car, subjected to inconveniences and annoyances when traveling, yea, subject to countless insults and humiliations in the South, I ask, "Why is it?"

I am educated and have over a century of free and respectable ancestry behind me. Why am I so treated in the South? Is it because I am connected with a race that is despised because of the color of its skin, the texture of its hair, the heaviness of its features; despised because it was until recently a slave race; despised because it does not possess wealth and has not made a contribution to civilization or played a part in shaping and moulding the world's history?

What am I to do? The most natural thing for me to do is to hoist the signal of distress and set up a pathetic howl and plaintive wail. But suppose the world turns a deaf ear to my cries and lamentations? And that is what it has done to the Negro. For the past twenty-five years, we have had our race conventions. We have met and passed resolutions. We have resolved and dissolved. And what has been the result? The petitions and entreaties of the Negro have been ignored and one Southern State after another has disfranchised and Jim-Crowed him.

1914

This Is Wholly Un-American

For years Harlem was a predominantly white suburb separated from New York City by farms and wooded lands. The few black families in Harlem were domestic servants who lived in or near their employers' homes.

By the end of the nineteenth century, the character of Harlem began to undergo dramatic changes. For one thing, many white families began moving to Washington Heights and other newly developed suburbs. The city continued to grow outward to Harlem. Increasingly Harlem became an area within the city rather than a suburb outside the city. With black migrants coming from the South to New York and with whites moving from Harlem to new suburban areas, realtors seized upon Harlem as a place with housing available for the black newcomers.

One of these realtors, Philip A. Payton, a black, approached the managers of an apartment house at 31 West 134th Street, east of Lenox Avenue. He offered to fill the apartment house with Negroes who would be willing to pay five dollars more per month on flats than the white tenants were then paying. The managers accepted Payton's proposition.

Old, white, established Harlemites did not welcome new black residents. They resented and fought their coming; they saw it as an "invasion." The presence of even one black family in a block, no matter how well bred or orderly, was enough to cause a wholesale flight of the block's white residents.

The following anonymous and undated letter was sent to a realtor. It reveals the intensity of feeling of the time. (Note the spelling of Realty in the address.)

Source: Original document in files of the New York Urban League.

Harry Bierhoff, President
The Rock Reality Company
345 Lenox Avenue, N. Y. C.

Dear Sir:

We have been informed of your intention to rent your house at West 117th Street to Negro tenants. This is wholly un-american, and is totally against our principles.

We ask you in a gentlemanly way to rescind your order, or unpleasant things may happen.

May your decision be the right one.

(Signed) K.K.K. Realm 7, Chapter 3

1915-1919

Help Wanted in the North

Dr. Emmett J. Scott, Secretary-Treasurer of Howard University, and a team of experienced social science researchers investigated the economic motives of the thousands of black workers who left Alabama, Georgia, Florida, and Mississippi. They concluded that because wages in the North were double and triple those in the South, many blacks headed for northern cities.

Attractive advertisements appeared in Negro newspapers with wide circulation in the South. The examples cited below are taken from the Chicago *Defender*. Although the wages offered in these advertisements seem low as compared to today's standards, they were unbelievably high to the southern black. In 1915, for example, wages of farm laborers in the South averaged seventy-five cents a day. For domestic service, women earned $1.50 to $3.00 per week plus board, while men received an average of $5.00 per week. In southern towns, the chief employment opportunities for blacks were in oil refineries and lumber mills, cotton compresses, railroad shops, and domestic service. Even skilled workers, such as carpenters and bricklayers, were paid just $2.00 to $3.50 per day.

Source: Scott, Emmett J. *Negro Migration During the War*. New York: Arno Press, 1969, pp. 17, 18.

Wanted—10 molders. Must be experienced. $4.50 to $5.50 per day. Write B. F. R. *Defender* Office.

Wanted—25 girls for dishwashing. Salary $7 a week and board. John R. Thompson, Restaurant, 314 South State. Call between 7 and 8 a.m. Ask for Mr. Brown.

Wanted—25 young men as bus boys and porters. Salary $8 per week and board. John R. Thompson, Restaurant, 314 South State Street. Call between 7 and 8 a.m. Ask for Mr. Brown.

Molders wanted. Good pay, good working conditions. Firms supply cottages for married men. Apply T. L. Jefferson, 3439 State Street.

Ten families and 50 men wanted at once for permanent work in the Connecticut tobacco fields. Good wages. Inquire National League on Urban Conditions among Negroes, 2303 Seventh Avenue, New York City, New York.

Molders wanted. A large manufacturing concern, ninety miles from Chicago, is in need of experienced molders. Wages from $3 to $5.50. Extra for overtime. Transportation from Chicago only. Apply Chicago League on Urban Conditions among Negroes. T. Arnold Hill, Executive Secretary, 3719 South State Street, Chicago.

Laborers wanted for foundry, warehouse, and yard work. Excellent opportunity to learn trades, paying good money. Start $2.50-$2.75 per day. Extra for overtime. Transportation advanced from Chicago only.

Apply Chicago League on Urban Conditions among Negroes, 3719 South State Street, Chicago.

Experienced machinists, foundrymen, pattern makers wanted, for permanent work in Massachusetts. Apply National League on Urban Conditions among Negroes, 2303 7th Avenue, New York City.

3,000 laborers to work on railroad. Factory hires all race help. More positions open than men for them.

Men wanted at once. Good steady employment for colored. Thirty and 39½ cents per hour. Weekly payments. Good warm sanitary quarters free. Best commissary privileges. Towns of Newark and Jersey City. Fifteen minutes by car line offer cheap and suitable homes for men with families. For out of town parties of ten or more cheap transportation will be arranged. Only reliable men who stay on their job are wanted. Apply or write Butterworth Judson Corporation, Box 273, Newark, New Jersey, or Daniel T. Brantley, 315 West 119th Street, New York City.

$3.60 per day can be made in a steel foundry in Minnesota, by strong, healthy, steady men. Open only to men living in Chicago. Apply in person, Chicago League on Urban Conditions among Negroes, 3719 South State Street, Chicago, Illinois.

1916-1918

Dear Sir: Letters From Migrants

No documentation of the exodus of Negroes from the South during World War I is more vivid than the letters written by the migrants themselves. Expressed in the participants' own words are their motives and aspirations, their hopes and fears. The pathos of the blacks' situation in America in the early twentieth century that gave rise to the movement, one of the most significant domestic events of our country's recent history, is in each one of these records of the past.

The following letters were collected under the direction of

Emmett J. Scott, an experienced social science researcher at Howard University.

Source: "Documents-Letters of Negro Migrants of 1916-1918." Collected under the direction of Emmett J. Scott. *The Journal of Negro History,* Vol. IV, 1919, pp. 294, 303, 315, 332.

New Orleans, La., April 23, 1917.

Dear Sir: Reading a article on the 21st issue of the Chicago Defender about the trouble you had to obtain men for work out of Chicago and also seeing a advertisement for men in Detroit saying to apply to you I beg to state to you that if your could secure me a position in or around Chicago or any northern section with fairly good wages & good living conditions for myself and family I will gladly take same and if ther could be any ways of sending me transportation I will gladly let you or the firm you get me position with deduct transportation fee out of my salary. as I said before I will gladly take position in northern city or county where a mans a man here are a few positions which I am capable of holding down. Laborer, expirance porter, butler or driver of Ford car. Thaking you in advance for your kindness, beg to remain.

Dyersburg, Tennessee, 5/20, 1917.

THE DEFENDER, NEGRO NEWS JOURNAL,

My dear Sir: Please hand this letter to the Agency of the negro Employment Bureau—connected with your department—that I may receive a reply from the same—I am a practical fireman—, or stoker as the yankee people call it—have a good knowledge of operating machinery—have been engaged in such work for some 20 yrs—will be ready to call—or come on demand—I am a married man—just one child, a boy about 15 yrs—of—age—a member of the Methodist Episcopal Church—and aspire to better my condition in life—Do me the kindness to hand this to the agent.

Houston, Texas, April 21, 17.

Dear Sir: As I was looking over your great newspaper I would like very mutch to get Some infermation from you about Comeing to your great City, I have a famile and Can give you good Referns about my Self. I am a Working man and will Prove up to what I say and would be very glad to Know from you, about a Job Allthough I am at work But, If I Could get Something to do I would be very glad to leave the South, as I Read in the Chicago Defender about Some of my Race going north and makeing good.—well I would like to be on the List not with Standing

183

my reputation is all O.K.
I thank you.

Mobile, Ala., April 25, 1917.

Sir: I was reading in theat paper about the Colored race and while reading it I seen in it where cars would be here for the 15 of May which is one month from to day. Will you be so kind as to let me know where they are coming to and I will be glad to know because I am a poor woman and have a husband and five children living and three dead one single and two twin girls six months old today and my husband can hardly make bread for them in Mobile. This is my native home but it is not fit to live in just as the Chicago Defender say it says the truth and my husband only gets $1.50 a day and pays $7.50 a month for house rent and can hardly feed me and his self and children. I am the mother of 8 children 25 years old and I want to get out of this dog hold because I dont know what I am raising them up for in this place and I want to get to Chicago where I know they will be raised and my husband crazy to get there because he know he can get more to raise his children and will you please let me know where the cars is going to stop to so that he can come where he can take care of me and my children. He get there a while and then he can send for me. I heard they wasnt coming here so I sent to find out and he can go and meet them at the place they are going and go from there to Chicago. No more at present. hoping to hear from you soon from your needed and worried friend.

1916

Let's Go Where Our Children Can Be Educated

Almost without exception, parents the world over want a good education for their children. Yet in the rural South, "colored schools" often were so inadequate that even learning basic reading and writing skills was difficult. Many black parents left the South, hoping that in the North their children might be educated.

The following excerpt is taken from an extensive study of Negro education made by Dr. Thomas Jesse Jones. It makes clear just how great the differences were between white and "colored" schools in Mississippi in 1916.

Source: U.S. Department of Health, Education and Welfare,

Office of Education. Jones, Thomas Jesse. *Negro Education,* Vol. II, Bulletin 30 Washington, D.C.: Government Printing Office, 1916, pp. 14-15.

The school population is 60 per cent colored. There are seven white and two colored schools. The average salaries paid to white assistant teachers is $75 per month. The average salaries paid to colored assistant teachers is $32.50 per month. The average number of pupils taught by white is 30 and the average number taught by colored is 100.

In the county there are no agricultural high schools or in fact high schools of any kind. The whites in the same county have an agricultural high school of "magnificent proportions" and "excellent facilities," a literary high school and about ten consolidated schools.

Negroes complain that the authorities are building white schools in communities where the negro population is five times as great. When they first sought to establish these consolidated schools, there was a provision that every one must pay taxes to support them. Negroes who were required to pay large taxes refused because they were denied the benefits of the schools. A law was passed with the provision that the majority of qualified electors in a county supervisor's district might secure one of these schools on petition to the Board of Supervisors and with the understanding that they would pay taxes. But negroes are not qualified electors and consequently have no schools.

In Liberty Grove the white school goes to the twelfth grade, with courses also in music. Automobiles bring the children to school and carry them back. The negro school in the same community has only one teacher getting $25 per month and teaching over 200 children. There are two large negro denominational schools, Jackson College and Campbell College, which serve to supplement the public schools provided by the city. . . .

The supervisor of white elementary rural schools in one of the States recently wrote concerning negro schools: "I never visit one of these (negro) schools without feeling that we are wasting a large part of this money and are neglecting a great opportunity. The negro schoolhouses are miserable beyond all description. They are usually without comfort, equipment, proper lighting or sanitation. Nearly all of the negroes of school age in the district are crowded into these miserable structures during the short term which the school runs. Most of the teachers are absolutely untrained and have been given certificates by the county board, not because they have passed the examination, but because it is necessary to have some kind of negro teacher. Among the negro rural schools which I have visited, I have found only one in which the highest class knew the multiplication table."

March, 1918

"We Want Them to Stay in the South"

One reason why blacks left the South between the years 1916 and 1918 was the increase of mob violence and lynchings, particularly in South Carolina, Georgia, and Tennessee. The colored press reported the atrocities and circulated these news accounts widely throughout North and South. Many public officials, including President Woodrow Wilson and the Governor of Georgia, denounced mob violence and called for a return to the rule of law. So did the authors of the following statement published in Nashville, Tennessee, in 1918. It was signed by Bishop Gailor, Episcopal Bishop of Tennessee, W. H. Litty, Mayor of Memphis, and by Bolton Smith and Charles Haase, two prominent white businessmen of Memphis.

Source: Haynes, George E. "Negroes Move North." *The Survey,* Vol. 40, No. 5, May 4, 1918, p. 119.

We are enlisting Negroes in our armies by the hundred thousand and sending them to France to fight for us. The Negroes furnish most of the labor for our farms and in our homes. We want them to stay in the South. Thoughtful Southern men, who know conditions, want to give the good, respectable Negro a fair deal, and protect him in his life, liberty, and property, and so encourage him to live and work among us. We believe that the mobs who are yielding to their mad passions are working a terrible injury to the peace and prosperity of our country, and especially to this section of it.

Some of us are determined, therefore, to create, if possible, a public opinion that is just and enlightened and that will frown down this evil; and with this view, we ask you to meet with some of your fellow citizens on Friday, March 8, at 5 p.m. in Committee Room A, Second Floor, Chamber of Commerce and discuss ways and means.

Three Hundred Years

The year 1919 was a very special one for black Americans. It marked the tercentenary, or 300th anniversary, of the importation of the Negro to the American colonies. All over the United States blacks observed this date. Programs, some lasting several days, emphasized the freshly awakened sense of racial harmony and importance of black people and their heritage in the development of America. Many speeches and papers cited Negro progress and achievements. Optimism—about relations between black and white and about the black man's future—was the sentiment of the hour. But the poet Lucian B. Watkins spoke of problems yet to be solved.

Source: Kerlin, Robert T. *The Voice of the Negro 1919.* New York: E. P. Dutton and Company, 1920, p. 41.

THREE HUNDRED YEARS

By Lucian B. Watkins
(Tercentenary, August, 1619-1919)

Three hundred years! Lord, these are they,
These toil-worn souls brief-sweet with play,
    These dream-charmed people, vision-eyed,
    Whose life-free goal is yet denied.
But these have heard the heavens say,
In answer to the prayer they pray,
    "No Christly cause can perish—nay,
    Though men be martyred, crucified—
Three hundred years!

March, 1925

A Great Future for Harlem

Black poet and author James Weldon Johnson was most enthusiastic about the future of Harlem when he wrote the following selection. At that time, so many black artists were at work in New York that the 1920's are aften called the years of the "Harlem Renaissance."

Source: Johnson, James Weldon. "The Making of Harlem." *The Survey Graphic Number,* Vol. LIII, No. 11, March, 1925, p. 639.

. . . There was considerable race feeling in Harlem at the time of the hegira [flight] of white residents due to the "invasion," but that feeling, of course, is no more. Indeed, a number of the old white residents who didn't go or could not get away before the housing shortage struck New York are now living peacefully side by side with colored residents. In fact, in some cases white and colored tenants occupy apartments in the same house. Many white merchants still do business in thickest Harlem. On the whole, I know of no place in the country where the feeling between the races is so cordial and at the same time so matter-of-fact and taken for granted. One of the surest safeguards against an outbreak in New York such as took place in so many Northern cities in the summer of 1919 is the large proportion of Negro police on duty in Harlem.

To my mind, Harlem is more than a Negro community; it is a large scale laboratory experiment in the race problem. The statement has often been made that if Negroes were transported to the North in large numbers the race problem with all of its acuteness and with new aspects would be transferred with them. Well, 175,000 Negroes live closely together in Harlem, in the heart of New York, 75,000 more than live in any Southern city, and do so without any race friction. Nor is there any unusual record of crime. I once heard a captain of the 38th Police Precinct (the Harlem precinct) say that on the whole it was the most law-abiding precinct in the city. New York guarantees its Negro citizens the fundamental rights of American citizenship and protects them in the exercise of those rights. In return the Negro loves New York and is proud of it, and contributes in his way to its greatness. He still meets with discriminations, but possessing the basic rights, he knows that these discriminations will be abolished.

I believe that the Negro's advantages and opportunities are greater in Harlem than in any other place in the country, and that Harlem will become the intellectual, the cultural and the financial center for Negroes in the United States, and will exert a vital influence upon all Negro people.

Blazing the Path of Thunder

Countee Cullen, the black poet, loved New York City. He was born there, and, after a year at Harvard and two years in France, he spent the rest of his life there as a teacher. Cullen's experiences and keen observations of Harlem and its people gave him great hope in the 1920's for an end to racial troubles in America. He shared the optimism of many during the "Roaring '20's" that Harlem would become a community where whites and blacks together would "blaze the path of thunder" and would show the rest of the country the way to this togetherness. Here is how he expressed his hopes.

Source: Cullen, Countee. "Tableau." From *Harlem Life: Seven Poems* by Countee Cullen. *The Survey Graphic Number,* Vol. LIII, No. 11, March, 1925, p. 648.

Tableau

Locked arm in arm they cross the way,
The black boy and the white
The golden splendor of the day,
The sable pride of night.

From lowered blinds the dark folk stare
And here the fair folk talk,
Indignant that these two should dare
In unison to walk.

Oblivious to look and word
They pass, and see no wonder
That lightning brilliant as a sword
Should blaze the path of thunder.

1920's

"Race" Records Become Big Business

Le Roi Jones, prize-winning and highly controversial black playwright, claims that the blues grew out of work songs which were a functional part of the black slave's life. However, the idea that blues as a form of music could be used to entertain people and that people would actually pay to see and hear blues performed, was a revelation. "And it was a revelation that gave large impetus to the concept of the 'race' record," said Jones.

Source: Jones, Le Roi. *Blues People: Negro Music in White America.* New York: William Morrow and Company, 1965.

Race records were commercial recordings aimed strictly toward the Negro market (what large companies would call their "special products division" today, in this era of social euphemism). The appearance and rapid growth of this kind of record was perhaps a formal recognition by America of the Negro's movement back toward the definable society. This recognition was indicated dramatically by the OKEH Record Company's decision to let a Negro singer make a commercial recording.

Strangely enough, the first Negro blues singer to make a commercial recording was not Ma Rainey or Bessie Smith, or any of the other great classic or country blues singers, but a young woman, Mamie Smith, whose style of singing was more in the tradition of the vaudeville stage than it was "bluesy". . . . Nevertheless, Mamie Smith and her recordings of Perry Bradford's "Crazy Blues" ushered in the era of race records.

> I can't sleep at night
> I can't eat a bite
> Cause the man I love
> He didn't treat me right.
>
> Now, I got the crazy blues
> Since my baby went away
> I ain't got no time to lose
> I must find him today.

. . . Of course, looking at the phenomenon of race records from a more practical point of view, as I am certain the owners of OKEH must have done, Mamie Smith's records proved dramatically the existence of a not yet exploited market. "Crazy Blues" sold for months at a rate of 8000 records a week. Victoria Spivey's first record, "Black Snake Blues" recorded six years later, sold 150,000 copies in one year. So it is easy to see that there were no altruistic or artistic motives behind the record companies' decision to continue and enlarge the race category.

Early advertising for the race records might now seem almost ridiculously crass, but apparently it was effective and very much of the times. This is an example taken from a Columbia Records advertisement that appeared in 1926: the song being advertised was something called "Wasn't It Nice?"

> There sure am mean harmonizing when Howell, Horsley and Bradford start in on "Wasn't It Nice." You're a-gonna think it's nice when you once get the old disc a-spinning. The boys are still going strong when they tackle the coupling "Harry Wills, The Champion." This trio sneaks right up on a chord, knocks it down, and jumps all over it.

The Negro as consumer was a new and highly lucrative slant, an unexpected addition to the strange portrait of the Negro the white American carried around in his head. It was an unexpected addition for the Negro as well. The big urban centers, like the new "black cities" of Harlem, Chicago's South Side, Detroit's fast-growing Negro section, as well as the larger cities of the South were immediate witnesses to this phenomenon. Friday nights after work in those cold gray Jordans of the North, Negro workingmen lined up outside record stores to get the new blues, and . . . the money rolled in.

1920's

Left Wing Gordon, A Black Man on the Lonesome Road

John Wesley Gordon, better known as Left Wing Gordon, or just Wing, got his nickname because he lost his right arm in an accident when he was eighteen years old. As a casual laborer and blues singer, he traveled from St. Joseph, Missouri, through thirty-eight states. As he explained to an interviewer, "I started travelin' when I wus 'leven years ol' an' now I'll be thirty this comin' August 26th. I didn't have no father an' mother, so I jes' started somewheres. I'd work fer folks, and they wouldn't treat me right, so I moved on. An', Lawd, cap'n, I ain't stopped yet."

Wing was typical of the tide of black laborers who were on the move in the 1920's and '30's—people moving from country to town, from town to town, from city to city, from state to state, and from South to North. Wing said that he never stayed in one place more than three weeks and certainly not more than four. Wherever he roamed he sang the blues. Here is one sample of Left

Wing Gordon's blues that tells of his life as a black man on the lonesome road.

Source: Odum, Howard and Johnson, Guy. *Negro Workaday Songs.* Chapel Hill: The University of North Carolina Press, 1926, pp. 211-212.

When I come from New York,
Walkin' 'long the way,
People pick me up
Jes' to get me to pay,
Ain't my place to live,
Anyway you can't stay here.

O Illinois Central
What can you spare?
Fo' my baby's in trouble
An I ain't dere.
Hey, Lawdy, Lawdy, I got crazy blues,
Can't keep from cryin'
Thinkin' about that baby o' mine.

Lawd I woke up dis mornin',
Found my baby gone,
Missed her from rollin'
An' tumblin' in my arms.

O Lawd, if I feel tomorrow
Lak I feel to-day,
Good God, gonna pack my suitcase,
Lawd, an' walk away.

I'd rather be in jail,
Standin' like a log,
Than be here
Treated like a dog.

Well, I woke up dis mornin',
Had blues all 'round my bed;
I believe to my sould
Blues gonna kill me dead.

O baby, you don't know my min',
When you think I'm laughin',
Laughin' to keep from cryin',
Laughin' to keep from cryin'.

The South Lingers On

> From farms and small towns of the South to the cities of the North came black peasants. After World War I, they poured into New York City's Harlem in increasing numbers.
>
> It was easier for the young to adjust to city ways than it was for their parents and grandparents. Many of the old folks longed for the more familiar life "down home." Some worried and even wept about what the city might do to their children, as Grandmother did about Jutie.

Source: Fisher, Rudolph. "The South Lingers On." *The Survey Graphic Number,* Vol. LIII, No. 11, March, 1925, p. 646.

It was eleven o'clock at night. Majutah knew that Harry would be waiting on the doorstep downstairs. He knew better than to ring the bell so late—she had warned him. And there was no telephone. Grandmother wouldn't consent to having a telephone in the flat—she thought it would draw lightning. As if every other flat in the house didn't have one, as if lightning would strike all the others and leave theirs unharmed! Grandmother was such a nuisance with her old fogeyisms. If it weren't for her down-home ideas there'd be no trouble getting out now to go to the cabaret with Harry. As it was, Majutah would have to steal down the hall past Grandmother's room in the hope that she would be asleep. . . .

Into the narrow hallways she tipped, steadying herself against the walls, and slowly approached the outside door at the end. Grandmother's room was the last off the hallway. Majutah reached it, slipped successfully past, and started silently to open the door to freedom.

"Jutie?"

How she hated to be called Jutie! Why couldn't the meddlesome old thing say Madge like everyone else?

"Ma'am?"

"Where you goin' dis time o' night?"

"Just downstairs to mail a letter."

"You casin' out mighty quiet, if dat's all you goin' to do. Come 'eh. Lemme look at you."

Majutah slipped off her pendants and beads and laid them on the floor. She entered her grandmother's room, standing where the foot of the bed would hide her gay shoes and stockings. Useless precautions. The shrewd old woman inspected her granddaughter a minute in disapproval, and then she asked:

"Well, whas de letter?". . . .

"Hello, Madge," said Harry. "What held you up? You look mad enough to bite bricks."

"I am. Grandmother, of course. She's a pest. Always nosing and meddling. I'm grown and the money I make supports both of us, and I'm sick of acting like a kid just to please her."

"How'd you manage?"

"I didn't manage. I just gave her a piece of my mind and came on out."

"Mustn't hurt the old lady's feelings. It's just her way of looking out for you."

"I don't need any looking out for—or advice either."

"Excuse me. Which way—Happy's or Edmonds?"

"Edmonds—darn it!"

"Right."

It was two o'clock in the morning. Majutah's grandmother closed her Bible and turned down the oil lamp by which she preferred to read it. For a long time she lay thinking of Jutie—and of Harlem, this city of Satan. It was Harlem that had changed Jutie—this great, heartless, crowded place where you lived under the same roof with a hundred people you never knew, where night was alive and morning dead. It was Harlem—those brazen women with whom Jutie sewed, who swore and shimmied and laughed at the suggestion of going to church. Jutie wore red stockings. Jutie wore dresses that looked like nightgowns. Jutie painted her face and straightened her hair, instead of leaving it as God intended. Jutie—lied—often.

And while Madge laughed at wanton song, her grandmother knelt by her bed and through the sinful babel of the airshaft, through her own silent tears, prayed to God in heaven for Jutie's lost soul.

"We Are Busy Now"

Jerome Dowd, a professor of sociology at the University of Oklahoma, wrote a book on race relationships. Dowd claimed that "the first step in the direction of good will and cooperation among the races of the world is that they come to know each other. In the high schools and universities of our country there should be courses offered dealing with the culture and contributions to civilization of the several great races of the world, especially of the races living under our flag."

The professor wrote the following descriptions of racial separation in the North in the 1920's.

Source: Dowd, Jerome. *The Negro in American Life.* New York: Negro Universities Press, 1926, pp. 39-40.

Not only in respect to their place of residence, but in nearly every other respect, the Negroes in the North tend to live apart from the whites. The degree of segregation generally varies with the mass of the Negro population. In cities where the number of Negroes is large the segregation is sharply limited, while in cities where Negroes are few there is much freer commingling with the whites. . . .

Very frequently embarrassment, lawsuits, and even acts of violence grow out of the unadjusted contacts of the Negro and Caucasian in the Northern states.

In Boston . . . several hotels, restaurants, and especially confectionery stores will not serve Negroes, even the best of them. The discrimination is not made openly, but a Negro who goes to such places is informed that there are no accommodations, or he is overlooked and otherwise slighted, so that he does not come again. Even Booker Washington was turned away from hotels in Boston and Springfield. Similarly there are numerous hotels in Chicago, Cincinnati, Columbus, Dayton, and other cities which refuse to admit Negroes.

Some years ago there was much newspaper comment over the refusal of a white maid in an Indiana hotel to make up a bed occupied by Booker Washington. Also, a few years ago, much ado was made over the refusal of hotels to receive Negro delegates at a Methodist General Conference held in Los Angeles. When I was living in Madison, Wisconsin, a Negro glee club visiting the city had to be provided for privately because no hotel would lodge them.

Restaurants adopt a variety of ruses to avoid Negro patrons. The Chicago *Tribune,* referring to a famous restaurant in that city, says: "When a negro entered and asked to be served, he was seated in the usual way at a table on which were no menu or price cards. Presently a price card was laid before him. And in that price card lay all the effectiveness of the strictest Southern 'Jim Crow' law. It read something like this:

Coffee, per cup .... $ .50
Coffee, with cream .... .75
Bread and Butter 1.00
Pork Chops .... 8.00 etc.

One glance at that card and its awful prices was usually enough to send the colored man hurrying out of the place!"

One summer evening at an open air restaurant in Chicago I saw a group of Negroes seat themselves at a table. After they had been tardily served, one of them arose and spoke to the proprietor in a complaining manner of the prices charged. The proprietor refused the overcharge upon the understanding that the Negroes would not return. Referring to the situation in New York, the *Sun* says: "In restaurants the waiters keep within the law. They do not say, 'We will give you no dinner,' but 'We are busy now.' And the Negro may look at his empty plate, if he will, from 6 o'clock until midnight, and the excuse will be the same."

November 13, 1929

"To You May My Heart Forever Cling"

Although thousands of blacks left the South for new homes in other sections of the United States, many left their hearts there.

Typical of the black migrants' yearning for the familiar land and loved ones they had left behind is that of Miss Annie M. Glover. She left St. Helena Island, South Carolina, in 1867, and lived and worked in Pennsylvania and Massachusetts for more than sixty years. Even though she sent money home to her parents regularly, she managed to save enough of her earnings to return "home" three different times during her life in the North. On her last visit, she wrote the following poignant tribute to the rural South she loved.

Source: Kiser, Clyde Vernon. *Sea Island to City: A Study of St. Helena Islanders in Harlem and Other Urban Centers*. New York: Columbia University Press, 1932, p. 247.

I love St. Helena for her natural beauty. I love her people for their unselfishness and hospitality.

When I last saw St. Helena her clear skies, her beautiful sunshine, her gray moss and live oaks, her vivid greens, her mockingbird singing on the wing enthralled me, and though I am more than a thousand miles from her I still see St. Helena.

> Home of the gray moss and the Live Oak,
> Land of sunshine and light,
> Free from the city's grime and smoke,
> Free from the city's horrors of the night,
> Land where the mockingbird sings on the wing,
> St. Helena
> To you may my heart forever cling.

> Annie M. Glover,
> November 13, 1929, West Medford, Mass.

1920's and 1930's

House Rent Parties and Chitterlin' Drags

Because the cost of housing was high and incomes of black migrants to northern cities generally low and hard to stretch to meet the costs of living, a unique form of entertainment known as "rent parties" began. Admission was usually twenty-five cents, and refreshments were sold. In this way, families hard pressed to pay their rents raised money at the same time that newcomers had a chance to enjoy themselves and meet their neighbors.

House rent parties or "chitterlin' drags," as they were sometimes called, continued through the Depression years. These parties gave urban blues singers and boogie-woogie pianists a chance to perform and become popular. As their popularity spread from the black community to other groups of people, recording companies recognized the growing market for "soul music." Many performers who began their careers at chitterlin' drags were asked to record. Phonograph records gradually began to replace live artists at many rent parties. Some of these people who started out at these neighborhood parties and went on to national fame are: Le Roy Carr, Jimmy Yancey, Cripple Clarence Lofton, Meade "Lux" Lewis, Cow Cow Davenport, Montana Taylor, Albert Ammons, Pete Johnson, Charlie Spand, Big Maceo Merriweather, Roosevelt Sykes, Tampa Red, Sonny Boy Williamson, Big Bill Broonzy, Memphis Slim, and Lonnie Johnson.

Here is an example of the kind of small card people often sent out to announce a rent party.

Source: Kiser, Clyde Vernon. *Sea Island to City: A Study of St. Helena Islanders in Harlem and Other Urban Centers.* New York: Columbia University Press, 1932, p. 45.

SHAKE IT AND BREAK IT. HANG IT ON THE

WALL, SLING IT OUT THE WINDOW, AND

CATCH IT BEFORE IT FALLS AT

A SOCIAL WHIST PARTY

Given by

Jane Doe

2 E. 133rd St. Apt. 1

Saturday Evening

March 16, 1929

Music by Texas Slim   Refreshments

1937

The Urban League Hails a Presidential Appointment

In 1911 Negro scholar Dr. George Haynes and several white reformers formed the Urban League in an effort to meet problems of the growing black populations in northern cities. Dr. Haynes believed that cooperation between black and white people was essential to improving living conditions and opportunities in business, education, and recreation of urban blacks. Of his plans for the Urban League, he said: "White people were to be asked to work with Negroes for their mutual advancement and advantage rather than working for them as a problem." In one of the League's publications this salute to President Franklin Roosevelt appeared.

Source: "A Presidential Appointment." *Opportunity: A Journal of Negro Life.* Published by the National Urban League. March, 1937, p. 69.

We salute President Roosevelt for his appointment of William H. Hastie to the post of District Judge of the Virgin Islands. By this appointment the Chief Executive of the U.S.A. has removed one of the taboos which have dogged the Negro since Reconstruction. The abstract right to hold public office is guaranteed to the Negro by virtue of his citizenship, and many Negroes have received Presidential appointments carrying no little responsibility. But it has generally been understood that the federal judiciary was verboten [forbidden] to men of Negro blood, a sort of unwritten law having the force of a tradition that received its validity from the myth and dogma of the Reconstruction.

The fact that the appointment is to the Virgin Islands where the population is small and overwhelmingly Negro does not lessen its significance. The important fact is that a Negro has been charged with the administration of the laws and statutes of the United States government. It may be many years before a person is appointed to a like position on the mainland. But the precedent has been established and the way will not be as difficult as it would have been if this appointment had not been made.

1937

What It's Like: a Poem

One day Waring Cuney, author of this autobiographical poem, happened to meet the black poet, Langston Hughes, on a streetcar in Washington, D.C. Although Cuney was already an accomplished singer, he began writing verse. His poetry was acclaimed immediately, perhaps because he expressed so well what it was like to be black in America.

Source: Reprinted with permission of the National Urban League, Inc., from *Opportunity: Journal of Negro Life.* Vol. XV, January 1937, p. 22.

COLORED

By Waring Cuney

You want to know what it's like
    Being colored?

Well,
It's like going to bat
With two strikes
Already called on you—

It's like playing pool
With your name
Written on the eight ball,—

Did you ever say,
"Thank you, sir"—
For an umbrella full of holes?

Did you ever dream
You had a million bucks,
And wake up with nothing to pawn?

You want to know what it's like
    Being colored?

Well,
The only way to know
Is to be born that way.

Section Nine

Black and White Together— The Drive for Civil Rights

1848 and 1888

Rights for Women, Too

Next to abolition of slavery and the struggle for equal rights for the Negro people, the cause closest to Frederick Douglass' heart was women's rights. Douglass was aware of the important roles women had played in antislavery activities. In his own newspapers and journals he regularly devoted space to the work of women.

Here is a description of some of Douglass' activities in the struggle for civil rights for women—both black and white.

Source: Foner, Philip S. *The Life and Writings of Frederick Douglass,* Vol. II, Pre-Civil War Decade 1850-1860. New York: International Publishers, 1950, pp. 16, 17.

While Douglass believed that the antislavery movement was doing much for the elevation and improvement of women, he understood fully the need for an independent, organized movement to achieve equal rights for women. On July 14, 1848, *The North Star* which featured the slogan, "Right is of no sex," carried an historic announcement:

A Convention to discuss the Social, Civil, and Religious Condition and Rights of Women will be held in the Wesleyan Chapel at Seneca Falls, New York, on Wednesday and Thursday, the 19th and 20th of July instant.

During the first day, the meetings will be exclusively for women, which all are earnestly invited to attend. The public generally are invited to be present on the second day, when

Lucretia Mott, of Philadelphia, and others, both ladies and gentlemen, will address the Convention.

Thirty-five women and thirty-two men, courageous enough to run the risk of being branded "hermaphrodites" and "Aunt Nancy Men," responded to the call for the world's first organized gathering for women's rights. Douglass was the only man to play a prominent part in the proceedings. . . .

In 1888, a few years before his death, Douglass recalled his role at the Seneca Falls Convention, and told the International Council for Women:

"There are few facts in my humble history to which I look back with more satisfaction than to the fact, recorded in the history of the Woman Suffrage movement, that I was sufficiently enlightened at the early day, when only a few years from slavery, to support your resolution for woman suffrage. I have done very little in this world in which to glory, except in this one act—and I certainly glory in that. When I ran away from slavery, it was for myself; when I advocated emancipation, it was for my people; but when I stood up for the rights of women, self was out of the question, and I found a little nobility in the act."*

*From *The Woman's Journal,* April 14, 1888

June 27, 1882

"I May Stand Alone Among Colored Men"

At the close of the Civil War, new black leaders came forward. Perhaps none was more remarkable than T. Thomas Fortune, who later became editor of the New York *Age* and known as the "Dean of Negro Journalism." Under his leadership, the *Age* demanded abolition of separate schools and fought for the adoption of a civil rights bill. It also carried on an effective crusade for the right of Negroes to serve in the Spanish-American War.

Fortune's editorials were widely quoted by white dailies. When Theodore Roosevelt was police commissioner of New York City, he once said, "Tom Fortune, for God's sake, keep that pen of yours off me." Later, when Roosevelt became President, he asked

Fortune to serve as his representative to investigate conditions in the Hawaiian and Philippine Islands.

Here in an excerpt from one of his early speeches, Fortune spells out his hope that blacks and whites would work together for civil rights.

Source: "The Colored Man as an Independent Force in Our Politics." Address delivered by T. Thomas Fortune before the Colored Press Association in Washington, D. C., June 27, 1882. Reprinted in Fortune, T. Thomas. *Black and White: Land, Labor, and Politics in the South.* New York: Fords, Howard, and Hulbert, 1884, pp. 116, 122, 129, 130.

I may stand alone in the opinion that the best of the race and the best interests of the country will be conserved by building up a bond of union between the white people and the negroes of the South—advocating the doctrine that the interests of the white and the interests of the colored people are one and the same; that the legislation which affects the one will affect the other; that the good which comes to the one should come to the other; and that, as one people, the evils which blight the hopes of the one blight the hopes of the other. . . .

It is not safe in a republican form of government that clannishness should exist, either by compulsory or voluntary reason; it is not good for the government; it is not good for the individual. A government like ours is like unto a household. Difference of opinion on non-essentials is wholesome and natural, but upon the fundamental idea incorporated in the Declaration of Independence and affirmed in the Federal Constitution the utmost unanimity should prevail. . . .

In a word, I am an American citizen. I have a heritage in each and every provision incorporated in the Constitution of my country, and should this heritage be attempted to be filched from me by any man or body of men, I should . . . stake even life in defense of it. . . .

Let there be no aim of *solidifying* the colored vote; the massing of black means the massing of white by contrast. . . . There can be no general elevation of the colored men of the South until they use their voting power in independent local affairs with some discrimination more reasonable than clinging to a party name. When the colored voters differ among themselves and are to be found on *both sides* of local political contests, they will begin to find themselves of some political importance; their votes will be sought, cast, and *counted.*

And this is the key to the whole situation; let them make themselves a part of the people. It will take time, patience, intelligence, courage;

but it can be done, and until it is done their path will lie in darkness and perhaps in blood.

1907

The Difference Between Being Worked and Working

Booker T. Washington was born into slavery in Virginia just four years before the Civil War began. He studied at Hampton Institute and then founded a school for Negroes at Tuskegee, Alabama. Washington lectured widely and received honorary degrees from a number of universities.

A contemporary black leader, W. E. B. Du Bois, criticized Washington's insistence upon the need for industrial education. He accused Tuskegee's founder of preaching a "gospel of Work and Money to such an extent as apparently almost completely to overshadow the higher aims of life." Du Bois advocated more academic-oriented, more challenging education for the "talented tenth" and a more aggressive drive for blacks' civil rights than Washington supported.

In 1907 these two chief contenders for leadership of their people were invited to be the William Bull Lecturers at the Philadelphia Divinity School. Here is part of what Washington said then in defense of his philosophy of education.

Source: Washington, Booker T. and W. E. Burghardt Du Bois. *The Negro in the South: His Economic Progress in Relation to His Moral and Religious Development.* Philadelphia: George W. Jacobs and Company, 1907, pp. 30, 31, 46-50, 53.

. . . In all my advocacy of the value of industrial training I have never done so because my people are black; I would advocate the same kind of training for any race that is on the same plane of civilization as our people are found on at the present time. . . .

One of the first and most important lessons, then, to be taught the Negro when he became free was the one that labor with the hand or with the head, so far from being something to be dreaded and shunned, was something that was dignified and something that should be sought, loved, and appreciated. Here began the function of the industrial school for the education of the Negro. This was the uppermost idea of General Armstrong, the father of industrial education for the Negro. . . . And in a large measure for the entire United States. For you must always bear in mind that, prior to the establishment of such institutions as

Hampton Institute, there was practically no systematic industrial training given for either black or white people, either North or South. At the present time more attention is being paid to this kind of education for white boys and girls than is being given to black boys and girls. . . .

When industrial schools were first established in the South for the education of members of my race, stubborn objection was raised against them on the part of black people. This was the experience of Hampton, and this in later years was the experience of Tuskegee Institute.

I remember that for a number of years after the founding of the Tuskegee Institute, objection on the part of parents and on the part of students poured in upon me from day to day. The parents said that they wanted their children taught "the book," but they did not want them taught anything concerning farming or household duties. It was curious to note how most of the people worshipped "the book." The parent did not care what was inside the book; the harder and the longer the name of it, the better it satisfied the parent every time, and the more books you could require the child to purchase, the better teacher you were. . . . I found some white people who had the same idea.

They reminded me further that the Negro for two hundred and fifty years as a slave had been worked, and now that the race was free they contended that their children ought not to be taught to work and especially while in school. In answer to these objections I said to them that it was true that the race had been worked in slavery, but the great lesson which we wanted to learn in freedom was to work. I explained to them that there was a vast difference between being worked and working. I said to them that being worked meant degradation, that working meant civilization. . . .

If you will excuse my making personal reference, just as often as I can when I am at home, I like to get my hoe and dig in my garden, to come into contact with real earth, or to touch my pigs and fowls. Whenever I want new material for an address or a magazine article, I follow the plan of getting away from the town with its artificial surroundings and getting back into the country, where I can sleep in a log cabin and eat the food of the farmer, go among the people at work on the plantations and hear them tell their experiences. . . .

Only a few days ago I heard one of these old farmers, who could neither read nor write, give a lesson before a Farmers' Institute that I shall never forget. The old man got up on the platform and began with this remark: "I'se had no chance to study science for myself," and then he held up before the audience a stalk of cotton with only two bolls on it. He said he began his scientific work with that stalk. Then he held up a second stalk and showed how in the following years he had improved the soil so that the stalk contained four bolls, and then he held up a third stalk and showed how he had improved the soil and method of cultivation until the stalk contained six bolls, and so he went through the whole process until he had demonstrated to his fellow farmers how he had made a single stalk of cotton produce twelve or fourteen bolls. At the close of the old man's address somebody in the audience asked what his name was. He replied, "When I didn't own no home and was in debt, they used to call me old Jim Hill, but now that I own a home and am out of debt, they call me 'Mr. James Hill.' "

1918

An Appeal to Conscience

In the famous *Plessy* v. *Ferguson* case of 1896 the Supreme Court ruled that separate facilities for blacks and whites were constitutional provided they were equal. As a result, "separate but equal" waiting rooms, rest rooms, swimming pools, and railroad cars were legal until 1954.

Some people attacked the existence of separate facilities on the grounds that facilities for whites were of better quality than those for blacks; others charged that the "separate but equal" doctrine was unconstitutional. However, Dr. Kelly Miller of Howard University attacked them on the grounds that they were not only un-American but absurd. Here is part of his reasoning taken from *Appeal to Conscience,* a book he wrote in 1918 and addressed to "right-minded America."

Source: Miller, Kelly, *An Appeal to Conscience: America's Code of Caste, A Disgrace to Democracy,* pp. 16, 17, 66, 67. New York: Copyright, 1918, by the Macmillan Company.

The more progressive and ambitious the Negro becomes, the less tolerable he seems to be to his white lord and master. The good old Negro slave who was ever faithful and loyal to the welfare of his lord and master was always acceptable to him. But his more ambitious son, with a college diploma in his knapsack, is "persona non grata" [unacceptable]. The Negro coachman can drive his white master to the depot, sitting side by side and cheek by jowl, with complaisant [agreeable] satisfaction; but a different situation is created should they become joint occupants of a settee in a railway coach, where each pays his own fare and rides on terms of equality. . . .

When the Negro contends for public equality, he is often accused of the desire to force himself into association wherein he is not wanted. If this were his motive, the accusation would be justified. If Negroes walk on the north side of the street on a summer's afternoon, it is not because they desire to force association with whites who occupy the same thoroughfare, but they are both seeking shelter from the scorching rays of the burning sun, and the fact that they are thrown together is incidental to their common quest of the same advantage. When the Negro seeks a residence where white people happen to live, it is not that he wishes to force himself into unwelcome association. The whites, representing the more numerous and wealthy elements of the population, are apt to occupy the more advantageous localities and sections.

The Negro is in quest of a fair chance to work out his own destiny, and to contribute his share to the common honor and glory of the nation. This he cannot do if handicapped and circumscribed by laws separating him from the rest of his fellow men. Already handicapped by tradition and environment, it is poor sportsmanship on the part of his white fellow citizens still further to handicap him in the race of life. Equality of opportunity is the most that the Negro asks, and the least that a democratic nation can afford to grant.

August 1, 1920

"Black Moses" and the World Convention of Negroes

Although he was born and raised in Jamaica and received some education in England, it was in the United States that Marcus Garvey became famous. In 1917 Garvey, often called the "Black Moses," came to Harlem. There he launched a movement to unite all "Negroes of the world."

Just four years after he arrived in New York City, Garvey had won thousands of followers. He had also become: President-General of the Universal Negro Improvement Association (UNIA); President of the Provisional Republic of Africa; President of the Black Star Line of Ocean-going Steamships; President of the Negro Factories Corporation; and Editor and Publisher of Negro World, a "newspaper devoted solely to the interests of the Negro Race."

As leader of the UNIA, Garvey called a "great world convention" of black men which convened at Liberty Hall in New York City. Three thousand delegates came from all parts of the world. On Sunday, August 1, 1920, a huge parade dramatically opened the convention of Negroes from all parts of the globe. Here is how one reporter described that event and its meaning.

Source: Talley, Truman H. "Garvey's Empire of Ethiopia." *The World's Work,* Vol. 41, No. 3 (January, 1921), pp. 264-265.

On the opening day there was held the great parade which resulted in much more than a spectacular display of pageantry. It was a panorama of patriotism. Fifty thousand Negroes of all ranks and stations in life and from every part of the globe—there were princes, high officials of various governments, and even a Haitian admiral—were in the line of march. There were twelve bands that were almost smothered in the enthusiastic tumult of the tens of thousands of participants and onlookers. Their colors—"black for our race, red for our blood, and green for our promise"—were everywhere to be seen intertwined with the Stars and Stripes, "like," recorded one Negro newspaper, "unto a benediction in the peaceful effect and calm it brought to the soul; the one emblematic of its peculiar liberal institutions that made possible such a demonstration as this parade, the other no less significant of the much larger and greater freedom that will come to every Negro in his own United States of Africa." Another observer wrote, "The insistent note of the parade was liberty and so insistent, indeed, was this appeal that white women were seen to cry as in imagination they beheld the Negro achieving that measure of success that they themselves under similar distressing conditions in other parts of the world are fighting to achieve. One emotional Irishwoman, as the parade traversed 125th Street, with tears upon her cheeks and in the anguish of despair, cried, "And to think, the Negroes will get their liberty before the Irish." Among the slogans emblazoned on standards in the march which enthused the thousands of dusky reviewers were, "Africa Must Be Free," "The Negro Fought in Europe, He Can Fight In

Africa," "Down With Lynching," "The New Negro Wants Liberty," "Freedom For All," "Africa a Nation, One and Indivisible," "Garvey, the Man of the Hour," "What of the New African Army?", "United We Stand for African Liberty," with an occasional "Long Live America."

Flushed with the fervor and the success of the opening procession, as many more Negroes as the 25,000 seats in Madison Square Garden could hold surged down town in an attempt to get within earshot of the opening night's verbal fireworks. Amid a most patriotically turbulent scene, with the three thousand delegates in their sectional seats after the fashion of a national political convention, the numerous dignitaries and officials in the Garvey cabinet arranged around the rostrum, and the rest of the balconied building teeming with thousands more of his color, Marcus Garvey arose to deliver the keynote speech. The throng, which had been singing "Onward Christian Soldiers" along with the music of the bands, grew silent. The hour indeed had come.

"We are met here tonight," was his orthodox beginning, "for the purpose of enlightening the world respecting the attitude of the new Negro. We are assembled as the descendants of a suffering people who are determined to suffer no longer. For three thousand years our forefathers and even ourselves suffered in this Western Hemisphere. For more than five hundred years our forefathers on the great continent of Africa suffered from the abuse of an alien race.

"We as new Negroes declare that what is good for the white man in this age is also good for the Negro. The white race claim freedom, liberty, and democracy. For that freedom, that liberty, that democracy, they drenched Europe in blood for four and a half years. In that bloody war, fought to maintain the standard of civilization and freedom of democracy, they called upon two million black men from Africa, from the West Indies, and from America to fight that the world might enjoy the benefits of civilization. We fought as men; we fought nobly; we fought gloriously; but after the battle was won we were still deprived of our liberties, our democracy, and the glorious privileges for which we fought. And, as we did not get those things out of the war, we shall organize four hundred million strong to float the banner of democracy on the great continent of Africa."

After the uproar from this pointed introduction had subsided, Garvey proceeded with what, from a study of his countless speeches and writings, stands as about the most representative presentation of his project.

"We have absolutely no apologies or compromises to make where Negro rights and liberties are concerned," he declared. "Just at this time as the world is reorganizing it is also reconstructing itself, and everywhere oppressed peoples are striking for and obtaining their rightful freedom. Negroes of the world shall do no less than also strike out for freedom. Liberty is the common heritage of mankind and as God Almighty created us four hundred million strong, we shall ask the reason why and dispute every inch of ground with any other race to find out why we also cannot enjoy the same benefits.

"We, as a people, do not desire what belongs to others. But others have sought to deprive us of those things which belong to us. Our fathers might have been satisfied to have been deprived of their rights, but we new Negroes, we young men who were called out in this war, we young men who have returned from the war, shall dispute every inch of right with every other race until we win what belongs to us.

"This convention is called for the purpose of framing a bill of rights for the Negro race. We shall write a constitution within this month that shall guide and govern the destiny of our four hundred millions. This constitution, like that of the greatest democracy in the world, we shall defend with the last drop of our blood. . . ."

January 19, 1922

Just Hanged Him

William Allen White was called "The Sage of Emporia." As editor and owner of the Emporia, Kansas, *Gazette*, he gained national recognition for his powerful and outspoken editorials. From a small country tabloid, the *Gazette* grew to one of the foremost newspapers in the country. An influential and liberal Republican, White supported both Theodore Roosevelt's Bull Moose Party and Herbert Hoover. His concern with political and social reform even prompted him to enter the political ring himself—in 1924 he ran for Governor of Kansas on an independent ticket. He lost the election but polled 149,811 votes.

One of the subjects of his editorials was the racial situation in America. White attacked the revived Ku Klux Klan and called for action to curb its activities. In this editorial, his words are the voice of conscience of the nation.

Source: *The Editor and His People: Editorials by William Allen*

210

White. Selected by Helen Ogden Mahin, pp. 324-325. Copyright, 1924, by the Macmillan Company.

JUST HANGED HIM

January 19, 1922.

It took twenty-two lines in the morning papers, including a three-line head, to tell the story of the hanging of Jake Brooks, of Oklahoma City, because he went to work in a packing house during a strike. The brevity was due to Jake's color. He was black. Custom makes that kind of a hanging unimportant in this country. We are as brutal and merciless with the black man as the Russians are with the Jews. And take it one year with another, we kill as many defenseless blacks as the Russians kill of the defenseless Jews in the pogroms.

It's a miserable business, this ruthless race prejudice; it is a blot upon our civilization, and all over the civilized world outside of America men scorn us for this, as we scorn the Russians for their barbarities, or the cannibals for theirs.

The day that Jake was being hanged the lower house of the Congress of the United States wrangled all day over the bill to make lynching a federal crime—and got nowhere. But that law must come, if we are to hold up our heads as Christian people in the civilized world.

Jake Brooks was a strike leader, and not in very big business; but he was an American citizen. And he did have rights as an American citizen, and to take him out and hang him for no other reason than that he was black—and at the bottom that's what hanged Jake, for the white strike breakers were unmolested—it's a horrible thing.

What a hell of fear and rancor and rebellion it must set to boiling in the hearts of black folks. God pity them, and sustain them, and finally help them in their bondage.

1931

Henry Ford Adopts "Inkster"

Early in its history, the Ford Motor Company "crossed the color line" as far as the right to work was concerned. It has been estimated that by 1940 approximately one-tenth or 10,000 of the available factory jobs were filled by blacks.

While few were employed at higher levels, a "Ford job" had

extraordinary lure for Detroit Negroes. Blacks eagerly sought work in the foundry or on the loading platform. Certainly the 200,000 residents of "Blackbottom" and "Paradise Valley" knew that there was no other large-scale employer of blacks anywhere in the area. Don Marshall, the Ford Company's chief Negro hiring agent, became a political force in his own right and was sometimes called the "unofficial mayor of Detroit's Harlem."

The Ford Company's reputation as a large-scale "race" employer is relatively well known. However, not many people know the story of how Henry Ford adopted the entire village of Inkster during the Depression.

Source: Sward, Keith Theodore. *The Legend of Henry Ford.* Copyright 1948 by Keith Sward. Reprinted by permission of Holt, Rinehart and Winston, Inc.

Inkster, adjacent to Dearborn, was a jerry-built community that had sprung up in past years to house Ford workers. Most of the inhabitants of the little colony were destitute Negro families. When Ford took over the community in November, 1931, it had been shorn of electric lights and police protection. The local bank had closed. Inkster's storekeepers were heavily in debt. Among the 500 Negro families in the village there were ten cases of rickets. . . .

All this was changed in a wink under the new management. The Ford people set up a public commisary. Other community services sprang to life. The 500-odd families in the drab, miniature city were decently housed and clothed. Their back bills were paid up.Inkster, in no time at all, became a shining little oasis, immune from the worst ravages of depression.

Not that Ford was out of pocket. In return for his communal services he hired every adult male in the village and put him to work at the Ford Motor Co., at a cash wage of 12 cents an hour. This money wage of $1 a day was carefully budgeted to meet the food requirements of every wage-earner's family. An additional $3 [per day] per man, subtracted from the prevailing $4 minimum then in effect at the Rouge [another Ford plant] was retained by the Ford Motor Co. as a check-off to pay for Inkster's rehabilitation. If about 500 of the villagers were so employed, Ford was reserving from their wages a daily fund of $1500. With that revenue he was paying Inkster's bills. . . .

The Inkster experiment had its merits. The rescue of the dismal little village was timely and beneficial. It was commercially intelligent. An eyesore to all who beheld it, the colony had been too close to the Rouge for comfort. The program of rehabilitation gave rise to reams of free publicity. It built good will for the Fords in the immense Negro population of metropolitan Detroit, and it paid for itself, in part at least, by means of the $3 daily check-off from the wages of the beneficiaries.

1933

Separate Ambulances

The following extract is taken from the Master's Thesis submitted by Rollin Chambliss, a Phelps-Stokes Fellow at the University of Georgia in 1933. Miss Carolina Phelps-Stokes gave the University of Georgia a permanent endowment so that it could appoint annually a Fellow in Sociology for the study of the Negro in the Departments of Sociology, Economics, Education, or History. Chambliss was a white scholar.

Source: "What Negro Newspapers of Georgia Say About Some Social Problems, 1933." A Master's Thesis by Rollin Chambliss. Phelps-Stokes Fellowship Studies, No. 13. Athens, Georgia: *Bulletin of the University of Georgia,* Vol. XXXV, No. 2, (November, 1934), p. 78.

It is not infrequent that hospitals refuse to accept Negro patients and that ambulances leave injured Negroes at the scene of an accident. An instance of this is shown in a report from Pensacola, Florida, December 4 (reported in The Atlanta *World,* a Negro Newspaper, December 4, 1933).

"Claude Kelly, returning from a fishing trip, was seriously injured after stepping from a car into the path of another car driven by a sailor from the Naval Air Station. . . . An ambulance from the Pow Funeral Home rushed to the scene, but could not take the victim to the hospital. The Goldstucker Brothers' ambulance was then called to take the wounded man where he might receive treatment. . . ."

The accident may not prove serious, but it does give us a vivid picture of America and its treatment of the Negro. . . . The sailor was extended every courtesy by police officers; yet the victim had to wait until a colored ambulance came to take him to a place for medical attention, when there was already on the scene an ambulance.

213

The Only Color He Saw Was Green

Branch Rickey, white president of the Brooklyn Dodgers, made sports history by bringing the first black player into Major League baseball. He selected Jack Roosevelt Robinson, an outstanding athlete at the University of California at Los Angeles, and sent him to their Montreal farm team for two years. Then, in 1947, Jackie Robinson began his long, colorful career as a scrappy player in the majors. His entry into what had been an all-white sports world was marked by rare, early instances of prejudice. Between 1947 and 1964, Robinson was named the National League's Most Valuable Player by the Baseball Writers' Association eleven times.

In the following excerpt, Whitney Young, a Negro civil rights leader, uses Robinson as an example of just how fast whites' attitudes towards blacks can change.

Source: Address by Whitney M. Young, Jr., Executive Director, The Urban League, at the opening session of the 100th Convention of the American Institute of Architects, Portland, Oregon, June 24, 1968.

Rickey solved the problem of attitudes and how long it takes. I disagree with you that it takes a long time to change attitudes. Doesn't take any time to change them overnight. When he brought Jackie Robinson to the Dodgers, there was this ball player that said I'm not going to play with that "nigger." He thought Rickey would flap like most employers. . . . But he didn't know Rickey very well. Rickey was kind. He said, "Give him three or four days." Well, at the end of a few days, Robinson had five home runs, stolen many bases. This fellow was reassessing his options—he could go back to Alabama and maybe make $20 a week picking cotton, or stay with the Dodgers and continue to work. And, now it looked like Jackie would get him into the World Series and a bonus of $5000—which he did. The only color he was concerned with was green.

"You Can Have a Private Room"

When Carl T. Rowan began writing a series of autobiographical articles for the Minneapolis *Morning Tribune,* he was unprepared for their popular reception. His columns entitled "How Far From Slavery?" elicited the greatest number of letters that the newspaper had received in its entire history. And the letters were nine to one in sympathy with Rowan. In his autobiography, called *South of Freedom,* Rowan compiled these newspaper articles.

For his crusade against racial discrimination, Rowan won the Service to Humanity Award of the Minneapolis Junior Chamber of Commerce, which also named him the "Outstanding Young Man of 1951."

Since the publication of *South of Freedom,* Rowan has served as United States ambassador to Finland and Chief of the United States Information Service. He was the first black man to sit on the National Security Council. One of the most active figures in the American public eye, Rowan continues to wage a relentless campaign against discrimination in any form.

In the following article he describes one of his early attacks on inequality.

Source: Rowan, Carl Thomas. *South of Freedom.* New York: Alfred A. Knopf, 1952, pp. 260-261.

Racism of the poorly concealed variety comes in many forms in the North, I remembered, and it is only a vigilant few who prevent the disease from spreading. It is common knowledge among Minneapolis Negroes, and a considerable number of whites, that Negroes are far from welcome in Charlie's Cafe Exceptionale, and that Negroes must be served in a private room, or, with only the rarest of exceptions, not at all.

One day I was asked to lunch with a few white friends. We called Charlie's for a reservation, and were informed that they didn't reserve tables for lunch, but that there was plenty of room. On our way to the cafe we discussed its racial policy and decided that two Negro members of our party should go in first. We did, and I asked for a table, informing the headwaiter that two others would join us later.

"There are no tables available. You may have a private room," he said.

"What do you mean, no tables?" I asked.

"All reserved," he said.

"But we were just informed a few minutes ago that you didn't reserve tables for lunch."

"Must have been a mistake. You can have a private room," he replied.

I rejected the private room and stepped toward the door so my friends would know to come in. They passed by as if they had never seen me before, and asked the waiter for a table.

"Oh, yes, your reserved table . . ." said the waiter, leading them into the dining room.

"What do you mean, reserved table?" asked the white couple. "Why is it you have a table for us but didn't for our Negro friends?"

The half-startled, half-angered waiter suddenly decided that he was mistaken about who they were. He thought they were another couple with a reserved table. They, too, would have to use a private room. We all walked out and went to another place where the food was no less tasty and the atmosphere, if not quite so ritzy, was less expensive.

The practice at Charlie's is no secret, not even among official Minneapolis. When Senator [Hubert] Humphrey was mayor of Minneapolis he became angered by reports of this policy and asked William Seabron, a Negro social worker, to have lunch with him. They went to Charlie's.

"I'll have my regular table," Humphrey said to the headwaiter, not even waiting to see if he would try the private-room story, and he and Seabron walked into the dining-room. That was the first, and last, known time that a Negro has eaten at Charlie's without being ushered into a private room.

This happens, not in Mississippi, but in Minnesota, at the top of the nation, as far as an American of any color can get from the Mason-Dixon line. And it is part of my report. It is more important, as a part of this final report to all Americans, because of the way citizens of the upper Midwest reacted to the report as run in the Minneapolis *Tribune.*

Reaction was overwhelmingly favorable—far more favorable than I had dreamed it might be. Less than an hour after the first edition was on the streets, a parking-lot operator called to let me know that he was "on you people's side." I could use his parking-lot without charge as long as I lived and was able to own a car. There were hundreds of letters to the paper, more than 500 to me personally. "Shame, shame on our nation," cried the vast majority of them. . . .

216

"You Folks Just Aren't Ready for Integration"

> Arna Bontemps, a noted black author, is a librarian and a professor of creative writing at Fisk University. In a speech he gave in Detroit, Michigan, in 1951, Bontemps told this anecdote about a black man's experience in the newly integrated restaurants of Washington, D. C.
>
> Source: Bontemps, Arna. "The Negro's Contribution Reconsidered." Speech delivered in Detroit, Michigan, February 19, 1951. Reprinted in Hill, Roy L. *Rhetoric of Racial Revolt.* Denver, Colorado: Golden Bell Press, 1964, pp. 191-192.

... When the restaurants in Washington, D. C., changed their policy about serving Negroes, I am told, a certain Negro who had been born and reared in that city heaved a sigh of satisfaction. This was something he had waited for and hoped for, but he had never really expected that he would live to see it. Now that it had happened, he resolved to test it himself. He would put on his best clothes and go to the best downtown restaurant he could find. But he wouldn't do it immediately. He didn't want to rush things. He wanted the proprietors to have enough time to make a complete change-over, to adjust their thinking, to get used to the new idea and to learn not to go to pieces when they saw a Negro enter the place. He could afford to be gradual about it. He decided to wait three weeks.

At the end of that period he was ready for this important experience. He found a restaurant that appeared to be the last word in exclusiveness, entered and followed the waiter to a good location. Everything was just as it should be. The waiter was courtesy itself. But a puzzled look came over the man's face as he examined the menu.

"Are you ready to order?" the waiter asked.

The customer was still poring over the beautifully printed menu.

"Don't you have any turnip greens?" he asked eventually.

The waiter became apologetic. "I am afraid we don't."

Another pause. "What about black-eyed peas?" the man asked.

"No black-eyed peas," the waiter said almost wistfully.

It was then that the poor man began to look downcast. "What about chitterlings?"

The waiter had to shake his head again. "We just have what's on the menu, sir."

"You folks," he said, more in sorrow than in anger, "you folks just aren't ready for integration."

His own readiness, it would seem to me, was attested by the fact that he was neither ashamed nor unprepared to make a positive contribution toward the improvement of native cuisine.

December 5, 1955

Montgomery's Moment in History

When young Martin Luther King first went to Montgomery, Alabama, in 1954, he was an unknown man anxious to do well in his first ministry. Daily he rose at 5:30 a.m. to devote three hours to his Ph.D. thesis. Then he plunged into his duties as minister of the Dexter Avenue Baptist Church.

Dr. King and his wife, Coretta, agreed that those two jobs were more than enough challenge for the time being. However, King was to become the leader of a great national effort to end "Jim Crow" laws, his name a household word around the world.

Dr. King was affronted by the segregated seating on Montgomery's buses. When Mrs. Rosa Parks was arrested for sitting in a "Whites Only" seat, King and other black leaders went into action. Under his leadership 50,000 Negroes "took to heart the principles of non-violence . . . learned to fight for their rights with the weapon of love. . . ."

Beginning December 5, 1955, the day Mrs. Parks was to appear in court, all Negroes were asked not to "ride the bus to work, to town, to school, or anyplace. . . . If you work, take a cab, or share a ride or walk." At most Dr. King hoped that 60% of Montgomery's black population would heed his call for "massive cooperation." But, instead, there was 100% compliance, and what happened in Montgomery turned out to be the beginning of a much larger struggle for civil rights everywhere.

In the following excerpt from one of his books, Dr. King describes the anxious first day of "Montgomery's moment in history."

Source: King, Martin Luther, Jr. *Stride Toward Freedom: The Montgomery Story*. New York: Harper and Row, Publishers, 1958, pp. 53-55 *passim.*, 63, 64, 70.

My wife and I awoke earlier than usual on Monday morning. We were up and fully dressed by five-thirty. The day for the protest had arrived, and we were determined to see the first act of this unfolding drama. I was still saying that if we could get 60 per cent coöperation the venture would be a success.

Fortunately, a bus stop was just five feet from our house. This meant that we could observe the opening stages from our front window. The first bus was to pass around six o'clock. And so we waited through an interminable half hour. I was in the kitchen drinking my coffee when I heard Coretta cry, "Martin, Martin, come quickly!" I put down my cup and ran toward the living room. As I approached the front window Coretta pointed joyfully to a slowly moving bus: "Darling, it's empty!" I could hardly believe what I saw. I knew that the South Jackson line, which ran past our house, carried more Negro passengers than any other line in Montgomery, and that this first bus was usually filled with domestic workers going to their jobs. Would all of the other buses follow the pattern that had been set by the first? Eagerly we waited for the next bus. In fifteen minutes it rolled down the street, and, like the first, it was empty. A third bus appeared, and it too was empty of all but two white passengers.

I jumped in my car and for almost an hour I cruised down every major street and examined every passing bus. During this hour, at the peak of the morning traffic, I saw no more than eight Negro passengers riding the buses. By this time I was jubilant. Instead of the 60 per cent coöperation we had hoped for, it was becoming apparent that we had reached almost 100 per cent. A miracle had taken place. The once dormant and quiescent Negro community was now fully awake.

All day long it continued. At the afternoon peak the buses were still as empty of Negro passengers as they had been in the morning. Students of Alabama State College, who usually kept the South Jackson bus crowded, were cheerfully walking or thumbing rides. Job holders had either found other means of transportation or made their way on foot. While some rode in cabs or private cars, other used less conventional means. Men were seen riding mules to work, and more than one horse-drawn buggy drove the streets of Montgomery that day.

During the rush hours the sidewalks were crowded with laborers and domestic workers, many of them well past middle age, trudging patiently to their jobs and home again, sometimes as much as twelve miles. They knew why they walked, and the knowledge was evident in the way they carried themselves. And as I watched them I knew that there is nothing more majestic than the determined courage of individuals willing to suffer and sacrifice for their freedom and dignity. . . .

Around nine-thirty in the morning I tore myself from the action of the city streets and headed for the crowded police court. Here Mrs. Parks was being tried for disobeying the city segregation ordinance. Her attorney, Fred D. Gray—the brilliant young Negro who later became the chief counsel for the protest movement—was on hand to defend her. After the judge heard the arguments, he found Mrs. Parks guilty and fined her ten dollars and court costs (a total of fourteen dollars). She appealed the case. This was one of the first clear-cut instances in which a Negro had been convicted for disobeying the segregation law. In the past, either cases like this had been dismissed or the people involved had been charged with disorderly conduct. So in a real sense the arrest and conviction of Mrs. Parks had a twofold impact: it was a precipitating factor to arouse the Negroes to positive action; and it was a test of the validity of the segregation law itself. I am sure that supporters of such prosecutions would have acted otherwise if they had had the prescience to look beyond the moment.

[Following Mrs. Parks' trial, Dr. King, Ralph Abernathy, and others met to form an organization to carry on the bus protest. Dr. King was elected President of this organization, and Ralph Abernathy headed a committee which drew up a resolution to be presented to a mass meeting that evening for approval. Mrs. Parks was present at the meeting. Ed. note.]

When Mrs. Parks was introduced from the rostrum by E. N. French, the audience responded by giving her a standing ovation. She was their heroine. They saw in her courageous person the symbol of their hopes and aspirations.

Now the time had come for the all-important resolution. Ralph Abernathy read the words slowly and forcefully. The main substance of the resolution called upon the Negroes not to resume riding the buses until (1) courteous treatment by the bus operators was guaranteed; (2) passengers were seated on a first-come, first-served basis—Negroes seating from the back of the bus toward the front while whites seated from the front toward the back; (3) Negro bus operators were employed on predominantly Negro routes. At the words "All in favor of the motion stand," every person to a man stood up, and those who were already standing raised their hands. Cheers began to ring out from both inside and outside. The motion was carried unanimously. The people had expressed their determination not to ride the buses until conditions were changed. . . .

The day of days, Monday, December 5, 1955, was drawing to a close. We all prepared to go to our homes, not yet fully aware of what had happened. The deliberations of that brisk, cool night in December will not be forgotten. That night we were starting a movement that would gain national recognition; whose echoes would ring in the ears of people of every nation; a movement that would astound the oppressor, and bring new hope to the oppressed. That night was Montgomery's moment in history.

September 24, 1957

Going To School With a Paratroop Escort

There were just nine of them—three boys and six girls. They had been selected by the school authorities to enter Central High

School in Little Rock, Arkansas, on September 3, 1957. Those nine were to be the first nonwhites to attend Central High.

Meanwhile, Governor Orval Faubus, a bitter foe of integrated schools, directed Arkansas National Guardsmen to surround the building and prevent the black students' entry. "Blood will run in the streets," he said, "if the Negro pupils should attempt to enter Central High." Angry mobs milled around outside the school; mass hysteria gripped the city.

Finally on September 24, President Dwight D. Eisenhower announced that he had federalized all 10,000 men in the Arkansas National Guard. He also authorized Charles E. Wilson, Secretary of Defense, to send in regular army troops to see that the integration orders of the United States District Court were carried out.

Secretary Wilson ordered 1000 black and white paratroopers from Fort Campbell, Kentucky, to go to Little Rock. Here is what happened the day the men of the 101st Airborne "Screaming Eagle" Division arrived. The story is told by Mrs. Daisy Bates, President of the National Association for the Advancement of Colored People State Conference of Branches, and a highly publicized leader of the integration movement in Arkansas.

Source: Bates, Daisy. *The Long Shadow of Little Rock: A Memoir.* New York: David McKay Company, 1962, pp. 104-106.

... Jeff, standing at the window, called out, "The Army's here! They're here!"

Jeeps were rolling down Twenty-eighth Street. Two passed our house and parked at the end of the block, while two remained at the other end of the block. Paratroopers quickly jumped out and stood across the width of the street at each end of the block—those at the western end standing at attention facing west, and those at the eastern end facing east.

An Army station wagon stopped in front of our house. While photographers, perched precariously on the tops of cars and rooftops, went into action, the paratrooper in charge of the detail leaped out of the station wagon and started up our driveway. As he approached I heard Minnijean say gleefully, "Oh, look at them, they're so—so soldierly! It gives you goose pimples to look at them!" And then she added solemnly, "For the first time in my life, I feel like an American citizen."

The officer was at the door, and as I opened it, he saluted and said, his voice ringing through the sudden quiet of the living-room where a number of friends and parents of the nine had gathered to witness this

222

moment in history: "Mrs. Bates, we're ready for the children. We will return them to your home at three thirty o'clock."

I watched them follow him down the sidewalk. Another paratrooper held open the door of the station wagon, and they got in. Turning back into the room, my eyes none too dry, I saw the parents with tears of happiness in their eyes as they watched the group drive off.

Tense and dramatic events were taking place in and around the school while the Negro pupils were being transported by the troops of the 101st Airborne from my home to Central High.

Major General Edwin A. Walker, operation commander, was explaining to the student body, in the school auditorium, the duties and responsibilities of his troops.

"... You have nothing to fear from my soldiers and no one will interfere with your coming, going, or your peaceful pursuit of your studies. However, I would be less than honest if I failed to tell you that I intend to use all means necessary to prevent any interference with the execution of your school board's plan. ..."

A block from the school, a small group of hard-core segregationists ignored Major James Meyers' orders to disperse peacefully and return to their homes. The major repeated the command when the surly crowd refused to disperse. He was forced to radio for additional help. About thirty soldiers answered the emergency call "on the double," wearing steel helmets, carrying bayonet fixed rifles, their gas masks in readiness, and "walkie-talkies" slung over their shoulders.

The soldiers lowered their rifles and moved slowly and deliberately into the crowd. The mob quickly gave way, shouting insults at the troops in the process. In a matter of minutes the streets, which for days had been littered with hate-filled mobs, cigarette butts, half-eaten sandwiches, and used flash bulbs, were strangely quiet.

At 9:22 a.m. the nine Negro pupils marched solemnly through the doors of Central High School, surrounded by twenty-two (Airborne troops) soldiers. An Army helicopter circled overhead. Around the massive brick schoolhouse 350 paratroopers stood grimly at attention. Scores of reporters, photographers, and TV cameramen made a mad dash for telephones, typewriters, and TV studios, and within minutes a world that had been holding its breath learned that the nine pupils, protected by the might of the United States military, had finally entered the "never-never land."

When classes ended that afternoon, the troops escorted the pupils to my home. Here we held the first of many conferences that were to take place during the hectic months ahead.

I looked into the face of each child, from the frail, ninety-pound Thelma Mothershed with a cardiac condition, to the well-built, sturdy Earnest Green, oldest of them all. They sat around the room, subdued and reflective—and understandably so. Too much had happened to them in these frenzied weeks to be otherwise.

I asked if they had a rough day. Not especially, they said. Some of the white pupils were friendly and had even invited them to lunch. Some were indifferent, and only a few had showed open hostility.

Minnijean Brown reported that she had been invited by her classmates to join the glee club.

"Then why the long faces?" I wanted to know.

"Well," Earnest spoke up, "you don't expect us to be jumping for joy, do you?"

Someone said, "But Earnest, we are in Central, and that shouldn't make us feel sad exactly."

"Sure, we're in Central," Earnest shot back, somewhat impatiently. "But how did we get in? We got in, finally, because we were protected by paratroops. Some victory!" he said sarcastically.

"Are you sorry," someone asked him, "that the President sent the troops?"

"No," said Earnest. "I'm only sorry it had to be that way."

1957

"I'm a Tennis Player, Not a Negro Tennis Player"

Althea Gibson was born in Silver, South Carolina, but grew up in New York City. She was a teenager when her athletic abilities were recognized and then developed by two tennis-playing Negro doctors, Hubert A. Eaton of Wilmington, North Carolina, and Robert W. Johnson of Lynchburg, Virginia. They helped Althea along the road from Harlem's 143rd Street to the courts of Wimbledon, England. There in 1957 Althea was crowned world tennis champion by Queen Elizabeth.

Following Althea's spectacular victory, President Dwight D. Eisenhower wrote these words to her:

Many Americans, including myself, have watched with increasing admiration your sustained and successful effort to win the heights in the tennis world. . . . Recognizing the odds you faced, we have applauded your courage, persistence, and application. Certainly it is not easy for anyone to stand in the center court at Wimbledon and, in the glare of world publicity and under the critical gaze of thousands of spectators, do his or her very best. You met the challenge superbly.

Althea's victory came at a time when the struggle for civil rights was foremost in the minds of many black Americans. However, Althea, always a strong individualist, had her own personal views.

Source: From pp. 158-159 in *I Always Wanted to Be Somebody* by Althea Gibson. Edited by Ed. Fitzgerald. Copyright © 1958 by Althea Gibson and Edward E. Fitzgerald. Reprinted by permission of Harper & Row, Publishers, Inc.

I am not a racially conscious person. I don't want to be. I see myself as just an individual. I can't help or change my color in any way, so why should I make a big deal out of it? I don't like to exploit it or make it the big thing. I'm a tennis player, not a Negro tennis player. I have never set myself up as a champion of the Negro race. Someone once wrote the difference between me and Jackie Robinson is that he thrived on his role as a Negro battling for equality whereas I shy away from it. That man read me correctly. I shy away from it because it would be dishonest of me to pretend to a feeling I don't possess. There doesn't seem to be much question that Jackie always saw his baseball success as a step forward for the Negro people, and he aggressively fought to make his ability pay off in social advances as well as fat paychecks. I'm not insensitive to the great value to our people of what Jackie did. If he hadn't paved the way, I probably never would have got my chance. But I have to do it my way. I try not to flaunt my success as a Negro success. It's all right for others to make a fuss over my role as a trail blazer, and, of course, I realize its importance to others as well as to myself, but I can't do it.

It's important, I think, to point out in this connection that there are those among my people who don't agree with my reasoning. A lot of those who disagree with me are members of the Negro press, and they beat my brains out regularly. I have always enjoyed a good press among the regular American newspapers and magazines, but I am uncomfortably close to being Public Enemy No. 1 to some sections of the Negro press. I have, they have said, an unbecoming attitude; they say I'm bigheaded, uppity, ungrateful, and a few other

225

uncomplimentary things. I don't think any white writer ever has said anything like that about me, but quite a few Negro writers have, and I think the down-deep reason for it is that they resent my refusal to turn my tennis achievements into a rousing crusade for racial equality, brass band, seventy-six trombones, and all. I won't do it. I feel strongly that I can do more good my own way than I could by militant crusading. I want my success to speak for itself as an advertisement for my race.

1960

We Stage a Nonviolent Sit-In

So that blacks might be served at lunch counters which were for "whites only," civil rights workers began a series of "sit-ins." The first one took place in Greensboro, North Carolina, in 1960. From that time on, sit-ins spread rapidly to hundreds of cities in the South. Whites and blacks together "sat in"—they pledged themselves to nonviolence no matter how provoked they were. More than 1600 of them were arrested for breaking city ordinances in the first six months after the initial sit-in. However, by the end of those six months, the sit-in technique had proved successful; the right of blacks to be served at lunch counters had been established.

This selection from *Our Faces, Our Words* by Lillian Smith describes what happened when some young blacks staged a sit-in. Lillian Smith is a southern white woman who is deeply concerned about race relations. Among her many literary works, probably the most soul-searching are *Strange Fruit* and *Killers of the Dream.* Both books were on best-seller lists for a number of years.

Source: Smith, Lillian. *Our Faces, Our Words.* New York: W. W. Norton and Company, 1964, pp. 29, 31, 32.

Well, we got going and sat in Walgreen's. Don't know why we picked that one but we did. Maybe because we knew it was a chain store and might be more sensitive to pressures—but I don't know, we actually weren't doing much thinking. We walked to the counter, sat down, opened our books. Bill opened the Bible—and read it, too. I had my physics textbook; read one paragraph sixteen times without knowing what was in it. The white girl behind the counter, awfully young, turned pink, then deathly white. She didn't say a word. Bill looked up, smiled, said quietly, "We'd like some coffee, please, and some doughnuts." She swallowed, swallowed again, shook her head. "I can't," she said. She wasn't mean. I felt sorry for her. "Please go away," she whispered, "they won't let me serve you." We sat there.

Pretty soon, two or three kids came in, stared at us, one sat down next to me, hummed something, got up, walked out. We kept on reading. Some more came in; we didn't turn around to see but they were making a lot of noise. Then it happened; that cigarette; the goon stuck the burning thing into my back. Sit tight, don't move, take it; this is nonviolence, I told myself, you have to take it. A white guy came in, knocked the cigarette out of the other guy's hand; there was scuffling back of me; I didn't turn. A cop came in. Walgreen's closed the counter. We left.

That's how it started. Three weeks later, the lunch counter opened to everybody. By then, we were sitting in at Kress's. There were about twenty-five or more students helping us now, and more high-school kids than we needed; the high-school kids just poured into the movement, completely unafraid, having a ball, but serious, too, deepdown.

We felt we had to hold meetings now to decide what to do, what not to do; we had to learn you can't lose your temper, you can't talk back, you can't hit back; you keep everything under control. Two of the college men couldn't make it; we told them to stay out of things until they could control their feelings. The high-school kids were cool, and they listened. "You got to feel compassionate toward the whites," a worker from CORE told us; at our request he had come to train us. So we talked about compassion, forgiveness, talked about absorbing evil through our own suffering. "You'll find it works," the CORE adviser told us; "if a white has any good in him, he'll respond to compassion and friendly talk; you got to remember that you can hate evil without hating the man who does the evil; it's like a doctor treating the evil of smallpox without hating the man who has it."

"Yeah," said one kid, "but you'd better fear that smallpox." Everybody laughed.

"Sure," said the teacher of nonviolence, "you've got to have sense; be wary, be shrewd, nobody was more shrewd than Gandhi, don't be reckless; but remember: negative nonviolence is not enough; it's got to be positive; you feel all the time that the other man, the one fighting you, can be redeemed; he's got to feel something good in you."

"I Do Not Think That We Have to Point Our Finger at the South"

Smug northerners who "pointed a finger" at violations of the black people's civil rights in the South were criticized by Senator Harrison A. Williams of New Jersey. Senator Williams suggested that Northerners themselves "get down to the day-to-day problems of discrimination" in their own communities.

Just about four years after the New Jersey lawmaker gave the following warning, riots in Newark left large areas of the city in smoking ruins.

Source: U.S. Senate. 88th Congress, First Session. *Hearings Before the Subcommittee on Constitutional Rights of the Committee on the Judiciary.* Bills Relating to Extension of the Civil Rights Commission, S. 1117 and S. 1219, May 21, 22, 23; June 5, 6, 12, 1963. Washington, D. C.: U.S. Government Printing Office, 1963.

All across this country we are faced with difficult problems involving civil rights. Minority groups of all types face hurdles placed in their way by jealous or fearful majorities. These extend not only to the well-known racial questions involving voting, employment, education, and public accommodation, but to a host of other questions stemming from ethnic or religious differences.

I do not think we have to point our finger at the people of Birmingham, or Oxford, or Auburn, or Albany, or Little Rock.

We can look at the North, at Orange, and Englewood, and Trenton, and Camden, and Newark, for in New Jersey we have this problem, too, and it extends from Cape May to Hoboken.

We are fortunate to have been spared violence, but some of our communities have segregation which limits the opportunities of the minority to obtain equal education. . . .

Prejudice has such a hold on some of our New Jersey unions that Negroes have an almost impossible time getting into the required apprenticeship programs.

I think there are less than 10 nonwhites among a total of some 4000 apprentices in New Jersey today. There is a difficult housing situation; cities like Trenton, where 25 percent of the city's population lives in substandard housing.

These people, most of them Negro, find their escape prevented by a combination of race prejudice and economic blockade which is, itself, the product of prejudice.

The housing situation is reaching the point of crisis. It costs Trenton, Camden, Newark, and other cities in New Jersey money to live with this prejudice. It shows up when twice as many nonwhite children drop out of school as the white children and when unemployment and welfare charges begin to mount to take care of them and their families.

Clearly, New Jersey has some deep-seated and massive problems in the field of civil rights. . . .

We simply have to get down to the day-to-day problems of discrimination in every community. We desperately need a program to tackle the daily, specific denials of civil rights that add up to the national disgrace about which we have all heard much too much. . . .

1966

We Need Police Protection

In St. Louis, Missouri, more than 12,000 people—almost all of them black—live in the Pruitt—Igoe Housing Project. Already a second generation is growing up in these bleak high-rise apartments of the inner city.

Some of the project residents went to Washington, D. C., to tell their story to a United States Senate Subcommittee: "[Ours] is a story which we hope will so mobilize public support and sentiment that the ugliness of Pruitt-Igoe can be changed. Our homes are a disgrace, a blemish on the face of this community . . . and our lives, our hopes, our dreams are, in some measure, limited by the physical and psychological conditions under which we live."

At a time when some blacks were crying "police brutality," Pruitt-Igoe residents pleaded for more and better police protection. Here is a summary of what the delegates from St. Louis' black community told a group of United States senators.

Source: U. S. Senate. 89th Congress, Second Session. *Federal Role in Urban Affairs: Hearings Before the Subcommittee on Executive Reorganization of Committee on Governmental*

Operations. Part 11. Washington, D. C.: Government Printing Office, December 6, 1966.

The St. Louis Housing and Land Clearance Authority employs a private watchman service to provide protection for all of the city's public housing complexes. Twenty-one private watchmen are retained for the seven housing projects. Two men are assigned to the thirty block Pruitt-Igoe area during each twenty-four hour period.

"The guards act as if they don't see a thing."

"We don't have any protection."

"Some of the police seem as if they are afraid to do anything about what they see going on."

... An elderly woman told an interviewer that she "would like to attend church much more but boys loitering in the center stairwell frighten her, and she is afraid to come home from church at night."

Many residents, especially women and the elderly, are virtual prisoners in their apartments once evening has come. They are afraid to leave; yet, if they remain inside, they are often disturbed by noisy groups of adolescents or children. "Dancing under the building should be stopped. I have called guards to stop it but they never come."

"Can't get in my door at night for girls and boys in the hallway. Men and young boys gambling in front of my door. I've asked them to move, they won't. Have called police, they don't come."

A Biddle Street respondent reported to the interviewer that she "can't come in the building from work for teen-age boys and young men gambling."

"If project police would be forceful to do their job, it would be better place to live at."

"Need more guards, some that is going to work and not flirt. They should walk and not ride and do something about what they see going on."

"The guard should check the building at least four times daily on foot. Also the guards should report or do something about the things they see going on."

Those hired to police, be they public enforcement officers or privately employed guards have been viewed by the poverty-stricken, ghetto-confined minority citizen as traditional enemies. The common accusation of "police brutality" or mistreatment at the hands of law officers is strangely absent from the Pruitt-Igoe tenants' complaints. Rather, police indifference to the plight of individual citizens is a common accusation; guards and public law enforcement officers ignore

230

the calls and complaints of tenants or respond to them hours after the initial report.

December 6, 1966

Why Blacks Riot

Bayard Rustin was asked to testify before a United States Senate subcommittee following rioting by blacks in a number of cities. The senators wanted to learn the causes of racial violence and to seek solutions to the discrimination and injustices faced by the Negro American.

At the time Rustin gave the following testimony, he was the Executive Director of the A. Philip Randolph Institute, an organization named in honor of the black leader of the Sleeping Car Porters Union who waged a long battle against discrimination in labor unions and industry. Formerly Rustin had been a field secretary for CORE (Congress For Racial Equality).

Source: U. S. Senate. 89th Congress, Second Session. *Federal Role in Urban Affairs: Hearings Before the Subcommittee on Executive Reorganization of the Committee on Governmental Operations.* Part 9, December 6, 1966. Washington, D. C.: Government Printing Office.

Senators . . . we face . . . fear on the part of the white community . . . and frustration on the part of many elements of the Negro and other minority communities. This becomes even more clear if one examines what happened on the streets of Chicago this summer, and compares it with the rioting that took place in other parts of the country. . . . We find ourselves in a society that is, in effect, teaching young Negroes to depend upon violence. I will give you two illustrations.

After the rioting in Chicago, a group of young Negroes sitting with Dr. [Martin Luther] King and me said the following:

You fellows have produced nothing. Dr. King has been here for a year. There has been no accommodation to him. But when we wanted sprinklers, we went out into the street, forgetting your nonviolence and your patience, and we tore up the street, and in

24 hours we had not only the eight dollar sprinklers we wanted, but we had, in addition to those sprinklers, swimming pools. Now, Dr. King, Daley [mayor of Chicago] hasn't given you a damn thing, but he has given us what we fought for.

Second illustration. Following the riot in Watts, Dr. King and I went there in the midst of the resultant chaos to do what we could. A young man stood up and talked about his group's manifesto, and quite unsuspectingly, I asked him if I might see a copy of this manifesto, whereupon he took out of his pocket a box of matches, lit one, held it up, and said:

"That is our manifesto, burn, baby, burn."

When we said to him: "But young man, what have you gained by this?," he said, "We asked the Mayor to come and talk with us, and he would not come. We asked the Governor to come, and he would not come. We asked the Chief of Police to come, and he would not come. But after we issued our manifesto, they all came!"

Then he whispered and said, *sotto voce* [very softly], but loud enough for all the teenagers to hear:

"And when you and Dr. King go out in the street, you better be careful, because they sent us so many damn sociologists, baby, so many economists, so many social workers, if you and King aren't careful, you will trip over them on the street."

If these two instances are not clear illustrations of the extent to which the conduct of the society creates and nourishes the despair and violence among Negro youth, then, I do not know of any.

I maintain, therefore, that unless a forthright master plan is executed, one sees the problems of housing, schools, jobs, and the psychology of the ghetto as a single problem, then this society will have to acknowledge that it is indirectly saying to the young dispossessed in this nation that if they want something, the only way they can get it is not to depend on leaders who are temperate leaders who advocate nonviolence, but that they themselves must take the law into their own hands.

This is a tragedy, and I ask you to see it as a tragedy which is being assisted and deepened by the inability of this society to produce or facilitate victories for the dispossessed so that they can maintain their faith in this nation, in law and order, and the cement of society, which is nonviolent action.

Senator Robert Kennedy: Mr. Rustin, you were sort of the

revolutionary of the 1950's, and it was really under your leadership that many of the present-day leaders developed. You taught them and worked with them. Could you discuss a little bit what the difference is in the attitude of the young man of the 1950's, the young Negro of the 1950's, and the young Negro of the year 1966, and what we . . . can anticipate in the future?

Mr. Rustin: I think, Senator, it was the objective situation which made the shift in the thinking of a limited number of young Negroes. . . . To try to be as sympathetic to them as I can . . . let us take Stokely Carmichael, as an example, jailed 28 times, beaten to the ground five times, thousands of dollars in bail, humiliated, stood by while Negro girls had their hair chopped, stood by while Negro girls had cigarette butts put . . . down their backs as they sat trying to eat in restaurants, having made all those sacrifices, and having seen children bombed in churches, 40 churches destroyed in a summer in Mississippi, he has every right to say he has done all he knows there is to do.

He then looks at the figures, seeing that unemployment is worse after all the sacrifice, that the ghettoes are fuller after all the sacrifice, and he says there is obviously something wrong with the established leadership, or these conditions would not get worse. . . .

If these conditions get worse, then they doubt that the South can ever solve the problem, and therefore, they do exactly what Marcus Garvey did in an earlier period. After World War I, Negroes really felt they were going to come back to the democracy they were fighting for. When they got back, they found that the Ku Klux Klan had moved from Georgia and Alabama to Indianapolis. They found lynching at its height. They found that Negroes were being driven off the land in the South. Now, after each of these periods of expectation, there follows a period of frustration, politics, and sloganism. Marcus Garvey said, "Let's build a black economy and then go back to Africa." Contradiction: Why build a black economy if you are going to go back to Africa? But frustration politics is by nature frustrated. Now, today, many young Negroes are saying, "We don't believe society can do this." I do not want to project, Senator, as to what the future will be. . . . The answer to your question is that if we come forward with victories, then the frustration politics will be limited. To the degree . . . that we muddle through and do not deal forthrightly with the problem . . . then the frustration politics will make life difficult for all of us. . . .

Senator Abraham Ribicoff: You know it is so hard to get across the concept that the poor numerically are more among the whites. When we think about many of these problems we are not just talking about Negroes. . . . We are talking about Puerto Ricans, Mexican-Americans, Indians, and so many poor whites who come off the farms into the cities and are just as lost and have just as many problems as the Negroes themselves. . . . We pay attention to the Negroes with this problem, but we shamelessly neglect the problems of other elements of our society who are in exactly the same boat.

Mr. Rustin: Agreed. . . .

1967

We've Never Met

For two years (1965-1967) the United States Commission on Civil Rights held hearings and open meetings in many of the nation's cities. The testimony given by persons living in black communities provided insight into how people felt about the conditions under which they lived. At hearings held in the Liberty Hill Baptist Church in the Hough area of Cleveland, a young Negro testified that he had never known a white person until he was fourteen or fifteen years old.

Source: United States Commission on Civil Rights. *A Time to Listen, A Time to Act: Voices from the Ghettos of the Nation's Cities.* Washington, D. C.: Government Printing Office, 1967, p. 9.

Well, I had never known a person of my own age who was white because I was raised in a predominantly Negro area. I was educated in a Negro school, I went to a Negro church, and everyone I came in contact with was Negro and I didn't know anything about a white person in as far as their actions—I didn't think they were different. I just didn't know them. I didn't think they even existed because I looked at my arm and my face, it was brown and I thought that was natural because everyone else around me was brown.

234

February, 1967

I Beg You to Come into the Delta and Try to Help Us

One fact-finding body after another discovered that the black man was as concerned about his right to work as he was about his civil rights. When the Commission on Rural Poverty, established by President Lyndon B. Johnson, held public hearings in Memphis, Tennessee, in 1967, there were many appeals for help. One of the more eloquent spokesmen was Amzie Moore, a black veteran of World War II. He told Commission members that his home, the Mississippi Delta, was supposedly the second richest spot on earth and yet his state was the poorest in the nation. Here is Moore's sworn testimony.

Source: *Rural Poverty: Hearings Before the National Advisory Committee on Rural Poverty,* Memphis, Tennessee, February 2 and 3, 1967. Washington, D. C.: Government Printing Office, 1967, pp. 27-29.

The plantation economy cannot help these people. We are looking to the Federal Government, to every agency of the Federal Government, to help us solve our economic problems. We have nowhere else to turn. We think it can be done, but we think that there is too much local control and not enough Federal supervision on a national level. Maybe I'm wrong, but that's how I feel and that is what I am saying.

I would like to say that this is not the only problem in my county. We have other problems, like health problems. For every one white child that dies in his first year, nine Negro kids die. We are at least five times above the national average in death, because in many the instances the mother is suffering from malnutrition; the kid had nothing to eat. These problems, it seems to me, should be solved because we are Americans and we are human beings, and being human beings we should really be treated like human beings.

Now, I don't know whether anybody really cares for the Mississippi Negro or not. I keep wondering about that. I keep asking myself that question. Do they really care? But I know one thing, that something is going to have to be done about the condition as it exists in the Mississippi Delta.

Yes, I know these people are farm people; they have never had any kind of skill. But I think they can be trained, because in 1942 when I went overseas to China, India, and Burma to fight for this country, quite a number of my people from Mississippi went into the factories in the industrial Middle West and North and West and learned to build planes and tanks and guns to defend this country. If they could do that, then they could certainly be trained for some kind of work now.

So I am suggesting that we move immediately to set up training programs in the Mississippi Delta to train people to be employed by industry that can be brought in. . . .

If there is food available, we suggest that you feed the poor. Now, we have spent quite a bit of money all over this world helping people. We built the economy of Europe, we are doing something in Asia, and now I suggest that we move around in our own backyard, right here in the Mississippi Delta, and try to eliminate the poverty and also find the cause of this poverty. I have always said it was the plantation economy that caused it, 50 years of plantation life, two generations back.

I appeal to you, I beg you, to please come into the Delta and try to help us.

1968

A Mayor Proclaims His City's Grief

A great, world-wide outpouring of anguish followed the assassination of the apostle of nonviolence, the Reverend Martin Luther King, Jr. In this proclamation of his city's grief, Mayor Joseph Alioto of San Francisco gave voice to the sentiments of most Americans.

Source: The San Francisco *Chronicle*, April 6, 1968.

As mayor of San Francisco I must give free voice to my heart tonight. And, as I do so I am speaking for every San Franciscan—man, woman and child.

The sentiments which are hereby expressed shall constitute a proclamation of the City of San Francisco. It is a proclamation not of material substance but spiritual in content. It concerns the souls of men, not their treasure they have laid up for themselves on this earth.

Slightly more than one day ago our nation suffered the loss by violence of one of the truly great Americans of this age. Dr. Martin Luther King had dedicated his work to non-violence. The role he played in the pageant of mankind was to assist his fellow citizens find richer lives.

He wished no man harm.

He wished no man misfortune.

He wished no man the agony of loneliness or the horror of hate.

Dr. King sought no selfish rewards for himself, no self glorification nor applause from the multitude.

His life was one of compassion toward his fellow man. He obviously was deeply moved by the teachings of our city's own patron saint—Francis of Assisi—whose warm and gentle life fashioned so deeply the spirit of our citizens. The entire world knows the philosophy of non-violence that so characterized the spirit of this remarkable man.

Therefore, as Mayor of San Francisco, I am taking upon myself the opportunity of expressing the shock and numbness that has befallen our entire city caused by the loss of the Reverend Dr. Martin Luther King.

Martin Luther King carried forward his crusade for brotherhood and peace among all men. Let us pray together that his country—and ours—will harvest a reward of non-violence—the concept for which this humble and great American gave his life.

Given by my hand,
Friday, April 5, 1968

Joseph L. Alioto (Signed)
Mayor

Section Ten

Black Power and Beyond

1943

What Is the Correct Name?

> Roi Ottley, a talented black writer, examined the perplexing question of just what name should be used to describe Americans of African descent. In 1943 he wrote *New World A-Coming* for which he was awarded a Life-in-America Book Prize. In that book he reveals that disagreements about "*the* correct name" have a long history. And the name controversy still has not been settled.

> Source: Reprinted with the permission of Farrar, Straus and Giroux, Inc., from *New World A-Coming* by Roi Ottley, copyright 1943 by Roi Ottley.

Early in its modern career, in the preparation of a style sheet, the Negro press attempted to settle a knotty problem—the issue being whether the race should be referred to as "Negro," "Colored," "Afro-American," "Aframerican," "African," "Race," or plain Black. . . . If white people are in doubt as to the acceptable term—the Negro writer and public speaker is in no less a quandary. I doubt very much that every Negro will be satisfied with my own use of the terms "Negro" and "Black" throughout this book.

For two centuries American Negroes called themselves merely "people of color," and even whites so designated them in the very earliest documents I have examined. The Dutch, Spanish, and English settlers leaned toward "black"—hence the term "Negro," which means black. In 1786, Jupiter Hammon, a slave on Long Island and the first Negro poet in America, addressed himself to "Negroes," but this term did not have real currency until the years before the Civil War. Absence

238

of color made one white, obviously. Sometimes "African" was used by Negroes, but this term was discarded when schemes were advanced to colonize Negroes in Africa. . . .

The issue finally came to a head in this century—coincidentally with talk about race pride. T. Thomas Fortune, editor of *The Age*, excluded "Negro" from his vocabulary because of the disagreeable connotation with the word "nigger"—which is perhaps the clue to the whole business. He is credited with being the originator of the term "Afro-American" which was adopted by the Murphy clan, founders of The Baltimore *Afro-American.* In Marcus Garvey's heyday, "African" and "Black" supplanted "Afro-American" for a time. The Chicago *Defender* meanwhile had a style sheet which excluded "Negro," "Afro-American," and "Black" altogether, and instead used "Race,"—as it does today—for example, one is a "Race man," or it is a "Race paper." *The Age* since Fred R. Moore's regime has used "Colored," which, of all the terms, has the nice sound of respectability and refinement. . . .

The *Voice of Ethiopia*—with eyes lifted toward an African utopia—complained that the word "Negro" signified nothing beyond the connotation of enslavement, and was an invention of white men to degrade the race. Every other race, it said, is known by the continent, land, or nation whence it came; therefore Negroes should be called "African" or "Ethiopian." For many years many literary folk liked "Aframerican," which has a melodious lilt, but this term has a derisive meaning to Negroes. . . . Many Negroes are indifferent to the whole matter. Yet I would say that generally the adjective "colored" and the generic designations "Negroes," "the Negro race," and "the Negro" are acceptable—but the use of "Negress," "Negra," and of course "nigger" are considered unforgiveable. However, the term "nigger" is used by Negroes quite freely when out of earshot of whites, sometimes having a good deal of affectionate meaning to them. . . .

1954

Haircut or a Shave?

Horace Revels Cayton was the grandson of Hiram Revels, one of the two Negro senators who served in the Congress of the

United States during the Reconstruction years. An outstanding sociologist, Horace Cayton is most famous for his book, *Black Metropolis,* written with St. Clair Duke, which describes the life of blacks in Chicago.

In his autobiography, Cayton cites an example of the confusion of blacks caused by the strange practices of discrimination. In the South where the "Jim Crow" laws were definite and familiar to all, even if the practice was not always the same from one city to another, the Negro from his childhood on could be fairly sure of what was permitted and what was not. In the North, however, there were no commonly known "Jim Crow" laws; discrimination depended upon individual whites' attitudes. To avoid anger and embarrassment, blacks often took it for granted that the owners of certain kinds of businesses would discriminate against them. In some cases they were wrong, as Horace Cayton reveals in this incident.

Source: Cayton, Horace R. *Long Old Road.* New York: Trident Press, 1965, pp. 368-369.

At that time I was living in Greenwich Village, and one of the things that irritated me most was that it was necessary for me to go all the way up to Harlem to get my hair cut. Leaving my hotel the next morning, I walked up to Union Square to take the subway, after buying my usual copy of The New York *Times.* On the train, still annoyed at having to make the long trip uptown and possibly missing an important meeting at the UN, I opened my paper to read that the Supreme Court had just ruled that segregation in the public schools was unconstitutional.

The magnitude of the decision shocked me; a large hole had been opened in the dike of segregation, and through it would soon pour a torrent. Would this widen the breach so that eventually it would cause the collapse of the whole structure? That the United States would find it impossible to maintain a caste society in this modern world desperate for freedom, I had realized. But the decision of the Supreme Court was something quite different. A long-overdue change was about to take place in America.

Then what was I doing, making this lengthy round trip to Harlem to get my hair cut? The Supreme Court had just ruled that I was an American citizen. I had the rights and privileges of a citizen, why not exercise them? I got off the train at Grand Central and walked into the well-appointed barber shop in the station. The barber came over to me, but before he could open his mouth I said brusquely, "Don't ask any questions, just cut my hair."

He drew back in surprise. "I merely wanted to know whether you wanted a haircut or a shave."

After this incident I threw over all my former compliance with any so-called color line and for the first time I felt free to go any place, providing I had money to pay the bill. Barbara and I, sometimes to attend UN functions, often just on our own, went to the better hotels and night clubs, and the most exclusive restaurants, and we met nothing but politeness. New York, at first hesitantly but soon quite willingly, had acknowledged the existence of nonwhite people. One now had to seek rather diligently to find any semblance of racial prejudice in any public accommodation.

June 6, 1959

"Mr. Johnson, Will You Please Read?"

When the North Atlantic Treaty Organization (NATO) Congress met to consider world problems, Mordecai Wyatt Johnson was asked to be a delegate. Dr. Johnson was then President Emeritus of Howard University and widely known for his wit and wisdom. Here is a part of the speech he delivered to the Atlantic Congress on the 15th anniversary of D-Day. It is an eloquent plea that peoples—black and white—who live in more advantaged nations help those in underdeveloped countries.

Source: Johnson, Mordecai W. "Speech to the Atlantic Congress," Delivered to the Atlantic Congress, Second Plenary Session, Saturday, June 6, 1959. Reprinted in Hill, Roy L. *Rhetoric of Racial Revolt.* Denver, Colorado: Golden Bell Press, 1964, pp. 245, 246, 251, 252.

Your Lordship, Mr. President, distinguished members of the NATO Congress: I am glad beyond measure to be here and to speak to you on behalf of the Fourth Committee, which has to do with the relationship between the NATO countries, the Atlantic Community, and the underdeveloped peoples.

I suppose one of the reasons why you have been so kindly constrained to invite me is because I am one of those under-developed peoples, (laughter) and you would like to hear about the world from the way it looks down under. I am indeed from among the under-developed peoples; I am the child of a slave. My father was a slave for twenty-five years before the emancipation; my mother was born in slavery; I have lived practically all my life on the territory of former slave states, so when you hear me talk you are dealing with the real under-developed thing.

Yet I have early in my life come into contact with what I conceive to be the noblest and best element in the Western World, namely those Christian educational missionaries who founded the first colleges and universities for Negroes. . . . When these men founded Howard University they put it on the cornerstone of the inherent dignity and immeasurable possibilities of the human individual as such, and they enrolled slaves and the children of slaves with their own sons and daughters without hesitation and without fear, being confident that on that campus they would be able to bring them all to maturity, to responsibility and democratic and Christian creativity. I am indebted to those men for the development of my powers . . . and for giving me the power to give my life away freely for causes that I love. . . .

May I say to you again, we have as yet been able to put no great world-encircling concept in the place of the colonial system to which we have been devoted for some 500 years and which is now fallen. What greater idea do we have now of a world encircling nature that we can offer these under-developed peoples of Asia and Africa, of which they can be members as we are, in which they can be respected just as we, they can move freely out of their own spontaneous enthusiasm just as we? I suggest that we do not have one yet. . . . And because we do not have it we are in some difficulty in approaching these Asiatics and Africans.

I have sat often in these meetings when we talk about what we want to do for them economically. And I have sat for a whole hour and heard us talk tactics, heard us talk self-interest, heard us saying that we must do these things in order to protect ourselves without one word of purehearted love for these people. . . .

When those early white men came to the place where I was to be educated they came to ask nothing, nothing. They looked at me when my trousers were not pressed, and my face was not clean, and said, "Mr. Johnson, will you read?" They knew I was no mister, but they knew what I could be, and they came there for only one purpose, for the joy that was set before them in making a man out of me and turning me loose in the world. I tell you that one of the great, great differences in our preparations is that we seem to have lost the power

242

to speak to these Asiatics and Africans that way. . . . There is as yet no substantial sum of money, and no substantial program developed for them purely out of the motive to make them free from the struggle of existence and to give them a chance to be men. . . .

1966

The Black Generation Gap

During the late 1960's and early 1970's, television, movies, and newspapers gave much attention to the so-called "generation gap." The trust that once existed between age groups was said to have evaporated. Those over thirty years of age and those known as "community leaders" were not to be trusted by the young any longer. In black communities as well as in white communities, the gulf of misunderstanding was widening.

In the following excerpt, A. Philip Randolph, President of the Brotherhood of Sleeping Car Porters and Vice President of the AFL-CIO, explains why he believes the attitudes of many black teenagers have changed. Randolph, a leader in civil rights movements for years, thinks Negro leaders should begin to develop a new generation of "ghetto leaders" among the young.

Source: U.S. Congress. Senate. 89th Congress, Second Session. *Federal Role in Urban Affairs: Hearing Before the Subcommittee on Executive Reorganization of the Committee on Government Operations.* Part 9. December 6, 1966.

. . . These teenagers who throw the Molotov cocktails, who set stores and houses afire, who turn over automobiles, who create disorder in the streets, and so forth, are unemployed. Teenagers with jobs don't go around throwing Molotov cocktails in store windows. They don't go around creating disorder, because they don't have the time and they don't have the will, if they have jobs.

The primary problem of the teenager is the lack of employment. When he receives employment, his whole reaction to the American community will change.

I may say to you that I have walked up and down the streets of Harlem for over 60 years, and I don't remember the time when I have met young men to whom I was unable to talk. I have attempted to talk to them about their life, about their future, their hopes, and their aspirations. What do they want? And they view you with cynicism and skepticism, if not disgust and contempt, and sometimes they end up with abuse. This is a change that has taken place in the psychology of Negro youth in the cities. I am alarmed about the change in the psychology of Negro youth, because here you have the foundation of the future generation, and these are young men who are certainly capable of being transformed. They are not hopeless, but they believe that society is against them. They believe that the promise of a job is merely a hoax. . . .

So that this is the condition that you have in every metropolitan center in the nation—young men walking the streets aimlessly, empty-minded, with souls that are hardened, and burning with frustration and anger, because they believe that there is no hope.

The Negro leadership today do not have the confidence of Negro teenagers. . . .

I believe that we have got to make leaders out of the ghetto workers, the ghetto people themselves. We have got to find a way of getting young teenagers, and help them to understand that they have leadership capacity to help their brothers, that everybody is not against them, and that opposition to white people merely because they are white is futile and has no meaning and has no hope.

Well, now, I am definitely of the belief that these youngsters can be rescued, but they have not been touched as yet. You go through Harlem or Detroit or St. Louis or Chicago. You will find them standing on the street corners, standing on the stoops, some shooting crap, some engaged in this and that thing, but not any work is visible. They have nothing to do, and this is the tragedy, because idle hands and idle minds naturally flow into antisocial activities.

Now the churches, they are doing what they can, but I don't think the churches are reaching them, because they simply look upon the preachers and the churches with a certain amount of contempt. They don't believe that the churches can do anything about the problem, and therefore they don't go into the churches. They are not in the Sunday schools. So they are the unreached.

We have got to reach the unreached. They are the young teenagers who represent the explosive force in every community, and with that chemistry of the loss of hope and the loss of jobs, or no possession of jobs, and with the belief that society is against them, that is the chemistry out of which you have social and racial explosions.

244

What Do the Words "Black Power" Mean To You?

In 1966 a prominent black civil rights leader coined a new slogan which excited great feeling among blacks and whites. Stokely Carmichael told his listeners to stop talking about "freedom" and to begin to demand "black power." As he put it; "The only way we gonna stop the white man from whippin' us is to take over. . . . We've been saying freedom for six years and we ain't got nothing. What we gonna start saying now is black power, . . . from now on when they ask you what you want, you know to tell them: black power, black power, black power!"

Carmichael's new slogan was echoed by Adam Clayton Powell, a black New York Congressman. Almost immediately radio and television transformed that term into household words. However, just what the term "black power" meant was not sharply defined, and debate rages to this day about the implications of that new rallying cry.

In an attempt to clarify the term, two University of Michigan political scientists surveyed public opinion in Detroit, Michigan, in 1967. They asked 394 whites and 461 blacks one simple, open-ended question: "What do the words 'black power' mean to you?" Whites were interviewed by whites, blacks by blacks. Here are some of the typical responses they received and the conclusions they reached as a result of their study. Quotations are identified by race, sex, age, and educational attainment for the benefit of the reader.

Source: Aberbach, Joel D. and Jack L. Walker. "The Meanings of Black Power: A Comparison of White and Black Interpretations of a Political Slogan." *The American Political Science Review,* Vol. 64. (June, 1970), pp. 370, 371, 372 *passim.*

Almost 40 percent of the whites believe black power means black rule over whites, while only 9 percent of the black respondents hold this view. . . . White people in this category usually refer to blacks taking over the entire country or even the world:

(white, male, 24, 12 grades plus) Black takeover—Take over the world because that is what they want to do and they will. There's no doubt about it. Why should they care? I'm working and supporting their kids. In time they'll take over—look at how many there are in Congress. It's there—when they get to voting age, we'll be discriminated upon.

(white, female, 28, 12 grades) They want the situation reversed. They want to rule everything.

(white, male, 32, 11 grades) The Negro wants to enslave the white man like he was enslaved 100 years ago. There will be no middle class, no advancement. He is saying, "If I can't have it neither can you." Everything will be taken away from us. We'll all be poor.

(white, female, 40, 12 grades) I don't like the sound of it. Sounds like something coming to take you over.

(black, male, 28, 12 grades plus) It means dominating black rule—to dominate, to rule over like Hitlerism.

(black, female, 38, 11 grades plus) It means something I don't like. It means like white power is now—taking over completely.

(black, female, 39, 10 grades) Nothing! Not a damn thing. Well, it's just a word used by people from the hate school, so it don't mean nothing to me.

(black, female, 60, 5 grades) It doesn't mean nothing. Biggest joke in the 20th century.

(black, female, 37, 9 grades) Black power and white power means the same to me which is no good. Man should be treated as a man.

(white, female, 53, 12 grades) Scare! Why should there be black power any more than white power? Don't the blacks agree that all races are equal?

(black, female, 47, 12 grades plus) That we should have blacks represent us in government—not take over, but represent us.

(black, male, 23, 10 grades) Getting in possession of something—like jobs and security.

(black, male, 36, 12 grades plus) Negroes have never been together on anything. Now with the new movement we gain strength.

(black, male, 28, 12 grades) Sounds frightening, but really is what whites, Jews, Arabs, and people the world over do—divided we fall united we stand.

(black, male, 42, 12 grades) Negroes getting together and forcing whites to realize our importance—our worth to the United States. Gaining respect and equality.

In summary, the vast majority of white people are hostile to the notion of black power. The most common interpretation is that it symbolizes a black desire to take over the country or somehow deprive the white man. Blacks, on the other hand, are almost evenly divided in their interpretations with 42.2 percent clearly favorable to black power and 49.6 percent defining it in an unfavorable way. Those blacks who are favorable to black power see it as another call for a fair share for blacks or as a rallying cry for black unity, while those who are negatively inclined tend to see it as empty and meaningless. Blacks certainly do not interpret the term the way the whites do. They do not see it as meaning racism, a general black takeover, or violence, and those few blacks who do define the term in this way are negative about such meanings. It is evident that "black power" is a potent slogan which arouses contradictory feelings in large numbers of people. Interpretations of the term may differ, but the slogan clearly stimulates intense feelings and may be exciting enough to move men to purposeful action. . . .

1966

"Operation Breadbasket"

Young Jesse Jackson was appointed by Martin Luther King to establish a "Breadbasket" office in Chicago in 1966. Operation Breadbasket's aim was to force businesses in Chicago's South Side to open new jobs for blacks who lived in the area. Jackson declared that there was power in the black pocketbook; he estimated that blacks spend about $36 billion per year as consumers. All they would need to do, he claimed, would be to unite and boycott firms that refused to hire blacks or to sell black products.

For sixteen weeks, Breadbasket conducted a drive against A. & P., which operated more than forty markets in Chicago's black neighborhoods. Finally the chain surrendered. It agreed to hire 268 additional blacks. Twelve of them were to be store managers and six to be warehouse supervisors. The chain also agreed to stock twenty-five black products, including Fresh Grove orange juice, Mumbo barbecue sauce, Staff of Life bread, and King Solomon spray deodorant. As the crowning touch of victory, Jackson won agreement from A. & P. that it would use black-owned firms for janitorial services, garbage removal, and rodent extermination.

Jesse Jackson is a well-educated young man who deliberately adopts a homey style of speaking to establish rapport with his audiences. He has abandoned suits and ties for casual clothing and an Afro haircut. In his travels throughout the nation, Jackson has organized other Breadbasket operations in Los Angeles, Milwaukee, Indianapolis, Brooklyn, Houston, and Cleveland. To date, none has been as successful as his Chicago venture. Here is a description of how Jackson continues to make Operation Breadbasket a power to be reckoned with in Chicago.

Source: "Jesse Jackson: One Leader Among Many." *Time,* April 6, 1970, p. 21. Reprinted by permission of *TIME,* The Weekly Newsmagazine; Copyright Time Inc. 1970.

Although Breadbasket has become linked almost solely to Jackson's name and image, it is far from a one-man show. Efficiently organized into functional divisions, it runs smoothly, even when Jackson is away, under the day-to-day administration of such able aides as the Rev. Calvin Morris, the associate director, and a lively woman minister, the Rev. Mrs. Willie P. Barrow.

Wherever he may travel during the week, however, Jackson inevitably returns to Chicago for the one big showpiece effort that keeps Breadbasket spiritually together; a three-hour Saturday morning (90 minutes of it broadcast locally by radio) in which black ministers mingle with black businessmen, tough youth-gang leaders sit beside aspiring politicians, and some 5000 of Jackson's fans shout their "Right on, Jesse!" and "Tell it, brother!" as he pitches for the current Breadbasket programs. He calls it "hustling time," and he sells pride as well as products. "I AM Somebody," he chants. "I AM Somebody," comes the crowd's ringing echo.

Jesse Jackson is somebody all right. He has a host of adoring admirers as well as caustic critics. . . .

May 15, 1967

"What Did He Do to be so Black and Blue?"

Black students from the lower socio-economic communities tend to do poorer work than their white classmates in the same school system. Of course, there are some important exceptions to that generalization. Nonetheless, scientific evidence shows that the difference in performance is *not* due to differences in intelligence between blacks and whites. Most educators believe that the black child does not perform as well as the white child in our public schools because he feels that his situation is hopeless. He lives in a white-controlled society. For the black student, all the evidence from the school environment seems to point to the conclusion that white is right and beautiful and that black is evil and ugly.

Huey P. Newton, the Minister of Defense for the Black Panther Party, makes a strong case for developing ways to change the black child's image of himself. Drawing upon the research of many educators, Newton argues that the need to build black pride is vital to the black people in America. This article originally appeared in *The Black Panther* newspaper.

Source: "Fear and Doubt" by Huey P. Newton, from his column "In Defense of Self Defense" in *The Black Panther*, May 15, 1967. Reprinted in U.S. Congress. Senate. 91st Congress, First Session. *Riots, Civil and Criminal Disorders: Hearings Before the Permanent Subcommittee on Investigations of the Committee on Government Operations*, Part 19, June 18, 24 and 25, 1969. Washington, D. C.: Government Printing Office, 1969.

The lower socio-economic Black male is a man of confusion. He faces a hostile environment and is not sure that it is not his own sins that have attracted the hostilities of society. All his life he has been taught (explicitly and implicitly) that he is an inferior approximation of humanity. As a man, he finds himself void of those things that bring respect and a feeling of worthiness. He looks around for something to blame for his situation, but because of negativistic parental and institutional teachings, he ultimately blames himself.

When he was a child, his parents told him that they were not affluent because "we didn't have the opportunity to become educated," or "we did not take advantage of the educational opportunities that were offered to us." They tell their children that things will be different for them if they are educated and skilled, but that there is absolutely nothing other than this occasional warning (and often not even this) to stimulate education. Black people are great worshippers of education, even the lower socio-economic Black person, but at the same time, they are afraid of exposing themselves to it. They are afraid because they are vulnerable to having their fears verified; perhaps they will find that they can't compete with white students. The Black person tells himself that he could have done much more if he had really wanted to. The fact is, of course, that the assumed educational

249

opportunities were never available to the lower socio-economic Black person due to the unique position assigned him in life.

It is a two-headed monster that haunts this man. First, his attitude is that he lacks innate ability to cope with the socio-economic problems confronting him, and second, he tells himself that he has the ability but he simply has not felt strongly enough to try to acquire the skills needed to manipulate his environment. In a desperate effort to *assume* self-respect, he rationalizes that he is lethargic; in this way, he denies a possible lack of innate ability. If he openly attempts to discover his abilities, he and others may see him for what he is—or is not, and this is the real fear. He then withdraws into the world of the invisible, but not without a struggle. He may attempt to make himself visible by processing his hair, acquiring a "boss mop," or driving a long car, even though he can't afford it. He may father several illegitimate children by several different women in order to display his masculinity. But in the end, he realizes that he is ineffectual in his efforts.

Society responds to him as a thing, a beast, a nonentity, something to be ignored or stepped on. He is asked to respect laws that do not respect him. He is asked to digest a code of ethics that acts upon him not for him. He is confused and in a constant state of rage, of shame and doubt. This psychological set permeates all his interpersonal relationships. It determines his view of the social system. His psychological development has been prematurely arrested. This doubt begins at a very early age and continues through his life. The parents pass it on to the child and the social system reinforces the fear, the shame, and the doubt. In the third or fourth grade, he may find that he shares the classroom with white students, but when the class is engaged in reading exercises, all the Black students find themselves in a group at a table reserved for slow readers. This may be quite an innocent effort on the part of the school system. The teacher may not realize that the Black students feared (in fact, feel certain) that Black means dumb and white means smart. The children do not realize that the head start the children got at home is what accounts for the situation. It is generally accepted that the child is the father of the man; this holds true for the lower socio-economic Black people.

With whom, with what can he, a man, identify? As a child he had no permanent male figure with whom to identify; as a man, he sees nothing in society with which he can identify as an extension of himself. His life is built on mistrust, shame, doubt, inferiority, role confusion, isolation and despair. He feels that he is something less than

250

man, and it is evident in his conversation: "the white man is THE MAN, he got everything, and he knows everything, and a nigger ain't nothing." In a society where a man is valued according to occupation and material possessions, he is without possessions. He is unskilled and more often than not, either marginally employed or unemployed. Often his wife (who is able to secure a job as a maid cleaning for white people) is the breadwinner. He is, therefore, viewed as quite worthless by his wife and children. He is ineffectual both in and out of the home. He cannot provide for or protect his family. He is invisible, a non-entity. Society will not acknowledge him as a man. He is a consumer and not a producer. He is dependent upon the white man ("THE MAN") to feed his family, to give him a job, educate his children, serve as the model that he tries to emulate. He is dependent and he hates "THE MAN" and he hates himself. Who is he? Is he a very old adolescent or is he the slave he used to be?

What did he do to be so BLACK and blue?

1967

Stokely Carmichael Tells Why He Went to Cuba

In the early summer of 1966, a black civil rights leader, James Meredith, began what he called a "march against fear" through the deep South. Not long after he started this courageous journey, Meredith was shot from ambush.

Immediately other black leaders took up the march that Meredith was unable to complete. One of these leaders was Stokely Carmichael, the newly elected chairman of the Student Nonviolent Coordinating Committee, widely known by its nickname "Snick." (In 1969, Snick changed its official name to Student *National* Coordinating Committee.)

Carmichael was arrested and jailed briefly. After his release, he began telling the crowds who gathered to hear him that they should seek "black power." The term he coined entered America's vocabulary; the cry of "black power" indicated the seriousness of the country's racial crisis. Black power, Carmichael said, meant that black Americans should build and control independent institutions, that they should seek to be "free of oppression."

In a manner reminiscent of Marcus Garvey, Carmichael sought to bring non-white peoples of the world together. In pursuit of that unity, he went to Cuba. While there he was interviewed by Mario Menendez, editor of the Mexican magazine, *Sucesos*. Part of that interview is reprinted below.

To understand Carmichael's point of view, it is important to remember that when Fidel Castro, the Cuban leader, came to a United Nations meeting in New York City a few years earlier, he stayed at the Hotel Theresa in the heart of Harlem. At one time, before Negroes were freely accepted in the downtown "white" hotels, the Theresa was "the place" for black travelers. For many black people, the most important fact about Fidel Castro was not that he was a Communist but that he had chosen to stay in a Harlem hotel close to the black people.

In the latter part of this selection, Stokely Carmichael explains what he sought to prove by his march through the South: that men must have a sense of self-worth or die.

Source: U.S. Congress. Senate. 91st Congress, First Session. *Riots, Civil and Criminal Disorders: Hearings Before the Permanent Subcommittee on Investigations of The Committee on Government Operations*. Part 19, June 18, 24, 25, 1969. Washington, D. C.: Government Printing Office, 1969.

Excerpt from Exhibit No. 417
Carmichael Interviewed by *Sucesos Magazine*
Havana in English to South America 2106 GMT 9 SEP 67 E

Excerpts of undated recorded interview given by Stokely Carmichael to Mario Menendez, editor of Mexican Magazine *Sucesos,* during Carmichael's stay in Havana.

Question. What is the Student Nonviolent Coordinating Committee?
Answer. The Student Nonviolent Coordinating Committee is the organization for which I work and is a group of young black people in the United States who decided to come together to fight racial and economic exploitation.

Question. When and why was it founded?
Answer. The Student Nonviolent Coordinating Committee was founded in 1960 by a group of young black students who felt the need to come together and actively fight against racial segregation in the United States. They came together because they felt the older organizations were not doing an effective job and were not actively participating. Most of them were taking their troubles to the courts and we felt that you could not take a problem of the whites' injustice to black people to the courts if those courts were all white. You would be taking an unjust problem to people who themselves were unjust.

It could not be solved that way. The only way to solve it was in the

252

streets. We used the name nonviolent because at that time Martin Luther King was the central figure of the black struggle and he was still preaching nonviolence, and anyone who talked about violence at that time was considered to have committed treason, so we decided that we would use the name nonviolent, but in the meantime we knew our struggle was not about to be nonviolent, but we would just wait until the time was right for the actual (word indistinct) name. We came together, we would coordinate activities between the students wherever we have a nonviolent demonstration.

But after one year many of us decided that demonstrations were not the answer. The only answer was organizing our people. So we moved into the worst state, Mississippi, and began to organize our people to fight. And we are now at the front where we are encouraging people to pick up arms and fight back.

Question. What are the political, social, and economic goals pursued by your organization?

Answer. Politically, we want black people in the United States to be free of oppression. We also want the peoples of the third world to be free from oppression, particularly Africa, Asia, and Latin America. We see that our freedom, our liberation, depends on these people and vice versa, their liberation depends on us, so we must wage the same struggle.

Politically speaking (words indistinct) in the United States we want the right to politically control the communities in which we live. In the United States we cannot do that. The communities in which we live, which they call ghettos, are politically controlled by whites. So in a real sense, we have colonialism inside the United States, just like colonialism in Latin American countries, or I should probably say all the Latin American countries, with the exception of Cuba, are controlled politically from the outside by the United States. Politically, we seek to free those colonies of any political intervention from the outside.

Economically speaking, we want our people to be able to enjoy life and to get all the things they need for a decent life without having to struggle as hard as they now do because they are economically exploited by the imperialist power structure of the United States, just as the colonies outside are economically exploited. We want to be able not only to control the resources inside our communities, but also we want to be able to divide those resources among the people of the [backward?] communities. We do not want to set up, for example, a black capitalist system. We want to economically destroy capitalism

253

because capitalism goes hand in hand with racism and exploitation. Wherever capitalism has gone, those two characteristics are sure to follow, racism and exploitation, so we must destroy the capitalistic system which enslaves us on the inside and the people of the third world on the outside.

Socially, I guess we want what most people want out of life: people who are happy and free and who can live [better?] than they now live and who make and participate in decisions that affect their lives, and never feel ashamed of the color of their skin or ashamed of their culture. In order for capitalism to exist it must make the people they conquer feel ashamed of themselves, ashamed of their culture, and what we want to do is to make our people unashamed (word indistinct) so that they can feel they are equal to anybody else psychologically, physically, and morally. . . .

Question. What made you come to Cuba?

Answer. Well, when the Cuban revolution was being waged I was a young boy but we were very interested in it. My interest was heightened by the fact that when the prime minister of Cuba, Fidel Castro, came to the UN he lived in Harlem with black people. He came to the Hotel Theresa, and that meant that our connection with Cuba became a real one in the sense that their prime minister, unlike all other prime ministers who come to the country, came to live in a ghetto with us while he stayed in the United States. And we have always felt that we owed something to Cuba, at least that same visit which they bestowed on us by their prime minister. . . .

Question. The fight you are developing in the United States signifies for people, for outsiders, that you have signed your death sentence. What do you think, or have to say, about that?

Answer. Brother Malcolm used to tell us that there were several types of death. I think a dehumanized people who do not fight back are a dead people. That is what the West has been able to do to most of us. They dehumanized us to the point where we would not even fight back. Once you have begun to fight back, you are alive, you are alive, and bullets do not kill you. If you do not fight back, you are dead, you are dead, and all the money in the world cannot bring you alive. So we are alive today, we are alive all over the world. All of our black people are coming alive because they are fighting back. They are fighting for their humanity. They are doing the type of thing that Fidel talks about. When you become alive, you want to live so much that you fight to live. See, when you are dead, when you do not rebel, you are not fighting to live, you are already dead. Well, we are alive and we love life so much that we are willing to die for it. So, we are alive. Death cannot stop us.

Summer 1967

Tampa's "White Hats" Restore Peace

More widespread and destructive civil disorders took place in the long, hot summer of 1967 than ever before in the nation's history. Racial disturbances exploded in 128 U.S. communities, reaching riot proportions in several cities—in Tampa, Cincinnati, Atlanta, Newark and Detroit, for example. Men killed and looted; at the summer's end over eighty people had been killed, and property damage was in the neighborhood of $50 million.

Americans called the disruptions by various names—"rebellion," "insurrection," and "civil war." However, even in the midst of the chaos and destruction there was a promising development in Tampa, Florida, which is described here.

Source: Muse, Benjamin. *The American Negro Revolution From Nonviolence to Black Power.* Bloomington, Indiana: Indiana University Press, 1968, p. 292.

The Tampa upheaval is of special interest because of a riot-quelling technique which it produced. Jim Hammond, the administrator of that city's human relations commission, went into the riot area and persuaded 120 Negro youths, some of whom had been rioting, to go to work as peacemakers. Organized in a City Youth Patrol, they were given white plastic helmets, from which they quickly got the name of "White Hats." Uniformed law enforcement officers tentatively withdrew and turned the job over to these amateurs. Talking in their own way and with only occasional rough handling, the White Hats restored peace to Tampa's Negro community in one night. Their five leaders were retained on the city's payroll at $76 per week for special liaison work. Florida's governor Claude Kirk paid a visit to Tampa a week later to publicly commend the White Hats.

A Black Man's Concern for Mexican-Americans

Concern for the rights of all men—not just black men—
prompted a Negro leader in the Southwest to appear on behalf of
Mexican-Americans before the United States Civil Rights Commission, an independent, bipartisan, non-political agency of the
United States government established by Congress in 1957.

In December, 1968, the Commission met for five days in San
Antonio, Texas. Its purpose was to collect information about the
civil rights problems of Mexican-Americans in the southwestern
states of Texas, Arizona, California, Colorado, and New Mexico.

Why did a black man speak for "brown" men? Here are the
reasons, given under oath by Richard L. Dockery, Southwest
Regional Director of the National Association for the Advancement of Colored People.

Source: U.S. Congress. *Hearing Before the United States Com-
mission on Civil Rights.* Hearing held in San Antonio, Texas,
December 9-14, 1968. Washington, D. C.: Government Printing
Office, 1969.

TESTIMONY OF MR. RICHARD L. DOCKERY, REGIONAL DIREC-
TOR, NATIONAL ASSOCIATION FOR THE ADVANCEMENT OF
COLORED PEOPLE, SAN ANTONIO, TEXAS.

MR. DOCKERY: I am Richard L. Dockery. I am a resident of San
Antonio, Texas, and I am the regional director for the NAACP in the
Southwest with offices in Dallas, Texas.

*MR. DAVID RUBIN, Acting General Counsel for the Commis-
sion:* And does your region include Texas and New Mexico?

MR. DOCKERY: Yes, it does.

MR. RUBIN: Could you tell us, Mr. Dockery, what kinds of problems are faced by Negroes in the Southwest? Let me ask you what
other States your region covers.

MR. DOCKERY: It covers the States of Louisiana, Arkansas, Oklahoma, Texas, and New Mexico.

MR. RUBIN: Could you give us some description of the problems
that are faced by Negroes in your region and particularly with respect
to Texas and New Mexico?

MR. DOCKERY: Well, I might itemize them in saying that we
encounter a serious problem of police brutality, and certainly the problem of unemployment and underemployment, inadequate housing,

inadequate schools and school buildings, facilities and curriculum, poor neighborhood recreational facilities, ineffectiveness of the local political structure and the grievance mechanisms.

There are in this area disrespectful attitudes by the Anglo-Americans. Discriminatory practices in the administration of justice, and some inadequacies in Federal programs, discriminatory consumer and credit practices, inadequate municipal services, inadequate welfare programs.

MR. RUBIN: Do you regard it as part of your job as regional director of the NAACP in Dallas to be concerned with the problems of Mexican Americans as well as the problems of Negroes?

MR. DOCKERY: Yes, it is. In fact, it is mandatory in my job description that I be concerned with equality, liberty, and justice for all Americans.

MR. RUBIN: Are there many Mexican Americans who are members of the NAACP?

MR. DOCKERY: Yes, we have a very large number of Mexican Americans who are members of the Association.

MR. RUBIN: Could you describe to us your involvement with the problems of Mexican Americans, particularly in Texas?

MR. DOCKERY: Well, in Texas, I have been involved in welfare programs, welfare problems, civil rights problems, evolving around Mexican Americans.

For example, in the Rio Grande Valley last summer, I was one of the first persons in the Valley. In Starr County—there are no Negroes in Starr County incidentally—but I was there because Americans were there and alleged that they had problems with civil rights.

I have been involved with the wage problems in the State with Mexican Americans. Basically Mexican Americans are sugar beet workers in this area; and of course, there is the problem of wages, and I have given testimony on this. I have worked with them on this. There has been discriminatory allegations in employment. And for the past 8 years I have worked with and for them on these problems in San Antonio and across the State.

MR. RUBIN: Do you believe that exposure of the problems that are faced by Mexican Americans in this country will benefit Negroes as well?

MR. DOCKERY: Without question. The death of discriminatory practices, correcting inadequacies for any minority group will undoubtedly help any other minority group. . . .

In my region I am also involved in a problem of Indian affairs. In

Oklahoma I have a tremendous problem with Indian affairs and in New Mexico the Indian affairs and the Mexican American affairs.

... We invite you back again, we leave a standing invitation to you, and I want to thank you very much for coming and giving me the opportunity.

CHAIRMAN HANNAH: Thank you Mr. Dockery. We are very grateful to you. . . .

1969

Let's Write Down Our History

James Forman, a black activist and former Executive Secretary of the Student Nonviolent Coordinating Committee ("Snick"), is well known for his dramatic presentation of demands for reparations owed black people. Forman has stated that white Christian churches and Jewish synagogues owe $500 million to blacks in America as "back pay" for past exploitation. The figure was later boosted to $3 billion. Forman is also interested in the heritage of his people and in preserving that legacy of black traditions. In a speech to a black political gathering, he made the following plea for his brothers and sisters to begin to write down their history.

Source: U.S. Congress. Senate. 91st Congress, First Session. Speeches of James Forman, contained in *Riots, Civil and Criminal Disorders: Hearings Before the Permanent Subcommittee on Investigations of the Committee of Government Operations.* Part 19, June 18, 24, 25, 1969. Washington, D.C.: Government Printing Office, 1969.

And now, brothers and sisters. . . . I repeat it is very important that we begin to write down our thoughts. We must get away from the oral tradition. It is extremely hard to pass on to future generations ideas and information if it is all in the oral tradition. For the six years I served as the Executive Secretary, I would make speeches and none of them would be written. That means that if something had happened to me, if I had been annihilated in battle, then whatever ideas I may have had would not be transmitted for they would have been lost. That is the problem with the Period of Reconstruction in our history. There were many strong black cats who were sheriffs and who were other lawmakers, but there is not much, if anything, written by them, nothing

258

that we can read and many of them could write. But as a people we have the oral tradition and they employed that, but for the future generation we must write. We must write from our own experience, for only we have all the insights into what we mean.

May 4, 1969

Not With Gun or Fire Bomb

To many persons Thurgood Marshall is "Mr. Civil Rights." Marshall was chief counsel for the National Association for the Advancement of Colored People when he won the Brown-Topeka case ending school segregation in 1954. In 1967 President Lyndon B. Johnson appointed him to the United States Supreme Court, the first black man to sit on the high court in American history.

When Dillard University in New Orleans celebrated its 100th birthday in the spring of 1969, Justice Marshall was asked to deliver the centennial address. He offered these words of advice for his audience, composed mainly of blacks.

Source: Excerpts from a centennial address delivered by Supreme Court Justice Thurgood Marshall at Dillard University on May 4, 1969. (The Justice had no prepared manuscript; he spoke from notes: His remarks were recorded by radio station WYLD, New Orleans.)

...I remember a Congressman, a Negro Congressman ... who said, "The trouble is that you don't follow the right theory. Don't get mad—get smart!"

I think of that when I think of violence for violence's sake.... I am a man of law, and in my book, anarchy is anarchy is anarchy! It makes no difference who practices anarchy. It's bad, and punishable, and should be punished....

I don't believe that everything that's black is right, and everything else is wrong. I think that we Negro Americans have just as many beautiful in mind and body, as well as skin, as any other group. And I am sure we have just as many stinkers as there are in every other group.... Likewise, I don't believe that you can use a color for an excuse for not doing what you know should be done. I don't think race should be an excuse not to take care of your children and bring them

259

up properly, even if they are still in segregated schools. I think that race is not an excuse for not keeping your house up properly. I say that because certainly pride of race is great. You find it more deeply seated in other ethnic groups than ours. . . . So there's nothing wrong with it, and I really think there's nothing new about it. But as you look around the world today, you'll find that anarchy is what's wrecking country after country, pulling down, tearing down, and building not. And in this country we don't approach it yet. But the seeds of it remain.

Nothing will be settled with a gun. Nothing will be settled with a fire bomb. And nothing will be settled with a rock, because the country cannot survive if it permits it to go unpunished. It's that simple. . . .

Sure you're frustrated. I am frustrated. There's hardly a person in the world today worth his salt who is not frustrated. The problems seem insurmountable. We've had those problems before, and we survived, worked them out. . . . Be willing to sit down and discuss the possibility of solution—the rule of reason, if you please.

Universities are the key to it. And the student owes it to his country to be ready and educated.

Black studies? Sure!

African culture? Sure!

African culture and black studies only? No!

You're not going to compete in this world with African culture alone. You're going to compete in this world when you get a brain exactly the same as the other one, and just hope yours is a little bit better. . . . But you don't make it just by saying, "Solely because I am black, I am better." You don't make it that way. . . .

But it takes no courage to get in the back of a crowd and throw a rock. Rather, it takes courage to stand up on your two feet and look anyone straight in the eye and say, "I will not be beaten."

Move, but move within the Constitution, and find new ways of moving nonviolently within the Constitution, bearing in mind that there are many of us in this country who are not going to let it go down the drain. We are not going to continue to stand for anarchy, which is anarchy, which is anarchy.

A New Day in a Mississippi Town

Charles Evers came home to Fayette, Mississippi, from Chicago in 1963 to take up the civil rights work of his slain brother, Medgar. Six years later Charles Evers became the first black mayor of biracial Fayette, a community once dominated by the Ku Klux Klan. He won election to the $75 per month mayor's post by a margin of two to one. Seventy-five percent of Fayette's 1600 citizens are black.

Upon his election, Evers promised: "We're going to make a model all-American city for this nation. We are going to make this city a good place to live, for black and white alike." Here is one reporter's eyewitness account of the celebration on the day Charles Evers was inaugurated as mayor.

Source: Copyright, Los Angeles Times. Reprinted with permission Los Angeles Times/Washington Post News Service.

Fayette, Miss.

Aaron Henry, the ubiquitous druggist who runs the NAACP in Mississippi, looked out over the crowd in the City Hall parking lot, sweating hard in the sweltering heat.

"Oh, my," he shouted, "this is some black power!"

Behind him on the rickety platform was the Honorable James Charles Evers, who was inaugurated at noon yesterday as the first black mayor in a biracial city in Mississippi since the Reconstruction aftermath of the Civil War.

In front of him were the all-black Fayette Board of Aldermen, black policemen, black justices of the peace, black constables and even a black Congressman (Charles Diggs of Michigan).

Across the street in the Confederate Memorial Park, black ladies sold tickets to the inaugural ball and ladled punch for the black crowds strolling in from Fayette's narrow streets.

Next to the statue of the Confederate soldier, a new memorial was ready for unveiling—a granite cenotaph inscribed with the name of Mayor Evers' brother, Medgar, who was assassinated for his civil rights activities several years ago.

A block away, bare-legged blacks in colorful African prints danced to the strange beat of African drums. They were guarded by expressionless white men from the Mississippi highway patrol.

"It's a new day," the new mayor declared and that was a fact.

When John Doar first came into this part of Mississippi for the justice department in 1961 he felt that he was in "mean country." Of the 10,000 people here in Jefferson county, 8000 were black but only two or three were permitted to vote.

The county was run, a Fayette newspaperman has said, by "a little clique" of whites who were "against progress for anybody white or black."

Doar and other justice department lawyers nibbled away at the racial problems of the area with investigations and school desegregation suits in adjoining counties. The big change did not come, however, until the passage of the Voting Rights Act in 1965.

Federal voting registrars moved into the area and in December, 1965, Charles Evers, working for the NAACP, moved in with them. He made Fayette his home, led marches, went to jail, and this spring was elected Mayor by a vote of 386 to 255.

"I hope," he said in his speech yesterday, "that the black and white people of Mississippi will understand that we've only done what God would want us to do—take part in our public affairs . . . some day, somehow, we all are going to be free and all men will be able to live on this earth without hating people and without discriminating against people. . . . "There will be no more hatred in Fayette, there will be no more guns carried around this town, there will be no more clowning and cursing in the streets and being disrespectful to people. We are going to have a clean and decent town."

However that may be, his administration had an impressive beginning. Most of the invited celebrities arrived—Shirley MacLaine, the actress; Raymond Burr, television's Perry Mason; Senator Edward Kennedy's brother-in-law, Stephen Smith; Whitney Young of the Urban League; numerous NAACP officials; and various politicians.

Leontyne Price, the Metropolitan opera soprano, flew down from New York to sing "The Star Spangled Banner" in the dust and heat with no accompaniment. She grew up in a Negro shanty 100 miles east of here at Laurel.

John Doar came back with other members of the Justice Department team that served under Robert Kennedy, among them Burke Marshall and Ramsey Clark, who was later attorney general.

The atmosphere was open and happy although for the past few days there had been an air of uneasiness in Fayette, a fear that the inauguration would be marred by bad trouble, perhaps an assassination attempt.

"It was almost paranoid," said Earl Graves, a young Negro urban planning consultant from New York who was in charge of the inaugural planning. "People thought there was going to be a man with a rifle in every tree."

Whether Evers in the days ahead will be able to work with whites as well as blacks and realize his hopes for Fayette as a "model city," is the subject of some controversy. There has been talk of a white exodus out of town. But Jim Walker, a member of the Mississippi state tax commission and the owner of the local newspaper, discounts those predictions.

"As far as I'm concerned," he said, "this means Fayette is on its way up and I think most other whites feel the same way. Up is the only way we can go because we've been down so far so long."

1969

White Power Failure

"Black Power" has been the natural result of "White Power failure" in the United States. That is the opinion of Joseph R. Washington, Jr., a professor at Beloit College in Wisconsin. Here is his explanation of "White Power failure."

Source: *Black and White Power Subreption.* Copyright © 1969 by Joseph R. Washington, Jr. Reprinted by permission of Beacon Press.

While I was researching this book, my ten-year-old son remarked, "Dad, you know the white man has everything going for him. Even Nature is on his side; he can bask in the sun and become as black as we are. If there is no sun, he turns on the electric lamp he invented and in midwinter becomes as brown as brown can be. He can even pass for a black man if he wishes. Dad, have you ever known a black, black man who became white and then black again?"

Of course, my son has a point. The difference between being black and being white is the difference between being powerless and powerful. There is another difference between blacks and whites which my son has yet to understand. Blacks have used their powerlessness with ethical effectiveness in the struggle for civil rights for all Americans, but they have not been ethical or effective.

The fact is that whatever improvement has come about in civil rights has been at the initiation of the powerless black minority. It would appear that the problem and its resolution are issues for blacks alone rather than issues for all. American white power has withheld civil rights from black Americans by demeaning the black man and depriving the black child. White America has been playing with black America, toying with black America. The 90 percent withheld civil rights from the 10 percent and now says to the 10 percent you can have as much civil rights as you can gain by pleasing or teasing us. It is the old elephant and mouse game. Black Americans have played the game with limited skill but with great earnestness only to discover the amount of civil rights gained is in proportion to the extent they, the mouse, scare the white elephant. There comes a time when limited skill and power-lessness versus gamesmanship and power becomes a dangerous game. The unskillful may forget it is powerless and act as if it possessed power. The powerful may not then react with skill but with all of its might. Frightened by the irritation in its trunk, the elephant first becomes resentful and then threatens to stomp. We are at the brink of a time when the powerless may go wild and the powerful may go mad. . . .

Put another way, we are engaged in a chess game, the rules of which whites made up, and they know all the possible moves that can be made by blacks. They are also in a position to check most moves made by blacks and do so as a defensive measure. But whites are somehow unable to move at their own initiative and easily win the game of democracy. As a result, a growing number of blacks and whites are saying that we not only have failed to achieve any real measure of civil rights, but that it is impossible to do so. For these Americans, the achievement of civil rights is no longer of moment. They are calling for an effective way for blacks and whites to live in peaceful coexistence, and whether it is ethical or not, it is believed that semi-separatism is the way.

January 5, 1970

First Day at School as the Only Whites

In 1954 the United States Supreme Court declared that segregated schools were unconstitutional. The court ordered states to

264

proceed "with all deliberate speed" to integrate their schools. Yet almost twenty years after that historic decision, the United States is still struggling with this issue—what integration in the public schools means and how to achieve it.

In the late '50's and early '60's, newspapers and television reported cases of one, two, or a few blacks enrolling in previously all-white schools—"token" integration. Ten years after the Brown v. Board of Education of Topeka decision, only three percent of the black school children in the South [states of Delaware, Maryland, Virginia, West Virginia, Kentucky, North Carolina, South Carolina, Tennessee, Georgia, Florida, Alabama, Mississippi, Arkansas, Louisiana, Oklahoma, and Texas] were going to public schools with white children.

In 1969, soon after he became Chief Justice, Warren Burger said that the rate at which integration had been proceeding was hardly deliberate and certainly not speedy. Accordingly, in October of that same year, the Supreme Court ordered that schools be integrated immediately. By December, 1969, almost twenty percent of black children in the South were attending desegregated schools.

As a result of the Supreme Court's 1969 order, thirty Mississippi school districts were required to shift students and teachers in the middle of a school year. The news media began reporting cases in which a few white children were the only members of their race attending "integrated" schools that were virtually all-black. Here is what happened to Annette and Tommy Brown, aged 11 and 9, on their first day in a school with 1500 black students in Woodville, Mississippi.

Annette Brown stood in the rain with her little brother, Tommy, biting her lips and waiting for a bus to take them home from their first day as the only white students in their county's public schools.

When the second semester began yesterday morning here in this rural town in southwestern Mississippi, all the other white children in Wilkinson county stayed home, waiting to begin their studies next week in a private school chartered after the Federal Courts had ordered this county and 20 other districts to integrate their education system immediately and completely.

"I can't figure it out," mused Dewitt Ginn, a Negro who serves as principal of the schools where Annette and Tommy enrolled. "Their daddy is like most white folks around here. Why should he send his kids to school with black kids!"

Annette had the answer.

265

"Daddy wanted us to go to a private school," she said. "But we didn't have the money."

So, yesterday morning, she took her seat in Virginia Wilkinson's 36-member sixth grade class, and her brother stored his books in a desk just down the hall with the 34 other fourth graders taught by Elizabeth Parker.

Except for two elderly janitors, the two young children of Mr. and Mrs. Burnell Brown were the only whites in a sprawling one-floor school where 1500 Negro students and teachers will study this year.

"I was afraid, yes, that's right," Annette said after class ended yesterday. She is 11. Tommy is 9.

Asked what she had feared, she said she didn't remember.

Tommy, unlike his sister, said he had not been afraid at all and "liked it pretty much."

The rain had begun before dawn yesterday and when the bells clanged in the corridors of the Wilkinson county training school, the 1391 black students and Annette and Tommy emerged boisterously into a school yard of mud and puddles.

A bit confused by the new surroundings, Annette and Tommy failed to board the bus that would take them to their rural home, several miles out of Woodville, where their father, like so many other men in this area, earns his living as a logger.

The Browns do not have a telephone and, for a moment, Annette was visibly shaken at the thought of being left behind. She stood alone, clutching her coat and hood tightly around her, and waited until she was told by two Negro girls that the bus would be back.

She walked slowly back toward the school and stood with her brother and a large group of Negro students. The rain, driven by a cold, brisk wind, blew through the shelter on them all.

"I don't know if we'll come back in the morning or not," she said. "Daddy will have to decide that tonight, I guess."

February 9, 1970

"The North is Guilty of Monumental Hypocrisy"

Between 1954 and 1970 most Federal court decisions and desegregation plans were directed to the South. However, many people in Congress and in news reporting charged that a double standard was being used. A report issued by the Department of Health, Education and Welfare in 1969 showed that seventy percent of the black children in the South were attending schools that were ninety-five to one hundred percent black. The HEW report showed that the North as well as the South would have to be concerned with school desegregation; fifty percent of the black school children in the North went to schools that were almost one hundred percent black.

Senator John Stennis of Mississippi introduced an amendment to a pending education bill. "If segregation is wrong in the South, it is wrong in the North," he declared. The Stennis amendment states that Federal desegregation policies should be uniformly applied throughout the nation, whether segregation is *de jure* or *de facto.*

De jure segregation is separation of blacks and whites "by law." Legal ways of separating people by color existed in the South until 1954. *De facto* segregation is separation of blacks and whites "as a fact." It results from nonlegal circumstances: residential housing patterns or zoning laws. *De facto* segregation has developed in the North in big cities. As blacks have moved to these urban centers, whites have moved out of the inner city. The migration of whites to the suburbs and the concentration of non-whites in urban ghettos creates neighborhoods that are almost white or nonwhite. Schools in these areas were built to serve their surrounding neighborhood. As the neighborhoods become predominantly nonwhite in the inner city or predominantly white in the suburban areas outside the city, so, naturally, do inner city schools become predominantly non-white and suburban schools predominantly white. While no law has created such segregated schools, such schools result from this separation of residence areas of whites and nonwhites.

In the debate in Congress over the Stennis Amendment, Senator Abraham Ribicoff, a liberal Democrat from Connecticut and a former Secretary of Health, Education and Welfare, startled his colleagues by agreeing with Stennis. Ribicoff's support marked a turning point in the debate and probably accounted for the passage of the Stennis Amendment. Here, in part, is Senator Ribicoff's indictment of the North.

Source: *Congressional Record:* Proceedings and Debates of the 91st Congress, Second Session. Vol. 116, No. 17. February 9, 1970, pp. S 1461-S 1463.

The Senator from Mississippi has argued that if segregation is wrong in the public schools of the South, it is wrong in the public schools of all other states. On this statement the Senator from Mississippi is correct. Therefore, I will support the Senator from Mississippi in his amendment, designed to apply the guidelines for desegregation uniformly across the whole nation.

The North is guilty of monumental hypocrisy in its treatment of the black man. Without question, northern communities have been as systematic and as consistent as Southern communities in denying the black man and his children the opportunities that exist for white people.

The plain fact is that racism is rampant throughout the country. It knows no geographical boundary and has known none since the great migration of rural blacks after World War II. . . .

Perhaps we in the North needed the mirror held up to us by the Senator from Mississippi, in order to see the truth. . . .

Our problem is not only the dual systems of education which exist nineteen years after the Supreme Court struck them down in 1954. The more fundamental problem is the dual society that exists in every metropolitan area—the black society of the central city and the white society of the suburb.

Massive school segregation does not exist because we have segregated our schools but because we have segregated our society and our neighborhoods. That is the source of the inequality, the tension and the hatred that disfigure our Nation. . . .

As long as we think the only problem is segregated schools we miss the point. . . . It is not the kids who are racists; it is the adults who are racists. I do not want to make the children innocent pawns. This is what we are doing. We think we can take a group of children, put them in a bus and take them five miles away to an atmosphere they do not like and do not know, and then think that we have solved the situation. . . . Until we take the races of the North and put them in this mess we are not going to solve the problem. As long as the North hides in lily-white suburbs, and as long as they say this is a Southern problem we are not going to attack the basic problem. The time has come for the North to take a look at itself in the mirror; it is not just the people in the South, in Georgia, Mississippi, and Alabama. It is time for us to solve our problem.

I am troubled over the fact that we in the North are so easy with solutions for problems and people 2000 miles away from where we live; yet we turn away—our faces, our minds, our heads, and our hearts— from problems that are blocks from where we live.

Unless we address ourselves, as a Congress, as a President, and as the people to the basic issue, this society of ours will be driven apart until there is no basis for a society to exist as a whole.

It has hurt me to see, suddenly, the whole ethnic problem, the black problem, the color problem, coming to the fore, when for many years we thought that a fluid society had finally been achieved and there were opportunities in this country for everyone, irrespective of race, color, creed, or religion. Yet, since 1954 I cannot say that the problems have become better. I must admit that I think they have become worse.

It would have been easy for me to be silent. But I woke up Sunday morning and felt that the time had come for us in the Senate to take a look at ourselves. We have plenty of problems. To look down our noses at the people of the South and come up with solutions for them, without having the guts to face up to our own problems, is the depth of hypocrisy. . . .

I make the prediction to those in the North that the southerners will solve the problems of black and white before we in the North will. We have a deep obligation, those of us in this body, if we love our States, and our country, and our people, to start talking frankly. . . .

March 24, 1970

A Man's Right and Ability to Choose for Himself

President Richard M. Nixon recognized that desegregating the public elementary and secondary schools is one of the most emotionally charged public issues of the early 1970's. For that reason, he issued a lengthy statement on desegregation. He declared: "The 1954 decision of the Supreme Court in *Brown* v. *Board of Education* was right in both constitutional and human terms." The President also said that desegregating schools was just one part of America's past, present and future commitment to a "free and open society." In this excerpt, President Nixon defines what he means by a free and open society.

Source: Text of a statement by President Richard M. Nixon on elementary and secondary school desegregation. Issued March 24, 1970.

The goal of this Administration is a free and open society. In saying this, I use the words "free" and "open" quite precisely.

Freedom has two essential elements: the *right* to choose and the *ability* to choose. The right to move out of a mid-city slum, for example, means little without the means of doing so. The right to apply for a good job means little without access to the skills that make it attainable. By the same token, those skills are of little use if arbitrary policies exclude the person who has them because of race or other distinction. . . .

An open society does not have to be homogeneous or even fully integrated. There is room within it for many communities. Especially in a nation like America, it is natural that people with a common heritage retain special ties; it is natural and right that we have Italian or Irish or Negro or Norwegian neighborhoods; it is natural and right that members of those communities feel a sense of group identity and group pride. In terms of an open society, what matters is mobility: the right and ability of each person to decide for himself where and how he wants to live, whether as part of the ethnic enclave or as part of the larger society—or, as many do, share the life of both. . . .

Instead of making a man's decisions for him, we aim to give him both the *right* and *ability* to choose for himself and the mobility to move upward. . . .

We must give the minority child that equal place at the starting line that his parents were denied—and the pride, the dignity, the self-respect that are the birthright of a free American.

We can do no less and still be true to our conscience and our Constitution. I believe that most Americans today, whether North or South, accept this as their duty. . . .

270

May 22, 1970

"Daddy, You Just Don't Understand"

With shouts of "soul power" and "I am Somebody," more than 300 demonstrators began a 110-mile "march against repression." The marchers—blacks and a few whites—began on May 20, 1970, from Perry, Georgia. Their destination was Atlanta, the state capital. They followed a mule-drawn coffin through what is popularly called the Black Belt of Georgia. The casket symbolized the deaths of twelve persons, black and white, at colleges in Kent, Ohio, and Jackson, Mississippi, which had occurred earlier in May. Officially "without incident," the march was a dramatic demonstration of commitments to change "the way it is."

Source: "Sixty Wesleyan Girls Join Protest on Third Day of March in Georgia." © 1970 by The New York Times Company. Reprinted by permission.

. . . On this, the third leg of the five-day walk from Perry, Georgia, to Atlanta, the marchers moved through the hot streets of this central Georgia city [Macon] about noon.

Later in the day, they reached Forsyth, a mostly white community of 3700 persons, said by the marchers to be one of the most racially conservative towns they are to pass through on their 110-mile march.

The mostly youthful marchers came singing and clapping through Macon's Negro community about noon. They called to other blacks to join them.

"Come and go with us," a marcher called to an elderly black woman watching from her porch.

"I can't walk that good," the elderly woman called back.

"Come and go as far as you can," she was urged.

The woman, holding carefully to a stair rail, moved down the stairs and into the street. She moved slowly. Young demonstrators opened the line of marchers and let her in. She walked for less than a block and then dropped out. Then the elderly woman urged others to join the march. "Go as far as you can," she told them.

Farther on, a middle-aged Negro man stood crying on the sidewalk. When he saw his daughter in the line of marchers, he called out: "Mildred, come out of there."

The girl, a student at Fort Valley State College, marched on. "Daddy," she said, "You just don't understand."

271

Black Men, Unite With Me

In the following excerpts from an open letter to blacks, Elijah Muhammad, leader of the Black Muslims, explains why he believes he is the most capable and trustworthy leader for the black people today. He warns that unless "all the little Black organizations" unite under his leadership into a "complete body of one," black groups will lose their power.

The Black Muslims are by far the largest and best known of the black nationalist organizations. Muhammad claims 250,000 followers in his "Nation of Islam." Most authorities, however, estimate Black Muslim membership to be around 100,000.

Elijah Muhammad was born Elijah Poole in the town of Sandersville, Georgia. For more than thirty years he has led the Black Muslims, a group absolutely against integration and against any blacks who advocate integration.

Source: "Muhammad Speaks" An Open Letter by Elijah Muhammad to Black Men, June 5, 1970.

Look how the devil is teaching our people division now. The devil goes and gets everyone whom he thinks is against me and the teachings and idolizes them in order for the Black people to idolize them. Look at how he names streets after Rev. Martin Luther King and Malcolm, because he was the devil's disciple. Rev. Martin Luther King was not the disciple of the Black Men. He preached integration with white people and to become white folk . . . and then the white man killed him. The white man does the same to you, although you [still] follow what the white man tells you to follow and you worship the white man.

Many times, I have reminded you that Rev. Martin Luther King was not trying to separate you from the enemy, but instead he was trying to unite you with the enemy. Rev. Martin Luther King was not seeking a home for you as Moses was seeking a home for Israel, who was oppressed in Egypt. In modern day America, I am seeking an independent home for you. . . .

The white man is right when he says that you are free. You are free, but if you go back to him for him to put chains on you again, he will do so.

Malcolm fell out from us a hypocrite. He went and joined white people and worshiped them and he got what he preached for. Now the white man names colleges after Malcolm only to get you to join in the philosophy he left behind . . . that white people are good. Malcolm went to Mecca and saw white people. And instead of joining in with the Black Man, he joined in with the white man, although he was taught the white man's birth and death and he preached it as long as he did not turn enemy against me. He turned enemy against me for he wanted my place over the people and he thought that by going over the earth and making mock of me, he would do just that . . . get rid of me. But the very people of Mecca and Egypt and other places he went, they are with me today. Here, in the United States of America, today, I have more followers than I had before Malcolm said a word.

You cannot disgrace one whom Allah [the Supreme Being in the Moslem religion] has taken for his Friend. . . . The white man teaches you to worship Malcolm in order to lead you astray against me. You come around trying to argue with us. I do not give 2 cents for you following Malcolm, if you want to follow him. You will get Divine Death and Destruction with no one to give you any honor and respect . . . only the devil whom you serve. The devil sets enemies and hypocrites for you to worship in order to pull you away from me. . . . This you will learn. . . .

If all the little Black organizations who are trying to do something for themselves would unite with me and make a complete body of one, we will most certainly have salvation in our hands at once. If we all want to be like Christianity, with each one sitting and enjoying his little part . . . one day they will lose their part. . . .

Your Brother,
Elijah Muhammad
Messenger of Allah to you all.

1970

Homecoming for the First Black Girl at the University of Georgia

In its 175-year history, the University of Georgia had never admitted a black student. Then, in 1961, two black honor students from Turner High School in Atlanta applied for admission. But Charlayne Hunter and Hamilton Holmes were not accepted, and they appealed to the courts. After eighteen months of litigation, the Federal court ordered the University of Georgia " . . . to approve the application of qualified Negro residents of Georgia." On January 9, 1961, the two black students finally were admitted.

Violent demonstrations by students and "outsiders" took place the following night. School authorities suspended the two blacks "in the interest of their personal safety." However, the court promptly ordered security measures strengthened and insisted that both Miss Hunter and Mr. Holmes be reinstated at once. Meanwhile, eight Ku Klux Klan members and two students were arrested.

Six years after she had graduated, Charlayne Hunter returned to the University of Georgia and then wrote an article about her homecoming, from which the following excerpts are taken. She is now a reporter for The New York *Times*. Hamilton Holmes was serving as an army doctor in Germany during 1970.

Source: Hunter, Charlayne. "After Nine Years—A Homecoming for the First Black Girl at the University of Georgia." *The New York Times Magazine*, January 25, 1970.

Several days after Hamilton (Hamp) Holmes and I entered the University of Georgia in 1961 under court order as its first two black students, I sat in a world history class, fighting desperately to stay awake and avoid confirming the stereotype that all blacks are lazy. The drowsiness was the result of my first few days on campus when white students, protesting our admission, rioted outside my dormitory.

Shortly after a brick and bottle had shattered the window in my room, sending chunks of broken glass within a foot of where I was standing, Hamilton, who lived off campus, and I were suspended for our "own safety." Our lawyers got the judge who had ordered us in to order us readmitted, but the girls who lived above me—I was the sole resident on the first floor—continued for a long time to pound the floor, night after night, late into the night, and I suffered the physical and mental exhaustion of those first few days throughout the winter quarter. Somehow, it was always in this mid-morning history class that I would find myself embarrassed as my head drooped and my eyes closed.

Almost nine years later, during my first visit to the campus since graduation, I entered that same classroom—this time wide awake, and found not a course in world history, but one in African history, part of

274

a new black studies program; and not one exhausted black girl, but five outspoken black men and women among the students and a young black man, with a heavy Afro haircut and wearing a turtleneck sweater, teaching the course. By the end of the hour, as the white students sat quietly taking notes, the black instructor was acting as a referee for two of the black students who were engaged in a vehement clash of opinion on the subject of pan-Africanism. . . .

After the class ended, I introduced myself to the black students sitting in front of me and invited them to have lunch with me. Anderson Williams joined us, and we drove to a steak house in town—one of many that did not serve black people when I graduated.

On the way out, Benny Roberson, a junior from Athens, majoring in anthropology, started to chuckle. "Charlayne Hunter. You know how I remember you so well? The day you entered Georgia and all that stuff was going on with you, I started getting ready to go to town, and my mamma said, 'Boy, you are not going nowhere near that town today.' And I sat back down. . . ."

It has been more than six years since I left the University of Georgia and the South, and I am still weighing the things I lost against the things I gained. At one point, I even spent six months in graduate school because I felt that I needed to fill in the gaps from the education I received from Georgia. Yet, before the six months were over, I realized that the education I received outside the classroom more than made up for what was lost inside. . . .

I remember resenting to the point of being rude that almost my only visitors in my dormitory were the girls whom no man would look at twice, the wallflowers who came because they had no Saturday dates, the overweight, the bookworms or the religious ones. Not that there weren't exceptions—and some wonderful ones. But the former were the rule. And often, listening to records at night and dancing with the closet door, I would ignore their knocks, because I found the whole charade disgusting.

And yet, I stayed, partly because I knew the world was watching. I think that, at that time, such a commitment was necessary. But the need is greater now, precisely because the world isn't watching. The movement of black students to black colleges is fine for those who can afford it. But Benny Roberson lives here in Athens, where there is no black college, and he can't afford to go out of town. Things for blacks may improve now, not because the world is watching, but because there are more Benny Robersons.

An African View: Turn Black Power Into Green Power

Black is beautiful. White is not ugly. Green, the color of money, money that can insure dignity, power, and economic well-being, is beautiful too. These were some of the thoughts of John J. Akar, Ambassador to the United States from the West African nation of Sierra Leone. The tall, handsome African wore his colorful ceremonial robes as he toured the United States and participated in celebrations during Afro-American Week. Here is some of his advice to Americans, whites as well as blacks.

Source: "The Economics of Blackness: An African View of It." © Chronicle Publishing Co. 1970, San Francisco.

You cannot solve racism by anti-racist racism. In Africa blacks are a majority. We have our nations and our expression of sovereignty is territorial. But here blacks are a minority and it is very different.

Militant American blacks have a very difficult time in Africa. Their revolutionary rhetoric and diatribes are meaningless to us. We have few problems of race; our problems are building up our housing, food, and health.

We are looking for economic self-sufficiency. American blacks should try to translate black power into green power. Black militants are dissipating their energies on rubbish, like all this business about "pigs." They should be working to beat the system at its own game so they could walk through the corridors of power and meet with whites as equals, not as antagonists.

Militancy is a phase, but there is no question it has achieved a lot. The system must be improved but not destroyed. White society must do some re-thinking so more conciliatory voices like Martin Luther King would be given greater hearing.

What concerns us in Africa is that ethnic groups like the Jews and the Irish count on ethnic communities in the U.S. to act as lobbyists and pressure groups for their interests.

We need American blacks to emerge as a strong political and economic force that can become Africa's great voice in the United States. Until this happens the African cause will get little sympathy in Congress.